Lean But Not Mean

Lean But Not Mean

Studies in Organization Structure

James C. Worthy

Edited by David G. Moore and
Ronald G. Greenwood

University of Illinois Press
Urbana and Chicago

© 1994 by James C. Worthy
Manufactured in the United States of America
C   5   4   3   2   1

This book is printed on acid-free paper.

Library of Congress Cataloging-in-Publication Data

Worthy, James C.
    Lean but not mean : studies in organization structure /
James C. Worthy ; edited by David G. Moore and Ronald G. Greenwood.
        p.   cm.
    Includes index.
    ISBN 0-252-02085-5 (cloth)
    1. Organizational effectiveness—United States. 2. Organizational
behavior—United States. 3. Industrial management—United States.
4. Industrial relations—United States. I. Moore, David G., 1918–   .
II. Greenwood, Ronald G. III. Title.
    HD58.9.W67   1994
    658.4'02—dc20   93-23550
                                                              CIP

To the men and women
with whom I have worked
who made every job I ever had
a richly rewarding experience

Contents

Preface   ix

Introduction, by David G. Moore   xi

Part 1   The Setting   1

1. The Organization Policies of General
   Robert E. Wood   3
2. Overview of the Research Program   11

Part 2   Studies in Human Relations   23

3. Early Studies of Employee Attitudes and Morale   27
4. Industrial Organizations as Social Systems   50
5. Development of the Organization Survey Program   55
6. The Organization Survey Program   62
7. Findings of the Survey Programs   70
8. Toward a Typology of Organizational Malfunction   81
9. Industry as a Social Science Laboratory   83

Part 3   Structure and Performance   89

10. The Ambiguous Legacy of Frederick W. Taylor   93
11. The Sears X-Y Study   117
12. The Sears Central Merchandising Organization   127
13. Evolution of a Structure   139
14. The Bureaucratic Dilemma   146
15. The Behavioral Dimensions of Span of
    Management Theory   149
16. The Critical Problem of Size   156

Part 4   Management Values   169

17. Democratic Principles in Business Management   173
18. Education for Business Leadership   184
19. Management's Approach to Human Relations   194
20. Labor Relations Policy   204
21. Overachievement at Work   206
22. A Working Philosophy of Personnel Management   209

Biographical Note, by Ronald G. Greenwood   213
Index   223

Preface

The papers presented here were written over a period of fifty years. All of them were "occasional," written for specific purposes or events or otherwise related to my work in industry, government, and education.

During my career I have written on a number of different subjects, among which are organization, human relations, personnel management, corporate social responsibility, business ethics, higher education, and religion. The papers included here are restricted chiefly but not entirely to organization, with special emphasis on organization structure and people in the structure. Most were written before "organization behavior" came to be recognized as a distinct subdiscipline of management.

The papers included were selected on a dual basis of historical interest and current relevance. Many of the problems discussed are closely similar to the problems of organization and behavior that trouble practitioners and scholars of management today. I sincerely hope that the findings of research and experience reported here, and the principles developed from them, will be as useful as when they were first recorded.

While the problems faced by management today are in many ways a reprise of those of a couple of generations ago, the settings in which they occur are often quite different. Throughout, the present tense, or other tense appropriate to the context, has been retained rather than the past tense, which would be used if the papers were written today. Also, those sensitive to such matters should bear in mind that in the 1940s and 1950s the masculine gender had not yet lost its generic status. More important, Sears, Roebuck and Co., while still one of the world's great business enterprises, is no longer the sole occupant of center stage in the merchandising field it was when many of these papers were written, and the Sears organization structure and patterns of leadership have changed in many important respects; the papers as written reflect the reality of their time.

The papers are organized by subject matter rather than by the order in which they were written. Most appear in condensed form to avoid repetition or eliminate administrative details no longer relevant. In no case have changes been made to reflect later experience or judgments.

I am deeply indebted to my two editors, Ronald Greenwood and David Moore, on whose scholarly judgment I have placed great reliance in selecting the papers for this collection; responsibility for final selections, of course, is mine alone. I have had the pleasure of knowing Moore for fifty years, including ten years in which we collaborated in the work at Sears that led to many of the papers in this volume. I have been associated with Greenwood in the affairs of the Management History Division of the Academy of Management for the last fifteen years, during which time I developed high respect for his historical judgment. I am most appreciative of Greenwood's generous biographical sketch and of Moore's informative introduction to the collection and his editorial notes for each of the four parts into which the collection is organized. I owe a special debt to Patricia L. Pronger of the Kellogg School staff for her work in transcribing many of the original papers to computer disks so that text could be submitted to the publisher in form appropriate to contemporary publishing practice.

And finally—again—I am indebted to my wife for her patience and understanding as I worked with my editors, often to the neglect of household chores, to put all of this together.

—James C. Worthy

Introduction

David G. Moore

If ever the title of a book were apropos its contents, *Lean But Not Mean* is apropos this collection of papers on management, some dating from as long as fifty years ago. Taken together, they are as relevant to the problems of management today as they were when they were written. Today, there is much wringing of hands over the decline in America's competitive position in the world economy, and "lean and mean" has become one of the popular nostrums for overcoming competitive failings. But the experience of one very large company demonstrates that a company can be lean *without* being mean; that in fact attention to humane values in managerial practice can be a major element of competitive strength.

"Lean" and "mean" may rhyme, but they don't work well together. A management that wants a lean organization cannot be mean in the way it runs that organization. A lean organization can operate effectively only if there is a high level of mutual trust and confidence in all internal organizational relationships, a working environment not likely to be characterized by the adjective "mean." A mean organization requires an extensive middle management hierarchy to police and enforce top management's dictates; a lean organization, on the contrary, requires a willingness on the part of top management to place significant reliance on the judgment and problem-solving capacities of those at operative levels, and for this purpose any extensive middle management structure is not only unnecessary but counterproductive.

In the 1940s and 1950s, there was no more successful company in America than Sears, Roebuck and Co. Far and away the dominant player in the mercantile field, Sears in 1954 accounted for over 7 percent of the country's retail sales in comparable lines of merchandise and just under 1 percent of the country's total gross national product. Despite its size, the company was exceptionally *lean*, with a minimum of middle management structure and the great bulk of people on the payroll engaged in one way or another actually serving customers rather than in staff and supervisory activities. But Sears was as remarkable for the high morale and esprit de corps of its work force as for its sales and profit performance; in point of fact, the economic power of the company rested in significant part on the loyalty and dedication of the men and women who comprised the far-flung enterprise.

During this period, Sears was headed by General Robert E. Wood, who was largely responsible for Sears' lean condition. He developed a highly decentralized management structure with few layers of supervision and decried the proliferation of middle level bureaucracy to replace the judgment of line management at lower levels. Worthy was employed by Sears during more than half the years of Wood's tenure as chief executive officer, and was in a position to observe at close hand the effects of Wood's executive methods and of the organization that developed under his leadership. In addition, Worthy was involved in the design and supervision of an extensive program of organizational and human resources research. He was able, therefore, to relate the findings from this research to the patterns of organization and management that had developed at Sears and to discover that a lean administrative structure was not only more efficient but could enhance rather than diminish employee morale.

Over the years, Worthy wrote and lectured extensively on his observations as a Sears executive and on the findings of the research program. A selection of these writings is presented in this volume. They are, as the reader will find, directly relevant to current efforts to restructure American corporate organizations, focused as they are not only on reductions in force at the worker level but on the elimination of layers of middle management and the bureaucratic structures that have proliferated as much in private industry in recent decades as they have in government. The cutbacks are painful to be sure, but they provide a propitious opportunity to develop new, more productive, and above all more flexible and adaptable organizations. The future belongs to business organizations that can serve a highly diversified, global market where entrepreneurship, adaptability, and creativity will play key roles.

In today's struggle to survive, the way in which individual corporations are organized and managed will be critically important. They must be designed to enhance employee initiative and creativity at all levels. There is much in Worthy's writings that bear directly on this issue, particularly in his exposition of the interplay between managerial assumptions about the work force, administrative hierarchies, patterns of managerial and supervisory control, departmentalization, job design, and employee initiative and productive effort. All of these considerations bear directly on the ability of a company to cope effectively with its external environment.

In broader perspective, Worthy's ideas are relevant to the problems of many nations of the world as old systems of organizations and governance break down. The breakdown has been both economic and political. Communist countries have demonstrated conclusively that control of the economy from the top, no matter how elaborate the central plans or the bureaucracy set up to carry them out, cannot orchestrate a workable system. There is clearly a need for decentralized control and decision making closer to the scene of action. But this cannot be achieved simply by denouncing communism, dictatorships, and entrenched government bureaucracies, acclaiming the virtues of the market system, and relying on Adam Smith's "hidden hand." Complex systems of manufacturing, distribution, and supporting services still need to be organized, and they need to be managed. Moreover, management and employees alike need to be stimulated and motivated.

It is natural for the emerging capitalistic countries to look to the United States for guidance in organizing and managing business enterprises in a free market economy. It is ironic that the search for guidance comes at a time when management and organization practices in the United States are themselves in a state of flux as a result of a number of factors—including the globalization of industry, increased competition, stifling debt from acquisitions and leveraged buy-outs, and concentration of stockholder power in giant mutual and pension funds. By comparison with present practices, the years in which Worthy wrote seem like a "golden age" of management in the United States, with its focus on organizational development and long-term growth and its search for a balanced approach to the interests of customers, employees, stockholders, and the community. These were the years in which a true profession of management appeared to be emerging. In contrast, today's focus on short-term profitability tends to narrow and distort top management's attention. Decisions are often made primarily to satisfy the investment community, with only secondary concern for strengthening the organization and the long-term development of the enterprise.

What better time to examine management practices in the United States! Are the management techniques of Japan and some Western European countries more effective than ours? If so, what have we lost in the last two decades that may have diminished our ability to innovate and compete?

Worthy lived and wrote about management and organization during the years following the Great Depression and extending through the 1980s. During this period he viewed management practices and organization behavior from the vantage points of business, government, politics, and academia. He wrote more than four hundred papers, most of which were originally in the form of speeches to diverse audiences, and often merely internal company memoranda. The quality of these speeches and memoranda is attested by the fact that many were published with little change from the original manuscripts. He also wrote five books, none of which dealt explicitly and comprehensively with his ideas about management and organization. The present collection represents an effort to assemble the best of Worthy's papers on organization theory in one volume. It is limited primarily to his views growing out of his business experience and research conducted under his direction at Sears during the 1940s and early 1950s and does not include any of his papers written at a later date on such subjects as business ethics, the public responsibilities of management, politics, and education.

Management in the Post-Depression Years

Many of Worthy's ideas may appear bold and unconventional today, but they received favorable attention at the time they first were published. Five major influences converged to shape management's thinking during that period. One was the shift in control over corporate assets from owner-stockholders to nonowner managers, first noted by Berle and Means in their widely read *The Modern Corporation and Private Property*,[1] published in 1932. With this newly acquired power came questions about the functions of executives. What were their responsibilities and to whom were they beholden in the exercise of their power over the economic assets of the nation?

The answer to these important questions was strongly influenced by the advent of a second major influence, the Great Depression. Business leadership, rightly or wrongly, was blamed for the hard times. Branded by President Roosevelt as "economic royalists," many business leaders grew increasingly aware of the fragile position of privately managed enterprises and the extent to which their very existence depended on public acceptance. This meant that management had to justify its role and prove that its power was legitimately held. One way to do this was to redefine management as a profession, to show that its decisions and actions were based on a special body of knowledge and experience that legitimized its authority. As such, management was like any other profession, such as medicine or law, that held a mandate to act in the public interest within the limits of its professional knowledge and judgment.

Some of the earliest efforts to create a profession of management go back to World War I, but the Great Depression provided a powerful stimulus to the endeavor. One of the most notable of these later efforts was that of Chester I. Barnard, president of New Jersey Bell. At the invitation of Harvard Business School professors, he presented a series of lectures on the executive's role based on an analysis of cooperative systems involving physical, biological, psychological, and social phenomena. He quite outdid the professors in the complexity and scope of his thinking, and his subsequent book, *The Functions of the Executive*,[2] became something of a classic. Other books on the management function began to appear in increasing numbers, some in the earlier tradition of basic management principles but others striking out in new directions like Simon's *Administrative Behavior*,[3] Gordon's *Business Leadership in the Large Corporation*,[4] Dimmock's *The Executive in Action*,[5] Drucker's *Concept of the Corporation*,[6] and of course his later classic, *The Practice of Management*,[7] to mention only the more notable.

Still another influence shaping the perceptions of business management during this period was World War II. The war brought together in the workplace Americans of all types—men and women, black and white, hill-folk and urban dwellers—and required that people get along together and cooperate for the larger good. In order to build more effective cooperation, management grew increasingly aware of the need to understand employees of diverse backgrounds whose values and behavior sometimes conflicted with what they were used to, and for this purpose the aid of specialists in social organization such as social anthropologists proved especially useful. But more than this, like all American wars, World War II was being fought for democracy and freedom. The incongruity of fighting for human rights of expression and freedom on an international scale while operating small tyrannies at the local factory level became apparent to many, especially as a new generation of managers began taking over from the old.

This led to a fourth factor that shaped management's interests

and values in the 1940s and 1950s. The new management was better educated than the old, especially the managers of the large, pub-
licly owned corporations. More than two-thirds of the executives
of the 1940s and 1950s were college graduates. Before the Great
Depression, perhaps only half as many had college backgrounds.
Better education meant broader points of view and understanding
and greater willingness to try new ideas.

The fifth influence was the rise of industrial unionism. The decisions of management were being directly challenged by union
leadership, and business leadership was responding by developing
new and more sophisticated personnel practices and in particular
searching for better understanding of the dynamics of work relationships. At the same time, new government controls required the
introduction of new personnel practices into the workplace.

Finally, from the end of the war on, business in the United States
was flourishing. Except for an occasional brief pause, the economy
grew steadily through the better part of three decades. This growth
impacted management in two ways. First, it focused attention on
growing the business and building and perfecting the organization
over the long haul as major management goals; profit making was
a consequence of effective organization and marketing strategies
rather than the proximate objective. Second, growth in both sales
and profits provided slack to permit greater management flexibility and the opportunity to experiment with new ideas.

Combining all these factors, small wonder that many executives
of the period were receptive to new ideas of broad and humane
scope. One cannot help comparing management in this post-depres-
sion, post–World War II era when Worthy was doing most of his
writing on organization with the present day. Some feeling for the
difference can be found in comparing books by business executives
in the 1950s with recent best-sellers. In the earlier period Ralph J.
Cordiner, president of General Electric, was writing about *New
Frontiers for Professional Managers*.[8] Roger Blough, chairman of
U.S. Steel, about *Free Man and the Corporation*;[9] Crawford H.
Greenewalt, president of DuPont, about *The Uncommon Man*;[10]
and T. V. Houser, chairman of Sears, about *Big Business and Hu-
man Values*.[11] More in tune with the spirit abroad in much of the
CEO world today is Allen Neuharth's *Confessions of an S.O.B.*[12]

A Personal Note

It has been a rewarding experience for me to have worked with
Worthy in reviewing his many papers and selecting those that best

represent his thinking about management and organization. It has been rewarding in part for the recollections it invoked of a stimulating and creative period in my own career. But the greatest reward has come from working with him again and being reminded of his qualities as a human being.

Not the least of these qualities has been his driving energy and ability to focus his efforts on the job at hand. I've never known anyone who worked harder and with greater efficiency than Worthy. One experience I remember vividly was at a convention of Sears personnel executives. Worthy was responsible not only for his own speech but for two others, one for his immediate superior, Clarence B. Caldwell, and the other for the vice president for administration, Fowler B. McConnell. It was the night before the big meeting. We had both suffered through a preliminary cocktail party and heavy dinner designed to loosen up the troops for the next day's big events. We were sharing a hotel room (Sears really knew how to save money in those days). I turned in, thoroughly "loosened up," by 11:00 P.M. while Worthy worked on into the night polishing the two speeches he had written for Caldwell and McConnell and finishing his own. Every so often, I would awaken, and he was still over there at the desk plugging away. I don't know whether he got any sleep that night, but those three speeches were ready to go by morning. And they were good speeches, designed to fit the style of each of the men for whom they were written.

Looking at the sheer quantity of speeches, articles, and books Worthy has turned out over the years, one would think he had nothing to do but observe life in the big corporation or big government and write up his ideas. Nothing could be further from the truth. Until recent years, Worthy was an active business executive or government administrator and did his writing on the side, evenings and weekends. For example, while the employee attitude and organization survey program in which I was involved and he was directing was going on, Worthy was revising Sears employee policies and setting up procedures for their administration, designing an entirely new compensation system for all Sears retail employees, developing a psychological testing program for executives, preparing training materials for first-line supervisors, serving variously as training director, labor relations director, and top staff assistant to the vice president and director of personnel, and I don't know what else. To make matters worse, he wrote all his own speeches, internal memos, and articles laboriously, letter by letter and word by word in longhand. It has only been in recent years that he discovered word processing. I often wonder how many new insights into organization and management we might have had if word processing had become readily available in the 1940s rather than the 1980s.

Another of Worthy's personal qualities that can be confirmed by anyone who has been associated with him is his abiding acceptance of and faith in people at all levels. He didn't have to hate management to love employees or hate employees to love management. While he had a deep respect for successful people in our society and its underlying meritocracy, he also respected the rights and dignity of those who were not all that successful. I remember on one occasion suggesting that Sears ought to do something for employees because it would likely increase their morale and efficiency. He said, "Can't we just do something for employees because it's the right thing to do?" To a great extent, Worthy's views on organization and management rest on his basic faith in people and their willingness to do the right thing if given half a chance.

I came to Sears fresh from Western Electric, where I had worked under the tutelage of Burleigh Gardner, a Harvard-trained social anthropologist, and had read everything that had guided the thinking of the Western Electric and Harvard group responsible for that program. In addition to my recently acquired knowledge of the Western Electric program and an M.A. in sociology from the University of Illinois, I had also minored in philosophy at both the A.B. and the M.A. levels and in fact did my honors paper on Bernard Bosanquet, a neo-Hegelian. Many of the ideas of neo-Hegelians and other idealistic philosophers are especially useful in analyzing the dynamics of ongoing organizations (as Mary Parker Follett found out). I am quite sure that Worthy and I got along as well as we did because he was a natural born moral philosopher who needed someone to bounce ideas off of. I happened to be well equipped to act as a sounding board, and fell right in with his style of thinking—Bernard Bosanquet and all. I can safely say that whenever I conferred with Jim Worthy I never had a small idea. He had a way of focusing on big issues, the bigger the better, and he carried you right along with him. Still does, for that matter!

Worthy has the ability to take ideas, study their implications, and systematically build a logically consistent conceptual framework that provides a prescription for action. This ability to sift through complex, disparate information and make sense of it is not an ability that is widely shared. When Worthy's natural philosophic bent and conceptual ability were coupled with the extensive factual data produced by the survey program that he directed at Sears over a period of almost fifteen years, he was able to bring together his considerable analytical skills with a great mass of live data about human behavior in diverse activities. It was a perfect combination and resulted, as already noted, in several hundred pages of analysis that together constitute a well-developed theory of organization and management.

Without Worthy, the Sears program would probably have been just another series of samplings of employee likes and dislikes, not too different from what others were doing at the time. It was his ability to analyze the implications of the survey findings that really mattered.

Concepts of Management and Organization

Although Worthy's writings speak for themselves, it will be useful to restate the main thrust of his theory in order to underscore the contributions he has made. Interestingly, one of the earliest papers in this collection, written in 1947, deals with the basic notion that most individuals and organizations have an inherent capacity to act responsibly and productively if the environment in which they are operating permits them to do so. "Our work at Sears," he said, "might be characterized as directed toward releasing the constructive forces within the groups comprising our organization." He went on to point out that factors external to the individual are the chief restraining influence. As he put it: "Many of industry's most serious problems are inherent in the structure of relationships within the organization and not in the individuals who comprise the organization." What a wonderful and refreshing approach! No blame! No dumb employees! No incompetent managers! Only people caught up in a particular web of interests and relationships that need to be understood and reckoned with.

In focusing on structure, Worthy was reflecting the findings of the Sears organization survey program, which underscored the importance of the nature of work, work relations, and hierarchical position as major factors in shaping human behavior at work. Probably for the first time in the study of human relations in industry, researchers were able to examine attitudes and relationships in many units involving the same work structure. They found that employees in the same jobs and status levels had similar attitudes and patterns of behavior from one location to the next. Appliance salesmen talked the same way in Keokuk as they did in Indianapolis and Birmingham. Researchers learned that the same tensions existed between service and sales personnel from one location to the next because of interests shaped by the nature of the work and the relationships between the two kinds of jobs. They discovered that the employee's place in the status system had a highly important influence on his or her attitudes toward the company. The reader could not come away from such studies without becoming aware of the importance of organization structure and the way it shaped job interests, relationships with others, potential for tension and out-and-out conflict, and degree of satisfaction with the organization for which employees worked.

These conclusions about structure were no surprise to social anthropologists who, following their mentor, A. R. Radcliffe Brown, focused on social structure as the major determinant of human behavior, but Worthy added considerably to the analysis. One fact from the very beginning stuck with him and challenged his thinking. The attitude surveys conducted at Sears over a period of years consistently found that larger units exhibited lower levels of cooperation and scored lower in employee morale than smaller units. In exploring the reasons for this, Worthy concluded that smaller size meant closer and more personal relations between management and employees, greater reliance on worker initiative, and greater informality in interpersonal relations that in turn led to improved understanding between employees and management, greater job freedom, a diminished sense of oppressive supervision and control, and more cooperative worker attitudes. Smaller size also meant reduced internal conflict and increased energy and ability to cope with problems as they arose. In short, it meant a better "integrated" organization in the psychoanalytical sense of an "integrated" personality—that is, a personality that has resolved its internal conflicts and is therefore better able to deal effectively with external problems and challenges.

If smaller size and closer, more personal relations between management and employees are major factors in employee morale and effective cooperation, it would appear that large, complex organizations are doomed to operate at lower levels of morale and management-worker cooperation. Not necessarily so, according to Worthy! Big organizations can be cut down to size through administrative decentralization. Here he was strongly influenced by observing the operations of General Wood's highly decentralized Sears organization. Instead of creating large, monolithic structures held together by formal systems and topside administrative controls, Worthy argued that management needed to establish more autonomous *internal* administrative units "as close as possible to the scene of action," and to delegate responsibility and authority to the lowest possible levels. He argued further that the operative reality of delegation depends not only on a superior's willingness to delegate but on the extent to which the structure of the organization makes it possible for the subordinate to exercise the powers delegated.

Effective delegation reduces the need for intervening levels of supervision, the special province of middle management. The burgeoning growth of administrative bureaucracies in American business during the last quarter century is one of the prime concerns for top management today, and Worthy's thinking on the relationship between delegation and structure should strike an especially responsive chord.

Further, in the interest of reducing organizational complexity, Worthy argued that overspecialization of jobs should be avoided to the greatest extent possible. Modern industry is characterized by excessive division of labor, often resulting in routine, uninteresting work requiring little skill. The difficulty is compounded when, as often happens, many of these unchallenging jobs are lumped together into departments where all employees are performing the same tasks. This concentration of routine, low-level activities tends to "destroy the meaning of the job" because it makes it difficult for workers to see a meaningful relationship between the work they do and the final product of the enterprise. Overspecialization also requires closer supervision and control in order to coordinate activities that have little inherent meaning to the participants, and this in turn requires additional levels of administrative bureaucracy to ensure coordination between functions that cannot occur naturally.

Overspecialization of both jobs and departments is ill-advised not only because it inhibits spontaneous cooperation, increases organizational complexity, and undermines employee morale, but because it runs contrary to the democratic values of our society. One of Worthy's early papers dealt explicitly with the issue of democratic values. In it, he calls attention to the discrepancies between American managers' typically unquestioning support of the virtues of free enterprise in society as a whole and the dictatorial ways they often run their own companies. As he put it, "It is easy for us in business to see the stifling effects of too much government control; what we often fail to see is that the essential principles we advocate for government apply equally to the internal organization and administration of our own businesses, and the violation of these principles produces within business itself the same stifling results, the same frustration of productive energy, that their violation in the larger field of government policy produces within the general economic system."

Sears' CEO, General Wood, was so taken with this idea that he had Worthy's paper distributed to all company officers with a memo stating that Worthy's views represented the official policy of the company. He went on to say that he wanted the officers to read every word and pass it along to their personnel people, retail and mail order managers, and factory managers and to see that the principles set forth were put into practice. I happened to be personnel manager of one of Sears' wholly owned factories at the time. The plant manager there was not exactly the reading type, and was thoroughly committed to the idea that freedom stopped at the factory gates. I saw in the memo and Worthy's paper a rare opportunity to call my boss's attention to other possibilities, so at our next staff meeting I reviewed Worthy's paper and asked for comments. The manager, who smoked cigars, spat with special force into his spittoon and growled, "The man's a communist." With which I asked, "Didn't you see the memo that came with it?" He said, "No!" So I read the General's memo. There was a moment's quiet and then the manager said, "Dave, the next time you pull a stunt like this you'd better be wearing armor."

Worthy had a unique opportunity to check his thinking against the reality of concrete employee behavior reported by the survey staff working under his direction. If I can put in a plug for more *qualitative* research in the organization behavior field, I would like to point out that there is no better way to evaluate one's thinking about people and organizations than to get out into the field and pay attention to what you hear and see. It is surprising how quickly your pet projections about what is going on out there are shattered when you come into contact with real people and real situations. Moreover, you become keenly aware of the complex factors that shape human behavior. Simplistic cause and effect notions go out the window. Your thinking becomes more comprehensive and therefore more realistic. There has been a recent revival of interest in qualitative approaches. I hope that interest continues. I hope, also, that there are a few James Worthys around to come up with meaningful interpretations of what it all means.

Manager Attitudes

Worthy was very much aware that effective organization depends heavily on the values of decision makers and particularly on their assumptions about human behavior. His views were strongly supported by a study he made of patterns of organization and administration in Sears' midsized stores. This study revealed marked differences in the way store managers viewed their employees. Their attitudes ranged along a continuum from trust and openness at one extreme to distrust and suspicion at the other. There was a tendency for managers toward the one extreme to be more "people oriented" and more ready to place confidence in their subordinates; these managers were more outgoing in their own behavior, more likely to be proud of their organizations, more concerned with the development and advancement of their employees, and more willing to delegate responsibility, give people their lead, and judge them by results. Managers toward the other end of the continuum tended to have less confidence in their subordinates, to be less ready to delegate responsibility, and more likely to think people had to be closely watched and controlled to ensure diligent performance and guard against mistakes. These managers organized and ran their stores in ways that made closer control possible. They had more supervisors, more formal rules, and more rigidly defined jobs, with seriously inhibiting consequences for employee initiative, adaptability, and creativity at the work level.

Worthy was fascinated by the writings of Frederick W. Taylor, founder of the scientific management movement, not only because Taylor's ideas were in many respects the antithesis of his own but also because of what they revealed about Taylor the man. In Worthy's mind, Taylor exhibited a compulsion for control not only of the workplace but of all aspects of his personal life, a characteristic similar to that of the store managers just described. Like these store managers, Taylor displayed a lack of confidence in workers and believed that every detail of how they did their work had to be determined by management. Taylor's philosophy of management was strongly influenced by his own personal insecurities. He was "fearful of the unknown and the unforeseen," and sought by every means possible to control all aspects of the work environment. In Worthy's view, many of the ills of modern industrial society derive from theories of organization that bear the imprint of Taylor's twisted personality.

As one consequence of his views on this issue, Worthy was concerned with what he saw as serious shortcomings in prevailing patterns of education for management. The problems faced by business executives are not narrowly confined to vocational and technical issues but are open-ended. The business leader works in a social and economic environment that is subject to constant and unpredictable change. The ability to cope with change requires a broader and deeper education than the narrow vocational training prevalent in schools of business as late as the 1950s; among other things, it requires better understanding of human motivation and behavior than that supplied by conventional economic assumptions. Worthy argued strongly for the introduction of the behavioral sciences into business curricula a decade before the well-known Ford Foundation and Carnegie Corporation reports made the same recommendations.

Contributions to Organization Theory

Worthy's work at Sears, as well as the research conducted by the Committee on Human Relations in Industry at the University of Chicago in the same period, is seldom included in the organization theory textbooks. There are several reasons for this, the most important of which is that Worthy's and the committee's work grew out of a social anthropological rather than the Max Weber tradition. W. Lloyd Warner, a Harvard social anthropologist, was instrumental in directing the Western Electric researchers to a social explanation of employee behavior[13] and supplied the methodological concepts used in the Bank Wiring Room study. These concepts provided the basis for analyzing the company as a social system. Warner later moved to the University of Chicago. Burleigh B. Gardner, one of Warner's students, followed him to Chicago and became research director in Western Electric's counseling program. I was fortunate in having the opportunity to work with Gardner before joining Sears, and introduced him and Warner to Worthy through whom they played an influential part in the Sears studies. There was thus a very direct connection between the later phases of the Western Electric research and that at Sears, and a solid anthropological foundation for both.

Organizational sociologists did not use the Western Electric research as their starting point but rather focused on the work of Max Weber, who was being introduced into this country by German refugees like Hans Gerth in the late 1930s, and there is little reference in the sociological literature to the work of social anthropology in the industrial field. Furthermore, the social anthropologists themselves did not pursue applied research in business and industry much beyond the 1940s; they appeared to lose interest in studying the social systems that evolved in modern American business organizations and turned to their more exciting field studies in developing countries.[14] As a consequence, most of the research includ-

ed in current organization theory texts has been undertaken by sociologists, behavioral scientists in the business schools, and social
psychologists. Worthy himself published fairly widely in trade and
business journals but to only a limited extent in academic media.[15]
He was not at the time pursuing an academic career and was interested chiefly in influencing management.

The present collection of Worthy's papers therefore serves as a
link between the work at Western Electric and current organization
theory. In an early unpublished paper written in 1943, he demonstrated a sure grasp of the concepts of social systems and functional analysis. With ideas gleaned from his reading of Roethlisberger
and Dixon and his frequent discussions with Warner and Gardner[16]
for an anthropological analysis of the modern factory as starting
points, Worthy proceeded to build a full-fledged theory of industrial organization as a social system. He had a clear understanding of
what he called the "functional unity" of business—that is, the way
in which one element of the organization affected every other element. He understood that an organization must be viewed as a
whole "since each particular relationship is interdependent with all
other relationships in the complex." He described the formal and
informal aspects of the social system that develops in a business
organization, or for that matter all goal-directed enterprises. He
viewed as one of the important tasks of management the harmo-
nizing of the formal and informal organizations. Above all, he understood how individual and group behavior is molded by organizational structure. Of particular importance was the individual's
place in the graded social system. He spoke of status symbols, of
status anxieties, and social distance, and demonstrated his clear
understanding of the interpretive concepts of social, or what was
then sometimes called functional, anthropology.

From this start, Worthy began to add his own evolving ideas
based on his experience and the organizational survey research at
Sears. One of his most important contributions was the introduction of dynamic analysis into what had been a very static field. Traditional management theory was based on so-called principles of
management, largely commonsensical judgments dealing with various aspects of organization. One that comes quickly to mind is the
principle of span of control, now more commonly known as span
of management, which holds that in order to provide effective supervision the number of subordinate managers reporting to a single
superior should be strictly limited, often to "not more than five or
six."[17] Worthy was at that time working in an organization where

five territorial vice presidents had from 150 to 250 store managers reporting directly to each of them with no intervening level of supervision. The question of span of control obviously needed rethinking and a more dynamic interpretation. Worthy contributed substantially to an understanding of how the key elements of organization interact and of the effect of different approaches to organizational design on the behavior of all members of the organization.

In particular, Worthy saw how structure shapes the nature and meaning of jobs. When an organization is set up along functional lines in order to enhance functional efficiency, the work itself is often too far removed from the *purpose* for which it is done. Not only individual jobs, but also the work of entire departments lose much of their meaning. Worthy's analysis of tall versus flat administrative structures and their relation to the types of controls exercised by management was most insightful, and his writings on the effects of administrative decentralization are the best in this area. For Worthy, one of the most important goals of management should be that of decentralizing authority and responsibility to the lowest feasible levels. He does not see decentralization as merely another administrative style to be used when the business environment is unpredictable and the technology required to produce particular results is not well understood. Major tenets of his thinking appeared to be: more minds are better than a few; problem solving should involve people at lower levels as well as high; decentralization requires job enlargement and makes jobs more meaningful; meaningful jobs mean higher morale and readier cooperation. In respect to these points, Worthy's writings of forty or fifty years ago strikingly anticipate current thinking about the need for greater employee involvement in planning and decision making at the workplace.

Worthy's analysis of "Organization X" and "Organization Y" anticipate McGregor's "Theory Y" and "Theory X."[18] This is not to suggest that McGregor took his ideas from Worthy, but it is useful to note that McGregor did not explore, as Worthy did, the implications for organization structure of managers' attitudes toward the workers in their employ, which is one of the most insightful of Worthy's contributions to organization theory.

The importance of jobs and work structure in shaping human behavior at the workplace is underscored in the findings of the Sears research. Of course, there was a good deal of research conducted elsewhere in this area, including especially William F. Whyte's study of the effects of job interests and work flow in the restaurant business,[19]

Walker and Richardson's *Human Relations in an Expanding Company*,[20] and later, Chapple and Sayles's *The Measure of Management*.[21] But once again the organization theory texts are lacking. The major textbooks in this field do attempt to show at a very abstract level the effects of various types of technologies on the administrative structures that develop, but seldom if ever show how technology and structure determine the content of jobs and patterns of work flow and what is actually going on in the organization.

The idea of building organizations that reflect the basic American values in which Worthy was so interested does not seem to concern the academic organization theorists even though it still remains a major challenge in our society. The basic question is: How do we apply democratic values in hierarchical, goal-oriented enterprises? The question is not even asked in modern texts, and yet it is fundamental.

Worthy's Role as an In-house Change Agent

One other observation that can be made of Worthy's work is that his writings were primarily directed to management while he himself was part of the management structure of a major corporation. As such, he was an active change agent (to use social anthropological parlance) within that organization from which vantage point he sought to improve his own management's understandings and behavior. It took courage to write some of the things he wrote since they often ran counter to current company practice and the prevailing wisdom of the time. He sometimes had to be somewhat more "delicate" in his approach than a disinterested outsider might have been. This led to perhaps his only stylistic fault: his periodic reassurance to his readers that he is not trying to destroy their favorite notions but to call their attention to other possibilities. The fact that so many of his ideas were accepted by the higher levels of Sears and other managements is testimony both to the quality of the ideas and to the quality of top business executives in America during the 1940s and 1950s.

Editorial Note

As indicated previously, the present collection of Worthy's papers is limited to those that grew out of his experiences primarily at Sears in the 1940s and early 1950s. While each paper is identified as to date of writing, related papers are organized into four major areas regardless of chronology. Part 1 provides background on Sears as an organization and General Robert E. Wood as a manager and an overview of the human relations research program that developed under Worthy's direction. Part 2 focuses directly on the research program and Worthy's interpretation of the results. Part 3 contains a series of papers written over the years in which Worthy further explores his concepts of organization structure and performance. Part 4 covers Worthy's observations regarding management values and their effect on organization structure and employee performance.

Together, the papers represent a significant contribution to management theory and practice.

Notes

1. A. A. Berle and G. C. Means, *The Modern Corporation and Private Property* (New York: Macmillan, 1932).

2. Chester I. Barnard, *The Functions of the Executive* (Cambridge: Harvard University Press, 1942).

3. Herbert A. Simon, *Administrative Behavior* (New York: Macmillan, 1948).

4. Robert A. Gordon, *Business Leadership in the Large Corporation* (Berkeley: University of California Press, 1945).

5. Marshall E. Dimmock, *The Executive in Action* (New York: Harper & Brothers, 1945).

6. Peter F. Drucker, *Concept of the Corporation* (New York: John Day Company, 1946).

7. Peter F. Drucker, *The Practice of Management* (New York: Harper & Brothers, 1954).

8. Ralph J. Cordiner, *New Frontiers for Professional Managers* (New York: McGraw-Hill, 1950).

9. Roger Blough, *Free Man and the Corporation* (New York: McGraw-Hill, 1959).

10. Crawford H. Greenewalt, *The Uncommon Man* (New York: McGraw-Hill, 1959).

11. Theodore V. Houser, *Big Business and Human Values* (New York: McGraw-Hill, 1957).

12. Allen Neuharth, *Confessions of an S.O.B.* (New York: Doubleday, 1989).

13. See David G. Moore, "The Committee on Human Relations in Industry at the University of Chicago, 1943–1948," in Daniel A. Wren and John A. Pearce II, eds., *Papers Dedicated to the Development of Modern Management: Celebrating 100 Years of Modern Management* (Ada, Ohio: Academy of Management, 1986).

14. See David G. Moore, "Industrial Anthropology: Conditions of Survival," *City & Society* 2:1 (June 1988): 5, 8.

15. Note in particular his "Organizational Structure and Employee Morale," in *American Journal of Sociology* (15 Apr. 1950).

16. See Burleigh G. Gardner, *Human Relations in Industry* (Chicago: Richard D. Irwin, 1945).

17. Cf. Lyndall Urwick, *The Elements of Administration* (New York: Harper & Brothers, 1943), 52.

18. Douglas McGregor, *The Human Side of Enterprise* (New York: McGraw-Hill, 1960).

19. William Foote Whyte, *Human Relations in the Restaurant Industry* (New York: McGraw-Hill, 1948).

20. F. L. W. Richardson, Jr., and C. R. Walker, *Human Relations in an Expanding Company* (New Haven: Yale Labor Management Center, 1948).

21. Eliot D. Chapple and Leonard R. Sayles, *The Measure of Management* (New York: MacMillan, 1961).

Lean But Not Mean

Part 1

The Setting

James Worthy's ideas emerged out of a fortuitous convergence of people and events at a particular time and in a particular setting. Of special significance was the Sears organization itself. By the late 1930s, when Worthy was first employed at Sears, the company was characterized by a radically decentralized management structure and minimal bureaucratic controls. The Sears organization differed sharply from the more traditional forms of organization and management prevailing at that time, which called for rigid topside controls, narrow spans of control, and multiple layers of supervision. For an inquisitive and thoughtful person like Worthy, Sears was a natural laboratory for observing new management ideas in action and studying their consequences.

Although Sears had a tradition of informality and organizational "looseness" under both Richard W. Sears and Julius Rosenwald, Sears' decentralized managerial structure at the time of Worthy's tenure reflected the policies of General Robert E. Wood, the company's CEO. "The General" was responsible for the conversion of Sears from a narrowly focused mail order company into a combined retail and mail order enterprise that rapidly developed into the largest and most profitable merchandising organization in the world. The early years of this growth were marked by organizational and administrative confusion that Wood handled in unique fashion.

Rather than impose stringent managerial controls to insure order, he took the drastic step of eliminating in one fell swoop virtually the entire middle management structure of the company and placed his reliance on getting capable people into the right places and, once there, holding them responsible for results but giving them wide latitude in the way they accomplished those results. During this same period, researchers at Harvard and Western Electric were reporting on the results of a series of studies of employee attitudes and behavior that began in the early 1920s and ended in the early 1930s. These studies directly challenged prevailing economic and industrial engineering assumptions about employee motivation. Of particular interest was the analysis of an industrial organization as a social system. The factory was not just a technological apparatus designed to create products and services for economic profit. It was above all a *human* organization in which expectations, motives, and satisfactions were psychologically and socially derived. Although Western Electric, Hawthorne Works, was very much a part of the Chicago scene, its research activities were not widely known in the business community. It took several migrant professors and researchers from Harvard to accelerate the diffusion of Western Electric concepts. W. Lloyd Warner, social anthropologist, and his student, Burleigh B. Gardner, both of whom were close to the Harvard Business School researchers, came to Chicago in the 1930s—Warner to a professorship at the University of Chicago and Gardner to a research position at Western Electric. They were joined later by William F. Whyte, another of Warner's students at Harvard. All of them participated in the development of the Committee on Human Relations in Industry at the University of Chicago, a major business-supported research effort to apply anthropological and sociological concepts to the analysis of employee behavior in industry.

The two papers included in part 1 of this collection are introductory and provide an overview, first, of the organizational setting at Sears largely created by the organization policies of General Wood and, second, of the human relations research program that developed under Worthy's direction both before and after collaboration with the Committee on Human Relations at the University of Chicago.

—David G. Moore

1

The Organization Policies of General Robert E. Wood

Robert E. Wood, West Point 1900, headed supply, manpower management, and other support services for the U.S. Army in the building of the Panama Canal and served as quartermaster general in the First World War. After a stint at Montgomery Ward following the war, he joined Sears, Roebuck in late 1924 and soon thereafter launched the company, until then strictly a mail order business, on an ambitious expansion program that in due course built Sears into the largest and most profitable merchandising organization in the world. Much of Wood's success is traceable directly to his innovative philosophy of organization and style of management.

For the purposes of this paper, it would serve no purpose to trace the variety of organizational arrangements tried during the first few years of Wood's and Sears' retail experience.[1] Suffice it to say, one arrangement after another was tried in an effort to find the form best calculated to achieve desired results. One consistent theme, however, ran through all the changes made: a tension between regional and functional executives on the one hand seeking to exercise closer supervision and control over the stores, and General Wood on the other seeking to hold overhead to a minimum and to allow maximum freedom and autonomy to individual store managers in the way they ran their stores.

General Wood's concept of organization was a concept of managerial decentralization: of delegating effective responsibility and authority as far down the line as possible, of placing well-qualified people in key positions at the scene of action, and of allowing them wide latitude for the exercise of initiative and judgment in the light of local circumstances. He had an abiding faith in the capacity of people of at least basic ability to rise to the needs of situations in which they were placed, and he had an equally abiding antipathy to unnecessary overhead expense.

Both predilections found dramatic expression when at the depth of the depression in 1932 he wiped out in one fell swoop the entire middle management structure that had grown up in the field and had all stores and mail order plants report directly to Chicago. In making this drastic move, which was opposed by virtually all his key associates, he was motivated not only by expense consider-ations but by a growing conviction that by making this move he would strengthen management at the operating level.

Wood's central concern was the building of merchandising com-petence *in the stores*. The retail system had expanded rapidly and its personnel was largely inexperienced, at least in the newly evolv-ing Sears way of doing things. One school of thought, espoused by many of his key people, argued for building well-qualified staffs at the district levels, "thus permitting the use of mediocre men in lesser positions."[2] But Wood didn't want "mediocre men." He wanted people of ability who could learn and grow on their own and who would develop into better managers because they were not held up by crutches.

The move took courage. Prior to that time, under the district structure, supervision of individual stores had been close and de-tailed, and decisions of even relatively minor import had to be cleared at the district level or higher. With dramatic suddenness, managers who had been accustomed to look to higher authority for much of what they did found themselves forced to act on their own and to take full responsibility for their actions; it was a case of sink or swim. Some managers sank, but a high proportion of them sur-vived and developed into a corps of exceptionally able executives from whose ranks emerged a generation of senior administrators and officers who carried the company to new and previously un-dreamed of levels of achievement.

Another revealing event occurred toward the end of the sharp 1937–38 recession. Sales and profits were down and a special com-mittee of senior executives brought in a report calling, among oth-er things, for closer supervision of the stores to keep local manag-ers from making the kinds of mistakes the committee had uncovered. In responding to the committee's report, General Wood gave what was perhaps the definitive statement of his managerial philosophy:

> We have a decentralized system of management for our stores, of which the manager is the key point. While our retail stores have devel-oped certain weaknesses during the past year, which have been brought out by the depression, I do not regard them as serious weaknesses. . . .

To make their stores successful in a decentralized system, it is essential that the responsibility be placed on the manager. He must decide just what merchandise to select from the offerings made to him, and just what price to put on this merchandise. If his initiative in this regard is removed and if he is visited constantly by supervisors and inspectors and representatives of the parent organization, it is only a matter of time before his morale will break down.

Having spent the greater part of my life in large organizations, I think I know their besetting weaknesses and the reasons for the decay of most of them. No organization is perfect, even the most efficient one. The easiest thing in the world is to find weaknesses in a large organization. The natural human tendency for the men at the top and the bright young members of their staff, if they discover a weakness, is to set up a system of checks and balances that will obviate the weakness, forgetting that in most cases the remedy finally turns out worse than the disease. While systems are important, our main reliance must always be put on *men* rather than on systems. If we devise too elaborate a system of checks and balances, and have too many inspectors going out as representatives of the parent organization, it will be only a matter of time before the self-reliance and initiative of our managers will be destroyed and our organization will be gradually converted into a huge bureaucracy.

I have faith in the great majority of our managers. I believe they will work out their own salvation with a relatively small amount of supervision from the officers and the staff. While system is important, I repeat that our main reliance must be on men rather than on systems, and the proper selection and training of managers is the most important work of the officers and the retail staff.[3]

Wood was convinced that no matter how wise and capable those on corporate or regional staffs might be, they could not do as good a job of running the stores from a distance as competent local management could do on the spot. Fundamental to his approach was a deep-seated reliance on the experience and good judgment of store managers, provided they had been properly selected in the first place. He did not want them subjected to too close supervision and control. He did not want them hemmed in by organizational supports on which they could easily become dependent. He insisted on giving them the autonomy they needed to deal with local problems and respond to local opportunities. To Wood, organization was not merely a means for directing and coordinating human effort but for fostering human growth. He conceived the task of building a business as essentially that of developing people. He did not want "mediocre men." He wanted the kind of organization that put a premium on finding good people and, once found, providing them a working environment that would bring out their best.

The structure he designed for this purpose has been characterized as "broad" or "flat," in contrast to the more "vertical" or "tall" structures with many organizational layers between top and bottom.[4] A striking fact about the Sears retail organization under General Wood from the early 1930s to the mid-1950s was that there were only four levels of supervision between the president of the company and salespeople in the stores: the territorial officers, zone or group managers, store managers, and department heads. This was remarkable for a widely dispersed enterprise that by the time of Wood's retirement in 1954 employed nearly 150,000 people in the retail stores alone.

Under Wood, Sears not only paid little heed but went directly counter to "span of control" theories that held that the number of subordinate executives reporting to a single superior should be severely limited to enable the superior to exercise the detailed direction and control generally considered necessary. On the contrary, key executives (especially at the officer and senior executive levels) were deliberately given *more* subordinates than they could control closely. The explicit purpose was to enforce maximum decentralization of authority and responsibility to successively lower levels of organization.

The purpose of maximum decentralization, in turn, was to build strength at all levels by creating a situation that put a premium on finding good people and giving them room to grow. There was not much organization structure on which people could lean; they had to rely largely on their own abilities. Their superiors could give them only limited help, but by the same token they could not unduly restrict the unfolding of their potentialities. Not all individuals could function effectively under this kind of management; it required large measures of self-reliance, self-confidence, and personal capacity. The system placed a premium on finding people with these qualities and tended to weed out those who lacked them in adequate degree. It was no place for "mediocre men."

The phenomenal success of Sears under General Wood's leadership was made possible in large part through the efforts of the highly capable men and women who grew up in this system. In a very literal sense, the business was built by building people. And a key element in building people was the simple, highly decentralized organization structure designed by General Wood for precisely that purpose.

In what some might characterize as circular reasoning, he saw clearly that if a highly decentralized system was to work, measures would have to be taken to assure that all key positions were filled by well-qualified people. If the reasoning was circular, the practice had something of the same kind of circular reinforcement as a particle accelerator in nuclear physics. People of high ability were required to make the system work, and the system enlarged the abilities of those who were in it. Not a bad arrangement, really.

To Wood, the process of managing was essentially the selection, placement, rewarding, and replacement of people. He expressed his thinking on this score late in 1931 in a memorandum to his territorial officers:

> I want to impress you with the vital selection of personnel. Our whole future depends on the proper selection, proper reward and proper elimination of personnel. You cannot personally remedy matters in any unit under your control. You haven't got the time. But you can remedy matters by getting the right men in the right place and I have not seen a single instance in any Territory, Mail Order House, District, or Store where the selection of right men did not almost immediately bring results. Put your personnel work first because it is the most important.[5]

Apparently because he saw the personnel function as so intimately a part of management, he at first refused to allow the territorial officers to have their own personnel staffs or to set up a central personnel office. However, at the time he wiped out the entire retail middle management structure he recognized that orderly provision had to be made for the handling of executive personnel and he at that time established the national personnel office reporting to the newly appointed vice president for retail administration and personnel.

After two abortive starts, Clarence B. Caldwell was appointed to the post of retail personnel director in 1933. Caldwell had had no experience with personnel work as such but he had been a successful store manager. Wood told him, "Hire whatever technical talent you need, but I want a man as personnel director who knows what it takes to be a good store manager." There thus grew up in Sears a tradition of personnel administration not as a technical specialty but as an integral part of the process of management. Because of the size to which the organization had grown it might be necessary to establish the function as a separate entity, but it could be and was staffed by people who were first and foremost proven managers who kept their personnel work in a managerial perspective.

Under Caldwell's leadership the personnel department developed into one of the strongest components of the parent organization. Initially the department was concerned almost exclusively with executive personnel matters and its energies were concentrated on the task of meeting the seemingly insatiable demand of the rapidly growing retail system for qualified store management talent. Executives with good Sears retail backgrounds were brought into the personnel department and assigned to the several geographic areas into which the company was divided. It was the task of these men to work with the stores and with the zone managers and territorial offices to build reservoirs of promotable people, to lay out job rotation schedules for them, to counsel with them and to evaluate their progress, and to participate in decisions regarding their advancement.

For administrative purposes, these activities were organized into the "Reserve Group Program." While an executive development program in every sense of the word, and a singularly productive one at that, the program made little use of formal training methods. Chief reliance was placed on hands-on job experience, and the program consisted of the planned rotation of Reserve Group members through those store activities deemed most important for their future careers. People were rotated through assignments not as "observers" but as fully responsible practitioners. Job vacancies were viewed not just as positions to be filled but as opportunities to provide valuable experience to people with promise.

It was Sears policy that decisions on the filling of all positions from the level of assistant store manager up required the concurrence of three persons: the superior to whom the position reported, that person's supervisor, and the personnel field man. The field man was only one of three, but his voice carried special weight. He, in effect, "controlled the inventory" because it was his records that were reviewed by the group making the decision and he was usually the only one of the three who had personal knowledge of all candidates under consideration. He was thus often able to say, "These two people are equally qualified for the job, but this one will work out better in this particular assignment than that one." The personnel field positions thus quickly acquired considerable power. Caldwell played much the same role in the filling of higher level executive posts, with an even greater augmentation of power. He and his key staff took pains not to abuse their privileged positions and as a result came to enjoy a unique degree of respect and confidence within the organization.

In the early days of Sears' retail system, chief reliance had been placed on recruiting experienced retail executives from outside the company. Beginning with Caldwell's appointment as retail personnel director, increasing emphasis was placed on promotion from within, and he frequently admonished the store managers to include in their hiring for rank and file positions at least a scattering of people who had potential qualifications to move to higher level posts. It was then the task of the personnel field men, in consultation with the store managers, to identify such promotable talent, to place them on the Reserve Group, and to move them to higher levels of responsibility as rapidly as they were ready. This relatively informal method of recruiting potential executive talent was supplemented by an aggressive college recruiting program.

At the start of the retail expansion, Sears was wholly dependent on outside recruitment for the filling of store executive positions. By about 1939–40, the company was fully self-sufficient in terms of promotable talent, able to meet even the severe losses to war industries and the military during the war; following the war, fortified by the return of executives and trainees, the program successfully staffed the tremendous retail expansion of 1946–54.

General Wood wrote late in his active career: "The only way for a large organization to function is to decentralize, to delegate real responsibility to the man on the job. But be certain you have the right man on the job."[6]

By establishing a strong central personnel department with primary responsibility for recruiting, training, placing, and moving executives, General Wood took the necessary steps to make sure he had "the right man on the job." Only thus could the highly decentralized system of management fashioned by Wood work successfully—and work successfully it did during Wood's long tenure and for many years thereafter.

Notes

Excerpted from a paper delivered at the 1978 meeting of the Academy of Management.

1. A perceptive analysis of the sequence of organizational changes is presented in Alfred D. Chandler, Jr., *Strategy and Structure: Chapters in the History of Industrial Enterprise* (Cambridge: M.I.T. Press, 1962), chap. 5. See also the author's *Shaping an American Institution: Robert E. Wood and Sears, Roebuck* (Urbana: University of Illinois Press, 1984).

2. Memorandum from G. E. Humphrey, June 6, 1930, quoted in Chandler, *Strategy and Stucture*, 252.

3. R. E. Wood, memorandum to officers and Retail Committee, October 27, 1938 (author's files).

4. See also chapter 7 of the author's *Shaping an American Institution.*

5. R. E. Wood, memorandum to territorial officers, December 21, 1931, quoted in Chandler, *Strategy and Structure,* 255.

6. R. E. Wood, *Ordinance* magazine, July-August 1951 (author's files).

2

Overview of the Research Program

Background

A significant amount of human relations research was conducted by Sears, Roebuck and Co. during the decade of the 1940s, with some carry-over into the 1950s. Much of this was done in cooperation with the Committee on Human Relations in Industry of the University of Chicago and with Social Research, Inc., a private consulting firm headed by the two principals of the Committee on Human Relations, W. Lloyd Warner and Burleigh B. Gardner, and largely staffed with personnel trained by the committee. The purpose of the present paper is to record Sears' participation in these collaborative efforts.

Sears, Roebuck Management

The Sears organization built by General Robert E. Wood was remarkable in many ways (Worthy 1984). Wood was an army man, trained at West Point and with a distinguished record as head of supply and manpower services in the building of the Panama Canal and as chief of the Army Quartermaster Corps during the First World War. Because of his experience in large-scale procurement, he joined Montgomery Ward in 1919 as merchandising vice president, a post from which he was summarily fired in the fall of 1924, chiefly for his insistent urging that the company add retail stores to its mail order operations, a course adamantly opposed by Ward's president.

The head of Sears, Roebuck, Julius Rosenwald, recognizing his good fortune in having a man of Wood's experience becoming unexpectedly available, hired him immediately, with a commitment to support his radical retail notions. Wood opened his first Sears store early in 1925 and others quickly followed. The venture was eminently successful, and three years later Wood was named president and chief executive. Under his leadership, Sears not only survived the Great Depression but learned from it many lessons that enabled Wood to build in a few years' time the largest and most profitable merchandising business the world had ever known.

Strong Personnel Function

For an army man, Wood had a curious distrust of authoritarian direction and control from above. His store managers, and to a considerable extent the department managers within the local stores as well, had wide discretion in the selection of merchandise to be carried, the quantities to be ordered, and the prices to be charged. To Wood, it was fundamental that managers at all levels worked best if they were held accountable for results but left free, within broad limits, in the ways they accomplished those results (Worthy 1984, chap. 7, "Organization Policies"). But Wood did not believe in blind delegation. For this kind of organization to work, special care had to be taken in the selection and placement of people, and this called for a strong personnel department.

Wood was also aware that a widely dispersed system of mail order plants and retail stores, each functioning with considerable autonomy, required that positive measures be taken to avoid friction and divisiveness between employees and management, to maintain high levels of morale, and to provide motivation for superior individual and group performance (Worthy 1984, chap. 9, "Employee Policies"). This, too, called for a strong personnel department.

In Clarence B. Caldwell, one of his best store managers, Wood found the man he needed to head that critical function. Appointed director of retail personnel in 1933, his responsibilities broadened in due course to include the entire company and he became one of the most influential and respected of all Wood's lieutenants. Encouraged by Wood to develop rational and soundly based policies for all aspects of Sears' personnel operations, Caldwell in 1938 established a research and planning function within his department, and it was my great good fortune to be hired for that responsibility.

With college majors in English and economics, I was not a trained management or research person. However, I had been an assistant deputy administrator of the National Recovery Administration, deeply committed to the humane values of the early New Deal, and after aiding in writing the history of NRA following its demise had served as personnel manager for a Milwaukee department store. I was attracted to Sears because it was obviously a fast-growing company with good opportunities for advancement, and because it was already gaining a reputation for excellence in management-employee relationships. I was also intrigued by the fact that General Wood was one of the few big businessmen who had been a strong supporter of President Roosevelt before breaking with him over his war policies. It seemed to me that Sears was the kind of company I wanted to work for. I was not disappointed.

Employee Attitude Surveys

One of the first undertakings of my new unit in the Sears personnel department was the design and implementation of a standard compensation plan for all retail employees. Other activities included studies of employee turnover and the demographic characteristics of company personnel, projections of future executive and employee requirements, designing better methods of selection and training, analyzing the operation of employee benefit plans, and exploring possible means for improving them.

Initiation of the Attitude Survey Program

A particularly significant phase of the work undertaken by the research and planning unit was the development of systematic means for assessing employee attitudes and morale. By 1939, General Wood and other senior Sears officers were growing increasingly uncomfortable with the fact that they no longer had the close touch with day-to-day affairs of the rapidly expanding retail system they once had had, and Caldwell and I were directed to come up with a means for providing "a reliable and continuing flow of information about . . . how we are getting along with our people" (Worthy 1984, 152; see also Jones 1952).

It seemed clear from the outset that the best way to find out what employees thought about their jobs and the company was to ask them, and for this purpose an outside firm, Houser Associates, was retained to design and administer questionnaires that employees answered anonymously (Houser 1938). By the end of 1939, a number of experimental surveys had been made of representative stores, and the results were encouraging. Wood and his fellow officers felt that a good start had been made and that the surveys were giving them at least some of the information they wanted. The project continued on a gradually expanding basis until Pearl Harbor, when it was suspended for the duration of the war.

Houser's approach was essentially that of traditional market research: count the number of people who respond in different ways to a series of questions. The results were interesting and useful as far as they went, but puzzling in many respects. Clearly, something more than counting was needed. As my staff and I studied the numbers, we became more and more convinced that social influences of some form were at work and that a sociological approach to the data might prove useful.

Interpretation of Survey Results

By fortunate coincidence, early in 1941 a young man with a master's degree in sociology from the University of Illinois applied to me for a job. He was David G. Moore, at that time a member of the personnel research staff of Western Electric Company. I was impressed by his ability to describe work relations phenomena in terms that seemed to make sense. I hired him at once and put him to work analyzing the data our employee attitude surveys were beginning to produce.

Moore organized the Houser data in new ways, with interesting results. While within all groups there were relatively normal statistical distributions, there were significant variations by age, sex, length of service, type of work, level of authority, size of store, size and economic base of city, geographical region, and so on. The data began to be more meaningful, but raised even more intriguing questions as to why there should be such large differences in the attitudes of different groups toward precisely the same thing.

As the survey data were studied further, it became increasingly clear that store organizations, and probably commercial and industrial organizations in general, were "social systems," and that the parts of the systems were closely interrelated. Compensation was not an independent variable, any more than hours of work, working conditions, or quality of supervision, and changes in any of these or in other significant elements in the working situation could not be made without affecting other elements and without modifying the whole. The importance of relationships and the analysis of attitudes and behavior in terms of group identity and organizational status loomed increasingly large in our thinking (Worthy 1943).

During this period, Moore often spoke to me about Dr. Burleigh B. Gardner, for whom he had worked at Western Electric. Gardner was a social anthropologist on the staff of William J. Dickson doing research on the Hawthorne counseling program, and Moore had been one of his assistants. From Moore's own training and from what he had learned from Gardner, he was convinced that some of the concepts of social anthropology, particularly those related to status and social class, would be useful in what we were trying to understand at Sears. Sometime in late 1942 or early 1943, Moore arranged for the three of us to have lunch at the Palmer House. That was the beginning of a long period of fruitful collaboration.

Shortly thereafter I met with Gardner and W. Lloyd Warner, who were then in the process of organizing the Committee on Human Relations in Industry at the University of Chicago. I was as well impressed by Warner as by Gardner, and the plans they had in mind held intriguing possibilities. Sears became one of the first corporate supporters of their new venture.

Postwar Planning

During the war years, General Wood directed his corporate staff departments to utilize whatever time they could spare from otherwise pressing duties to prepare for the period of peace that would eventually come. Among other things, the personnel department addressed the subject of improving the employee survey program, and the services of the Committee on Human Relations were engaged for that purpose.

The new survey program drew heavily on Warner's and Gardner's comprehensive grasp of the concepts of social anthropology and their experience with the methods of field research. Gardner's involvement in the nondirective interviewing program of Western Electric was also useful. Because Sears planned to use its program company-wide rather than at a single plant as at Western Electric, reliance could not be placed on nondirective interviewing alone; there were simply too many people and too much geography to cover.

The program as it finally emerged ready for use as soon as the war was over combined questionnaires and interviews. A simplified questionnaire was administered to all employees in a store or other company unit, and the statistical results analyzed to make tentative identification of areas that appeared to represent problems. A team trained in nondirective techniques then interviewed executives and employees in the unit itself, and others likely to have knowledge of the problems, to learn more about what caused them. The questionnaires were used somewhat as "geiger counters" to locate areas meriting closer investigation, which might be certain departments, or particular classes of employees, or some aspect of company policy or local practice, or perhaps some recent event. In addition to locating areas of difficulty, the questionnaires also gave some indication of what the difficulties might be. Armed with information such as this, the interviewers knew where to look and what to look for (Worthy 1947, 1950).

Although Gardner was deeply involved in designing the survey program and he and his committee staff in training survey teams and interpreting survey results, most of the actual survey work was conducted by members of the Sears personnel staff. Gardner was convinced from his extensive contacts with Sears employees in the course of developing the program that their level of confidence in the integrity of the company was sufficiently high that it would not be necessary for the questionnaires to be administered and the interviews conducted by staff of the Committee on Human Relations or by an outside firm, as had been done before the war with Houser Associates. This was a wise move because work as a member of survey teams proved to be valuable training for future personnel and store executives.

The New Survey Program

By this time Moore, under my general supervision, headed the Sears personnel research and planning staff and was in immediate charge of the survey program. His training as a sociologist, his experience with the personnel interviewing program at Western Electric, and his continuing collaboration with Gardner and Warner enabled him to provide the creative direction the program required, including training the program staff and interpreting survey results. Under Moore's leadership and with Gardner's aid, the staff developed high orders of analytical skill, and learned to use the questionnaire results much as a doctor uses tests as part of his procedure in diagnosing patient ills.

At one point, thought was given to the possibility of developing "a typology of the malfunctioning of organizations" that might be useful in diagnosing organizational problems. This possibility was suggested by the frequency with which profiles of questionnaire and interview data tended to form patterns that began to grow familiar, and the tendency for certain kinds of problems to occur in identifiable syndromes (Worthy, April 1950). Unfortunately, because of other research demands this possibility was not systematically pursued, although recognition of regularities definitely enhanced the skills of the interviewing teams.

The survey program was undertaken initially for the straightforward purpose of finding how well employees liked their jobs and whether there were factors in the work situation causing dissatisfaction. The assumption was that once any such factors were discovered, necessary corrective action could be taken and all would be well. This assumption proved only partially valid, because in the new survey program we soon learned that many employee relations problems could not be understood, much less influenced, except in terms of the broader context of the organization in which they had developed.

Gradually, the scope of the surveys was expanded to include the functioning of the unit (store, factory, and so on) as a whole and the entire pattern of technical processes and formal and informal relationships that comprise the unit. In recognition of this broader scope, the name of the program was changed from "morale surveys" to "organization surveys," and rather than simply discovering causes of employee dissatisfaction the purpose became to analyze strains or cleavages within operating units that might impede their functioning. In this context, determining levels of morale served chiefly as an aid in locating problem areas for further study by a field survey team (Worthy, January 1950).

A major early conclusion of the survey program was stated in a 1949 memorandum to Clarence Caldwell: "High morale is a by-product of sound organization. It is not a result that can be achieved by and for itself; above all, it is not a result of 'being nice to people' or plying them with favors. High morale is not something to be achieved at the expense of good operating results. The same policies, attitudes, and practices which are best calculated to produce good operating results are precisely the policies, attitudes, and practices which produce high levels of employee morale" (Worthy 1949).

Ancillary Values

In addition to its other values, because of the manner in which it was organized and administered the survey program developed into one of the company's most effective general executive training tools. Care was taken from the outset to keep the program from being perceived as threatening, and in point of fact the surveys were conducted primarily for the benefit of the manager or other executive in direct charge of the unit involved. Surveys were concerned not merely with identifying the existence and origin of difficulties; their primary purpose was problem solving, and to this end great reliance was placed on the local executives themselves rather than on the survey team. The central objective was to give the responsible executive a better understanding of the way his organization was functioning, the various influences at work in his particular situation, and the ways these were impacting the attitudes and behavior of his people. At the same time, an effort was made to give the executive a more effective way of thinking about both his organization and its problems, with the expectation that with a better way of thinking about both he would be in a better position to take constructive action directed at the root of difficulties rather than at their superficial symptoms (Worthy et al. 1947).

After a survey was completed and its results analyzed, the member of the personnel staff under whose direction it had been conducted would meet with the executive responsible for the unit and his staff. After reviewing the survey findings, the local executives would be questioned as to what interpretation might be put upon them, and a discussion would follow as to the best means for dealing with whatever problems had been uncovered. The survey "report" generally consisted of a memorandum to the manager saying, in effect, that "in our meeting we agreed that such and such things required attention and that such and such action would be taken." The local executives were thus intimately involved both in identifying problems and in designing solutions. It was an interesting example of the "case method" of teaching, with the considerable pedagogical advantage that the "case" was not some abstract problem but the company unit for which the executive himself was personally responsible. The learning results were impressive.

The program proved valuable in many other ways as well. It provided management with insight and understanding it could have gained in no other way of the actual state of affairs within the very large and widely dispersed organization into which Sears by the late 1940s had grown. It produced a comprehensive body of factual material by which management was able to refine and improve personnel policies under the rapidly changing conditions of the postwar period. In some ways, its most valuable contribution was the message it carried to employees of management's concern for running the business in ways that would serve their needs as well as the company's.

The survey program developed into an invaluable administrative tool, and with modifications is still being used by Sears as a significant feature of that company's widely admired personnel system.

Social Research, Inc.

Sears' work with the Committee on Human Relations in Industry went beyond the survey program, and heavy demands were placed on the committee's resources. We at Sears became increasingly impatient with the difficulties and delays of working through university channels. Our primary interest was in solving problems, and sometimes fast action was needed. But to start a project, it was necessary first to prepare a detailed written plan, which then had to be reviewed by university authorities and finally converted into a contract to be signed by appropriate officers of the university and the company. Weeks and sometimes longer were required to get projects under way, and while this might have been fast by university standards it was often exasperatingly slow by our needs. Early in 1947, therefore, I urged Gardner and Warner to establish an independent consulting firm with which we could deal. With Clarence Caldwell's and General Wood's ready approval, I offered them a contract that would underwrite the basic expenses of their new firm for its first two years of operation.

Thus was born Social Research, Inc., with Warner as chairman and Gardner as president. Warner continued for several years longer as professor at the University of Chicago, until moving to Michigan State in 1959 to introduce the study of social sciences into that university's School of Business. Gardner severed his formal connection with the university to devote himself full time to SRI, as the new firm quickly became known. He was succeeded as executive director of the committee by William Foote Whyte, who served in the post until 1948 when he accepted a professorship at Cornell University.

With Whyte's leaving, the Committee on Human Relations in Industry was disbanded. It had operated for a total of only five years, but those years had been remarkably productive, particularly in demonstrating the utility of applying the concepts of social anthropology to the practical problems of business and industry. And those concepts themselves were greatly enriched by exposure to modern forms of economic organization rather than to those of primitive societies, which had previously been the discipline's primary focus of attention.

Work with Social Research, Inc.

The work and influence of the committee did not die with it. Relieved of the burden of university red tape, Sears' work with Gardner and Warner through Social Research, Inc., grew apace.

Some of the more significant aspects of that work during the years 1947–52 included studies of special problem groups such as low status employees, commission salesmen, warehouse workers, and veterans returning from military service. A study of relationships between the company's sources of supply and its buying organization was particularly useful, as was an analysis of internal relationships within the buying organization itself. A study of the social class background of upwardly mobile employees proved useful in refining the company's recruitment and executive development policies.

In the course of several studies on a variety of subjects, attention was given to factors shaping the size and structure of administrative units within larger components of organization, and the influence of such factors on decision making processes (Worthy 1952). All told, an extensive number and variety of projects were undertaken in cooperation with Gardner and Social Research, Inc., for the purpose of improving the effectiveness of the company's organizational and managerial practices and for enhancing the quality of management-employee relationships.

While some of the results of this work were published, most of it was not. Unlike studies conducted under university auspices, which typically have publication of some kind in view, studies conducted in collaboration with SRI were basically done for administrative purposes, that is, to provide officers and executives with information and proposals that would be helpful in the discharge of their managerial responsibilities; many "reports" were simply in the form of memoranda. When a study had served the particular purpose for which it was made, it was usually filed away and attention turned to other more immediately pressing projects. Sponsored work with the Committee on Human Relations was essentially "scholarly," while that done with SRI tended to be much more along "consulting" lines. Fortunately, some of the more important results of this work found its way into Moore's doctoral dissertation (Moore 1950), and to that extent gained a measure of permanence it would not otherwise enjoy.

Conclusion

This study was in effect the climax of the collaboration between Sears, Roebuck and Social Research, Inc., as successor to the Committee on Human Relations in Industry. Social Research continued under Gardner's leadership to operate as a successful consulting firm until 1985, but did little further work of importance for Sears in the areas of organization structure and employee behavior. To a very large extent, the close collaboration that had characterized the

1940s had depended on the personal relationships between Gardner, Moore, and myself, and while the three of us to this day enjoy each other's friendship we have had little opportunity to work together for many years.

Moore left Sears in 1950 to complete his doctorate at the University of Chicago, and went on from there to a distinguished academic career. At the beginning of 1953 I joined the Eisenhower Administration as Assistant Secretary of Commerce. By this time, Clarence Caldwell's health was failing, General Wood was soon to retire, and there was a change in the leadership of the personnel function. In light of the results of the studies just described, it came as no surprise that important changes in managerial style ensued. The new style was effective in many ways, and served Sears well for many years thereafter. But it left no room for the kind of objective research in organizational behavior that had characterized the preceding ten years. It had been a productive ten years, and perhaps had gone as far as it was practical at that time to go.

Note

Excerpted from "Human Relations Research at Sears, Roebuck during the 1940s: A Memoir," in Daniel A. Wren and John A. Pearce II, eds., *Papers Dedicated to the Development of Modern Management* (Ada, Ohio: Academy of Management, 1986).

References

Gardner, Burleigh B. and David G. Moore. 1950. *Human Relations in Industry,* 2d ed. Homewood, Ill.: Richard D. Irwin.

Houser, J. David. 1938. *What People Want from Business.* New York: McGraw-Hill Book Company.

Jones, Virginia. February 1, 1952. "Sears Employee Attitude Program," *Personnel Report No. 52.* Sears, Roebuck and Co., Personnel Department (Sears Archives). Jones was a member of the employee survey staff from its earliest days.

Moore, David G.. 1950. "Proposal for Ph.D. Dissertation" (Sears Archives).

———. 1954. *Managerial Strategies and Organizational Dynamics in Sears Retailing.* University of Chicago, unpublished Ph.D. diss.

Worthy, James C. August 4, 1943. "Social Aspects of Industrial Relations." Chicago: Sears, Roebuck and Co., Personnel Department (Sears Archives).

———. October 1947. "Discovering and Evaluating Employee Attitudes." New York: American Management Association, *Personnel Series Number 113.*

———. February 18, 1949. "Factors Contributing to High Morale among

Sears Employees." Chicago: Sears, Roebuck and Co., memorandum to C. B. Caldwell (Sears Archives).

———. 1950. *Attitude Surveys as a Tool of Management.* New York, American Management Association.

———. January 1950. "Factors Influencing Employee Morale," *Harvard Business Review* 28:1.

———. April 1950. "Organization Structure and Employee Morale," *American Sociological Review* 15.

———. 1952. "Some Aspects of Organization Structure in Relation to Pressures on Company Decision-Making," *Proceedings*, Industrial Relations Research Association, Fifth Annual Meeting.

———. 1959. *Big Business and Free Men.* New York: Harper & Brothers.

———. 1984. *Shaping an American Institution: Robert E. Wood and Sears, Roebuck.* Urbana: University of Illinois Press.

———, Burleigh B. Garner and William Foote Whyte. April 1, 1947. "Methods and Techniques for Building a Cooperative Organization." Chicago: University of Chicago, Industrial Relations Center, Executive Seminar Series on Industrial Relations.

Whyte, William Foote. 1952. *Modern Methods in Social Research.* Washington, D.C.: Office of Naval Research.

———. 1959. *Man and Organization.* Homewood, Ill.: Richard D. Irwin.

Part 2

Studies in Human Relations

The survey program at Sears proceeded through three phases: the pre–World War II employee attitude surveys conducted by Houser Associates, the interim field studies conducted during the war by Burleigh B. Gardner and the Committee on Human Relations in Industry of the University of Chicago, and the postwar organization surveys conducted by Sears in collaboration with the Committee on Human Relations in Industry and Social Research, Inc., of Chicago.

The results of the prewar attitude surveys were summarized by Worthy in 1942 in a paper entitled "Early Studies of Employee Attitudes and Morale." By the start of the war, Houser surveys had covered more than 36,000 Sears employees—about one-third of Sears' total employment. At the time, it was probably the most extensive employee attitude survey ever conducted. By present standards, the statistics included in this report are relatively unsophisticated. However, many of the differences in levels of morale reported are more significant than their small numerical magnitude might indicate because the data represent large employee populations and not statistical samples. Of particular interest is Worthy's concern at this early date with the effects of organization size and complexity and job status on employee attitudes and performance.

During the war, Sears' human relations research was confined to a few field studies conducted by Burleigh B. Gardner, then director of the Committee on Human Relations in Industry of the University of Chicago. These studies were essentially demonstration projects designed to show the usefulness of anthropological field methods and analytic concepts in the study of employee behavior and management-employee relations. Worthy was strongly influenced by these studies and reveals the direction of his thinking in a paper written in 1943 entitled "Industrial Organizations as Social Systems." Later, in a presentation made at a seminar at the University of Chicago in 1947, entitled "Development of the Organization Survey Program," Worthy briefly described the field approach taken by Gardner and the way in which the nondirective interview process itself helped reduce employee tensions and improve relations between management and employees. Worthy was struck by the "self-healing" effects on an organization of nondirective interviewing and saw a parallel with the nondirective approach used by Carl Rogers in individual psychotherapy. This 1947 paper also provides background on the development of the third phase of Sears' human relations research, namely, the organization survey program.

That program, beginning in 1946 and extending through 1952, represented the culmination of more than a decade of human relations research at Sears conducted under Worthy's direction. The program combined quantitative questionnaire surveys with qualitative anthropological field methods and provided an opportunity to relate overall morale as measured by the questionnaire with detailed, nondirective interview materials and field observations. The results of surveys, conducted in more than five hundred Sears operating units throughout the country, underscored the significance of organization structure in shaping employee attitudes and behavior at all levels, and provided Worthy with a wealth of data to support his developing ideas and sharpen his thinking.

Three papers are presented in Part 2 that outline Worthy's interpretations of the survey data. "The Organization Survey Program" describes the design and use of the questionnaire, the function of the interview, and Sears' philosophy regarding the use of the results in strengthening the local operating unit. "Findings of the Survey Program" analyzes the influence of supervision, wages, hours, benefits, and working conditions—commonly viewed as the most important factors shaping employee attitudes—and concludes from the Sears studies that these are chiefly important not only in economic terms but for the message they convey to employees about management's attitudes toward its work force. This paper also examines the influence on employee attitudes and behavior of organization size and structure and the way work is organized and controlled. His discussion of administrative decentralization and differences between "tall" versus "flat" structures is significantly relevant to present-day concerns with excessive growth of middle managements and the traumatic down-sizing now being forced on many companies by competitive cost pressures. "Toward a Typology of Organizational Malfunction" speculates on the possibility of developing typological concepts that would be useful in diagnosing organizational ills in somewhat the same manner psychiatrists use typologies of personality malfunction in diagnosing and treating personality ills.

At a special meeting in 1949 of the American Psychological Association, the Society for the Psychological Study of Social Issues, and the newly organized Industrial Relations Research Association, Worthy had a chance to stress the need for a broad interdisciplinary approach to the study of human relations at work, and for that purpose he urged closer collaboration between academic scholars and practicing managers who must deal with problems in holistic fashion rather than in terms of specialized academic disciplines. He makes a persuasive case that this fact makes industry a uniquely fruitful laboratory for social science research.

—David G. Moore

3

Early Studies of Employee Attitudes and Morale

As one of the larger employers of labor in the United States, with an average of about 110,000 employees on the payroll, Sears, Roebuck and Co. has a vital interest in maintaining high levels of employee morale as a critical factor in company success. In an organization of this size with operating units spread across the country, the need to find and eliminate causes of employee dissatisfaction are too important to be left to chance. With this in mind, the officers of the company in 1939 authorized a series of surveys of employee attitudes and morale on the assumption that the best way to locate and identify causes of discontent would be to go to the employees and ask. Houser Associates, an independent agency specializing in this type of work, was retained to administer the surveys. By the beginning of 1942, when survey work was temporarily discontinued because of the onset of war, 158 Sears stores and other operating units and more than 36,000 employees had been covered. The present study summarizes the methods used in these surveys and the chief findings to date.

The questionnaires used consist of approximately seventy questions and take from a half to three-quarters of an hour to complete. Every aspect of employee experience in working for Sears is covered, and multiple choice responses are provided, ranging from completely satisfied to totally disssatisfied. In each store and other company unit surveyed, employees are called together in groups on company time. The head of the unit (store manager, etc.) introduces the Houser representative, explains the purpose of the survey, and leaves the room; no company executive is present while the questionnaires are being answered. Completed questionnaires are placed in a "ballot box" for shipment directly to Houser offices in New York. Employees are assured of complete anonymity, and the frankness of the opinions expressed is evidence they have few doubts on that score.

The questions used in different types of company units vary slightly according to type of unit:

"A" stores are large retail department stores located chiefly in major urban centers;

Unattached "B" stores are smaller stores, usually located in communities of 25,000–150,000 population, and reporting directly to company headquarters in Chicago;

Group "B" stores are also smaller stores, but usually located in outlying sections of major urban centers and reporting to a local district manager (typically the manager of the "A" store in the same city);

Pool stocks are central warehouses servicing a number of retail stores;

Control stores are mail order plants, all much larger than the largest "A" store.

Surveys have been well distributed geographically, in rough accordance with the distribution of the general U.S. population; as indicated in table 3.1 (see appendix 2 for all tables), the only major geographical deficiency in coverage is that for "A" and "B" stores on the Pacific Coast.

The "Morale Score"

The "morale score" is an overall measure of the employee's attitudes toward the company and his or her work as revealed by answers to a series of ten general questions (appendix 1). These ten questions are identical in all essential respects for all Sears units and with those used by Houser for other clients; this permits comparison of the scores of different company units and of Sears scores with those of other companies. There are five possible answers to each of the ten questions, and each has a weight determined by Houser in accordance with accepted methods of item analysis and scale construction. Values are set on a scale of 0 to 100 so that an employee who answers all ten "morale" items in the way most unfavorable to the company receives a score of 0 and one who checks only the most favorable responses receives a score of 100. The score for individual employees is the sum of the values of the ten answers checked. After calculating individual scores, it is a matter of simple arithmetic to determine average scores for the entire group tested, for various subgroups, and for any desired classification or grouping of operating units. The averages shown hereafter in this paper were arrived at in this manner.

These averages are not shown as percentages. The values used in scoring the responses to the ten questions are set arbitrarily on a scale of 0 to 100 simply as a matter of convenience. There is no proof that zero on the scale represents the lowest possible state of morale or that 100 represents the highest. The score reflects intangibles that are not susceptible to absolute measurement. The resulting figures must therefore be regarded as relative rather than absolute. The morale score concept rests on the commonsense assumption that an employee whose answers are generally favorable toward the company has higher morale than one whose answers are generally unfavorable. Examination of the ten morale questions themselves and the range of possible answers provides strong support for that conclusion. It is important that this assumption be kept in mind and that any conclusions reached from the morale scores themselves be checked against the wording of the ten key questions.

Scores by Type of Unit

The validity of the morale score is attested by its sensitivity to varying situations. Among the 158 operating units covered before the surveys were discontinued because of the onset of war, average unit scores range from a low of 58.0 to a high of 88.7, a difference of more than 30 points. Between these extremes, average unit scores tend to distribute themselves along a fairly normal curve of probability (table 3.2).

These data disclose very different patterns for different type units that become even more apparent when the averages for each type of operation are considered (table 3.3).

The relative standing of the various types of unit corresponds closely with the prior judgment of Sears management and reinforces a well-established belief that morale is lower in "warehouse type" operations (mail order plants and pool stocks) than in the retail stores. There is also a presumption that morale decreases with increasing unit size, and this is confirmed by the data of table 3 showing "A" stores as a group with significantly lower average morale than the smaller "B" stores and the mail order plants ranking well below the much smaller pool stocks.

Distribution of Unit Scores

Any average, of course, conceals a pattern of individual differences. Table 3.4 shows the percentage distribution of individual scores for 11,243 employees in forty-five "A" stores. If these data were presented in chart form, a definite skew to the right would be evident. Only 8.7 percent of all employees have individual morale scores of less than 50 and slightly less than half score 75 or more. Examination of the wording of the morale questions shown in the appendix suggests meaningful interpretations. Each question has five optional answers varying from extreme disfavor to extreme favor, with the middle answer designed to reflect a "just so-so, neither particularly good nor particularly bad" level of attitude. The employee who checks this middle response on each of the ten items has a score of 50. One who checks the next-to-best response (one step above the middle) on each of the ten questions has a score of 76. Thus the average company-wide score of 70.2 reflects an average attitude that corresponds closely with the next-to-best position.

Examination of the wordings of the questions, as well as the distribution of individual morale scores, indicates that the attitudes of Sears employees are substantially more favorable than unfavorable.

Scores of Selling and Non-Selling Employees

Further examination of the "A" store data suggests other interesting patterns. The primary employee classification in the retail industry is "selling" and "non-selling." The difference in the average morale of these two basic groups in the "A" stores is fairly substantial, given the large number of employees surveyed (table 3.5). There are equally significant differences in the distribution of individual morale scores between the two groups. From table 3.6 it will be noted, among other things, that 40.0 percent of all non-selling employees had individual scores of less than 70, whereas only 29.3 percent of all salespeople have scores below this point.

The following factors help explain the lower relative morale of non-selling employees:

1. *Relative Prestige of Selling and Non-Selling.* By and large in the retail industry, salespeople enjoy a "social status" superior to that of behind-the-scene employees. Many non-selling jobs (laborers, stock boys, markers) require little skill, and others (carpenters, electricians, janitors) even though skilled are "overall" rather than

"white collar." There are exceptions, as in the case of auditing employees for whom transfer to a sales job would be resented as a demotion, but for the most part employees themselves consider non-selling work as lower in prestige than selling (a saleswoman, for example, might refuse temporary work in the marking room even when the only alternative is a lay-off or part-time work because of slack on the selling floor).

2. *Monotony of Work.* Selling tends to be more exciting and stimulating work than wrapping packages. On the selling floor there is constant contact with other people, the challenge of a rapid succession of customers, the spirit of competition with other salespeople. Behind the scenes there frequently is only the drab succession of endless bales of merchandise to be opened, counted, and stored away, endless bundles to be wrapped.

3. *Job Selectivity.* Because of the varying requirements of and conditions inherent in the two types of work, there tends to be a natural process of selection that at least to some extent explains the difference in overall morale. People who are naturally more outgoing tend to drift into sales careers where their pleasant spirits are an asset. Although a high degree of congeniality is a basic requirement for almost every type of retail work, the quality of "good naturedness" is not quite so important in the display technician as in the clothing salesman.

4. *Working Conditions.* The working environment of selling employees is generally better than that of non-selling employees. Salespeople work in the presence of customers and their physical surroundings are designed to be attractive to customers; employees behind the scenes frequently work under less desirable conditions of lighting, ventilation, housekeeping, and so on.

5. *Quality of Supervision.* To some extent, non-selling employees do not enjoy as satisfactory a level of supervision as salespeople. In part, this condition undoubtedly results from the nature of retailing itself. The primary function of a retail store is to sell merchandise, and store executives are likely to be more immediately engrossed in daily sales performance than in the many collateral functions that help keep selling activities running smoothly. A problem on the sales floor is noted immediately and corrected promptly. A problem in the shipping room or in the adjustment department may go unnoticed for weeks. The relatively greater preoccupation of store executives with the selling floor helps explain the higher morale of the selling force as compared with the less frequently noticed non-selling group.

Attitudes toward Supervision, Pay, Hours, and Workload

The special importance of supervision in accounting for the difference in the morale of selling and non-selling employees is brought out by comparison of the responses of the two groups to specific items in the questionnaire involving supervisory relationships, as shown in table 3.7.

On all of the points shown, selling employees respond in a substantially more favorable manner than do non-selling employees. Whatever the cause, behind-the-scenes personnel feel that they have less opportunity to talk with the store executives about their work, that they know less of how well they stand in the organization, that good work on their part is less frequently recognized, that their grievances are less likely to be heard fairly and sympathetically, and that they take part less creatively in the organization as witness their relatively unfavorable responses to the two questions on suggestions.

Non-selling employees also respond much less favorably than do selling employees to questions dealing with pay, hours, and workload (table 3.8).

These data show that non-selling employees are much less satisfied with their pay than are salespeople. In part, this feeling may result from a comparison with factory and other non-retail jobs, many of which are fairly similar to non-selling retail work and which, on the whole, provide somewhat higher compensation (particularly since the defense program began). On the other hand, it may be that the dissatisfaction of employees with such intangibles as quality of supervision expresses itself in dissatisfaction with such tangibles as pay, hours of work, volume of work, and so on. This question is the subject of analysis below, which looks more closely at subgroups of employees.

Morale Scores of Selling Employees by Functional
Classification

The sales force is made up of employees of varying status. *Division managers* (heads of the selling departments) are at the top of the scale. Aside from personal selling, their duties include selection of merchandise from prepared listings, determination of prices, arrangement of displays, and supervision of salespeople. Their responsibilities are executed under the direction of the store merchandise manager, operating superintendent, and personnel manager. On the whole, division managers are older and more mature, with longer service, and are substantially better paid than salespeople. For the most part they have advanced to their positions from the ranks of salespeople. They participate in staff meetings and aid in the planning of sales promotions and other vital phases of store work.

"Big-ticket" salesmen sell major appliances, furniture, rugs, and other higher-priced merchandise. They are paid on a "commission" basis: a percentage on personal sales with a guaranteed minimum weekly "drawing account." Their income is greater than that enjoyed by other salesmen and often exceeds that of division managers of small-ticket divisions. The commission basis of compensation promotes often intense personal competition between individual big-ticket salesmen and tends to develop lone-wolf attitudes. Because their incomes are dependent on their personal sales, they usually spend fairly large amounts of time outside regular hours calling on prospects and developing new business.

"Small-ticket" salespeople comprise the remainder of the store's regular sales force. These are the "clerks" of a typical department store.

"Extras" are part-time employees, used only in the small-ticket divisions, who are called in to help handle peak traffic loads (Saturdays, special sales events, and heavy selling seasons).

Tables 3.9 and 3.10 disclose interesting differences in the levels of morale of these four categories of selling employees.

The high morale of division managers shown in these data is easily explained. They not only enjoy higher levels of income but occupy a favorable position in the store's social scale. They are in close and constant contact with store executives and participate actively in store councils. They have clearly defined responsibilities and the success or failure of their efforts is readily apparent from regular monthly statements for their divisions.

The more striking feature of tables 3.9 and 3.10 is the lower ranking of big-ticket salespeople. Despite their higher level of earnings, their attitudes toward the company and their jobs are less favorable than that of any other sales group—even the lowly "extras." The explanation for this anomaly probably lies in the competitive nature of their work, their relations with fellow salespeople, and the long hours they typically spend on their own time in outside selling.

Finally, the comparatively high morale of employees in the extra category was unexpected. They are the least well-paid of any employees, their hours are irregular and intermittent, and they work under the trying conditions of peak traffic periods. Offsetting these factors, however, is the company selection policy with respect to the part-time force. Insofar as possible, employees for this kind of work are picked from groups who were not dependent on their income for their livelihood: housewives, people with other jobs who have free evenings and Saturdays, and others anxious to pick up a little extra money.

Variations of Morale Scores by Sex, Age, and Service

An interesting finding of the studies is that women register higher morale than men almost throughout the Sears organization. This is particularly true in the case of selling work, as indicated by table 3.11.

The relatively more favorable attitudes of women is even more striking if selling employees of the same functional level are compared by lines of merchandise handled, as shown in table 3.12.

The only exception to the tendency toward higher morale on the part of women is among office employees in the non-selling classifications. Table 3.13 provides two particularly interesting contrasts:

1. Men score higher in the two types of work in which men are in the minority (customer service, etc., auditing, etc.).

2. Women score higher in the three types of work in which women are in the minority (porters, etc.; unclassified; receiving, etc.).

A possible explanation is that the minority sex in the work group tends to enjoy a favorable position among fellow employees that is reflected in higher job satisfaction.

Small but meaningful differences also appear when morale scores are analyzed in terms of age and length of service as shown in tables 3.14 and 3.15.

Further insight into age and service differences can be gained from considering the several functional groupings that, as already seen, show significant differences in average morale scores. Division managers, for example, who have the highest morale of any functional group are also older and of longer service, on the average, than any other functional group. Non-selling employees, on the other hand, tend to be younger and of shorter-service. Table 3.16 provides information about one aspect of these comparisons by analyzing morale in terms of *both* functional group and length of service.

Further data comparing morale scores by age and functional group have not yet been generated, but table 3.17 presents an interesting analysis in terms of age and length of service.

A review of the data presented in tables 3.14, 3.15, 3.16, and 3.17 leads to the following provocative conclusions:

1. Very young employees (those under 20) start their working lives with fairly good morale, but that slips badly during their twenties and climbs slowly back thereafter.

2. Regardless of age, employees tend to start with the company in a burst of enthusiasm that soon begins to cool and keeps cooling until they accumulate between three and five years of service, at which time their feelings toward their work begin to improve until, beyond the five-year mark, their enthusiasm has almost but not quite regained the level of their earliest novitiate.

Comparison of "Previous Experience" Groups

To further investigate the relation between morale and experience, the small-ticket selling group (exclusive of division managers and extras) was segregated according to responses to the question, "Have you ever worked for other companies or stores, or is this your first job?" Results are summarized in table 3.18. The interesting feature of this table is the lower average morale of employees who worked before coming to Sears but are now in retailing for the first time. Because of the definite pattern in scores by length of service already shown, scores were calculated for three "experience" groups by length of Sears service (table 3.19). In each of the groups shown, salespeople who had other jobs before but for whom Sears provided the first job in a store have relatively lower morale scores.

Not only do those in each length of service group whose previous experience was outside retailing have lower scores than other employees in the same service group, but their average continues to decline with longer service rather than tending to recover beyond a certain point. The data on this question are not conclusive because too few cases in the "over five years" bracket are available to permit reliable analysis. The scarcity of cases, however, is in itself significant: apparently few of those with no previous retailing experience survive the five-year mark.

Conclusion

From the data produced by the surveys, it is clear that purely material factors such as wages, hours, and physical working conditions are of less importance to employee morale than intangibles such as quality of supervision, recognition of performance, and fairness of treatment. This is not to say that wages, hours, and working conditions are unimportant, but simply that in themselves they are not enough. The findings suggest that too much attention has been concentrated on the tangibles of employer-employee relationships to the neglect of the perhaps more important intangibles. Giving workers more pay for fewer hours may be spectacular, but giving them courteous and considerate treatment and the respect due them as individuals may be less spectacular yet bring dividends in loyalty and cooperation that cannot be bought.

Appendix 1: Answers to the Morale Questions

The ten questions on which the morale score of the pre–World War II employee attitude surveys were based, and the percentage answers of 11,243 employees in forty-five "A" stores, follow:

1. Generally speaking, how does Sears compare as a place to work with other companies that you know about or have worked for?

One of the VERY WORST	.3%
WORSE than average	1.2
Just AVERAGE	20.0
BETTER than average	35.8
One of the VERY BEST	41.9
Unanswered	.7

2. How much does the top management of the company care about the welfare of people in jobs such as yours?:

LESS than ANY other company	1.0%
LESS than MOST other companies	4.1
About the SAME as most others	33.9
MORE than MOST of the others	37.8
MORE than ANY of the others	22.2
Unanswered	1.1

3. Would you rather work for some other company or store instead of Sears if you could get a job at the same pay for which you feel equally qualified?

I would rather work in ANY of the others	1.0%
I would rather work in ALMOST ANY of the others	1.9
SOME of the others	14.4
VERY FEW of the others	27.5
NONE of the others	54.4
Unanswered	.9

4. If you have ever been dissatisfied with your job here, how often was it the company's fault?

It was the company's fault in practically EVERY case	4.0%
MORE THAN HALF the time it was the company's fault	5.8
About HALF THE TIME	14.9
Considerably LESS THAN HALF the time	14.4
It was HARDLY EVER the company's fault	29.5
Have NEVER been dissatisfied	29.1
Unanswered	2.3

5. How much does the management of this store do to have good working relationships between you and the people with whom you work?

As LITTLE as possible	4.4%
LESS than one could expect	5.9
About AS MUCH as one could expect	45.2
MORE than one could expect	21.7
A GREAT DEAL MORE than one could expect	21.9
Unanswered	.9

6. To what extent are you made to feel that you are really a part of the organization?

Practically NO WAY at all	2.7%
To a SMALL DEGREE	8.8
To a FAIR DEGREE	24.5
To a LARGE EXTENT	22.9
In EVERY WAY possible	40.6
Unanswered	.4

7. How fair is the top management of the company with employees in jobs such as yours?

RARELY fair	2.0%
OCCASIONALLY fair	4.4
About HALF the time fair	5.0
USUALLY FAIR	34.5
Practically ALWAYS fair	53.4
Unanswered	.6

8. How fair do you feel the people immediately above you are in their treatment of you?

RARELY fair	1.6%
OCCASIONALLY fair	4.1
About HALF the time fair	10.8
USUALLY fair	31.7
Practically ALWAYS fair	52.1
Unanswered	.2

9. In your opinion, are there other companies which treat their employees better than SEARS does?

ALL of the others are better	.2%
MOST of the others are better	5.4
About the SAME	24.1
This company is BETTER than MOST others	44.1
This company is BEST of ALL	25.3
Unanswered	.8

10. Are you reasonably sure of being able to keep your job as long as you do good work?

Doing good work doesn't have ANYTHING to do with holding my job	2.8%
Holding my job depends a LITTLE on how good work I do	3.6
If I do good work I can be FAIRLY SURE of holding my job	21.2
As long as I do good work I can be ALMOST CERTAIN of holding my job	30.2
As long as I do good work I can be VERY SURE of holding my job	41.8
Unanswered	.4

Appendix 2: Tables

Table 3.1. Geographical Distribution of Morale Surveys by Type of Operation.

Geographical Area	"A" Stores		Unattached "B" Stores		Group "B" Stores		Pool Stocks		Control Stores		All Types of Operations	
	U	E	U	E	U	E	U	E	U	E	U	E
New England	2	406	19	1,016	5	79	1	90	1	1,443	28	3,034
Middle Atlantic	11	2,788	15	645	5	110	4	317	1	3,503	36	7,363
East North Central	20	5,327	16	1,357	8	217	4	332	1	5,428	49	13,161
West North Central	6	1,363	4	279	2	54	1	71	2	2,031	15	3,798
South Atlantic	3	807	5	459	2	49	—	—	1	1,541	11	2,858
East South Central	3	730	—	—	4	98	—	—	1	1,325	8	2,153
West South Central	5	1,151	—	—	—	—	—	—	1	1,027	6	2,178
Mountain	1	141	—	—	2	48	—	—	—	—	3	189
Pacific	—	—	—	—	—	—	—	—	2	1,727	2	1,727
All Areas	51	12,716	59	3,756	28	655	10	810	10	18,025	158	36,461

Key: U = units; E = employees

Table 3.2. Distribution of Average Morale Scores by Type
of Operation

Morale Score Interval	Number of Units Having Average Morale Scores within Designated Intervals					
	"A" Stores	Unattached "B" Stores	Group "B" Stores	Pool Stocks	Control Stores	All Units
85–89	—	4	3	—	—	7
80–84	11	21	8	—	—	40
75–79	15	22	7	—	1	45
70–74	15	11	9	5	2	42
65–69	8	1	—	3	3	15
60–64	2	—	1	1	2	6
55–59	—	—	—	1	2	3
Total units	51	59	28	10	10	158

Table 3.3. Average Morale Scores by Type of Operation

Type of Store	Number of Units	Number of Employees	Average Score
"A" Stores	51	12,716	74.2
Unattached "B" Stores	59	3,756	79.5
Group "B" Stores	28	655	77.9
Pool Stocks	10	1,310	68.3
Control Stores	10	18,025	64.9
Total	158	36,462	70.2

Table 3.4. Distribution of Individual Morale Scores for 11,243
Employees of 45 "A" Stores

Morale Score by Intervals	Number of Cases	Percent of Total	Cumulative Percent
0–9	4	.0	.0
10–13	8	.1	.1
14–17	10	.1	.2
18–21	21	.2	.4
22–25	32	.3	.7
26–29	57	.5	1.2
30–33	83	.7	1.9
34–37	109	1.0	2.9
38–41	165	1.5	4.3
42–45	206	1.8	6.2
46–49	280	2.5	8.7
50–53	326	2.9	11.6
54–57	452	4.0	15.6
58–61	533	4.7	20.3
62–65	688	6.1	26.5
66–69	843	7.5	34.0
70–73	845	7.5	41.5
74–77	1,004	8.9	50.4
78–81	1,169	10.4	60.8
82–85	1,161	10.3	71.1
86–89	1,084	9.6	80.8
90–93	935	8.3	89.1
94–97	850	7.6	96.6
98–100	378	3.4	100.0

Table 3.5. Comparison of Average Morale Scores for Selling and
Non-Selling Employees at 45 "A" Stores

	Number of Employees	Average Morale Score
All selling employees	6,365	76.4
All non-selling employees	4,878	72.1

Table 3.6. Distribution of Individual Morale Scores for Selling
and Non-Selling Employees at 45 "A" Stores

Morale Score by Interval	Number of Cases		Cumulative Percent	
	Selling	Non-Selling	Selling	Non-Selling
0–9	1	3	.02	.1
10–13	6	2	.1	.2
14–17	3	7	.2	.2
18–21	12	9	.3	.4
22–25	11	21	.5	.9
26–29	27	30	.9	1.5
30–33	44	39	1.6	2.3
34–37	44	65	2.3	3.6
38–41	78	87	3.6	5.4
42–45	92	114	5.0	7.7
46–49	138	142	7.2	10.6
50–53	163	163	9.7	14.0
54–57	211	241	13.0	18.9
58–61	269	264	17.3	24.3
62–65	328	360	22.4	31.7
66–69	439	404	29.3	40.0
70–73	470	375	36.7	47.7
74–77	557	447	45.5	56.3
78–81	665	504	55.9	67.2
82–85	699	462	66.9	76.7
86–89	661	423	77.3	85.3
90–93	597	338	86.6	92.3
94–97	580	270	95.8	97.8
98–100	270	108	100.0	100.0
Total	6,365	4,878		

Table 3.7. Percent of Employees Responding to Questions
in Manner Indicated

	Selling	Non-Selling
Access to store executives 13. I have a chance to talk to the following store executives once in a while, or regularly, about my work and tell them what things I like about my job and what things I do not like:		
Store manager	57	42
Superintendent	64	52
Personnel manager	78	61
Knowledge of standing 12. I am told fairly well, or fully and completely, by the store executives as to how well they like my work and where they think I need improvement.	57	50
Recognition of good work 34. When employees do some unusually good work, they usually, or always, get recognition or praise for it.	55	46
Grievances 53. If I had any cause for dissatisfaction, I would have a reasonably good, or very good, chance of getting a fair hearing and a square deal from the store executives.	74	66
Encouragement to offer suggestions 20. Employees get good encouragement, or are encouraged in every way, to offer suggestions for new or better ways of doing the job.	66	59
Credit for suggestions 21. If I were to make a good suggestion for a new or better way of doing a job, I probably would, or would be sure to, get credit for it.	81	76

Table 3.8. Percent of Employees Responding to Questions
in Manner Indicated

	Selling	Non-Selling
Pay comparisons in store 22. The pay for my job is about the same as, or higher than most, or higher than any, other jobs in this store of the same importance or difficulty.	76	59
Pay in other companies 23. The pay for my job is about the same as, or higher than most, or higher than any, other jobs of the same sort in other companies or stores.	75	60
Pay increases 30. When a person in a job such as mine deserves an increase in pay, he usually gets it within a reasonable time, or always gets it as soon as he deserves it.	49	41
Working hours 26. My present daily working hours are satisfactory.	80	74
Work load 18. In general, the amount of work expected of me is reasonable.	85	77

Table 3.9. Comparison of Average Morale Scores for Selling
Employees by Classification at 45 "A" Stores

Classification	Number of Cases	Average Score
Division managers	1,291	80.0
Big-ticket salespeople	1,302	74.6
Small-ticket salespeople	2,548	75.4
Extra salespeople	1,224	76.5
Total	6,365	76.4

Table 3.10. Distribution of Individual Morale Scores for Selling
Employees by Classification at 45 "A" Stores

Morale Score Interval	Cumulative Percentages				
	Division Managers	Big-Ticket Sales	Small-Ticket Sales	Extra Sales	Total
0–9	—	—	.04	—	.02
10–13	—	.1	.2	.2	.1
14–17	.1	.2	.2	.2	.2
18–21	.2	.4	.5	.2	.3
22–25	.3	.6	.7	.2	.5
26–29	.6	1.2	1.3	.4	.9
30–33	.9	2.1	2.1	1.0	1.6
34–37	1.5	3.3	2.8	1.2	2.3
38–41	2.7	4.4	4.2	2.2	3.6
42–45	3.8	6.4	5.8	3.0	5.0
46–49	4.9	9.1	8.7	4.2	7.2
50–53	6.5	12.1	11.5	6.8	9.7
54–57	8.6	15.8	15.0	10.8	13.0
58–61	11.5	20.7	19.5	15.0	17.3
62–65	15.0	26.8	24.8	20.6	22.4
66–69	21.0	33.8	31.7	28.4	29.3
70–73	27.9	40.6	39.1	36.8	36.7
74–77	35.6	50.2	47.6	46.2	45.5
78–81	45.5	60.4	57.5	58.7	55.9
82–85	56.2	69.9	69.0	70.6	66.9
86–89	69.4	79.9	78.1	81.0	77.3
90–93	80.9	88.9	86.9	89.7	86.6
94–97	93.4	96.4	96.0	97.9	95.8
98–100	100.0	100.0	100.0	100.0	100.0

Table 3.11. Comparison of Morale Scores by Sex and
Functional Group

Functional Group	Average Morale Score		
	Male	Female	Difference
All employees	73.6	75.5	1.9
All selling employees	74.7	78.9	4.2
Division managers	79.1	81.6	2.5
Big-ticket salespeople	74.1	81.2	7.1
Other regular selling	73.0	77.7	4.7
Contingent and extra selling	73.1	77.8	4.7
All non-selling employees	71.8	72.3	.5
Regular non-selling	72.0	72.3	.3
Contingent and extra non-selling	71.1	72.5	1.4

Table 3.12. Average Morale Scores by Sex and Job Classification
for Regular Salespeople Only, Exclusive of Division Managers
and Extras

Job Classification	Average Morale Score			Difference between Male and Female
	Male	Female	Total	
Draperies, yard goods, domestics	74.7	80.2	79.4	5.5
Corsets, infants' wear, lingerie, hosiery, accessories, ready-to-wear	—	77.8	77.8	—
Housewares, lamps, china and glassware, toys	73.4	76.7	76.5	3.3
Shoes, men's and boys' furnishings and clothing	75.6	80.0	76.4	4.4
Furniture, rugs, radios	75.3	82.9	76.2	6.6
Vacuum cleaners and sewing machines, stoves, washers, heating, refrigerators	73.6	78.2	73.8	4.6
Stationery, jewelry, drugs, notions, candy, tobacco	66.9	74.2	73.6	7.3
Sporting goods, hardware, auto accessories and tires, electrical fixtures, building materials	72.4	78.9	73.0	6.5

Table 3.13. Average Morale Scores by Sex and Job Classification
for Non-Selling Activities, for Regular Non-Selling Employees
Only

	Average Morale Score			Difference between Male
Job Classification	Male	Female	Total	and Female
Porters, cleaners, matrons, watchmen	72.9	80.0	74.1	7.1
Customer service, unit control, cashier, personnel	74.5	73.9	74.0	-0.6
Non-selling activities not otherwise classified	73.5	73.9	73.6	0.4
Maintenance, mechanical service, delivery	73.0	—	73.0	—
Receiving, marking, stock, shipping	70.6	74.6	71.7	4.0
Auditing, credit, telephone, stenographic	74.5	70.8	71.1	-3.7
Service station, tire and battery service	70.1	—	70.1	—

Table 3.14. Average Morale Scores by Age Groups

Age	Average Score
Under 20 years	74.1
21 to 25 years	72.7
26 to 35 years	74.5
36 to 45 years	76.9
Over 45 years	78.1

Table 3.15. Average Morale Scores by Length of Service

Length of Service	Average Score
Under six months	76.2
Six months to one year	74.9
One year to three years	74.1
Three years to five years	73.1
Five years and over	75.8

Table 3.16. Average Morale Scores by Functional Group and Length of Service

Functional Group	Under 6 Months	6 Months– 1 Year	1–3 Years	3–5 Years	5 Years & Over
Division manager	79.9	78.7	80.6	80.2	80.3
Big-ticket salespeople	78.4	75.5	75.0	73.1	75.0
Small-ticket salespeople	78.8	78.6	75.6	74.0	76.1
Extra salespeople	78.4	76.8	74.3	75.5	75.1
Regular non-selling	76.7	73.5	72.3	70.5	73.0
Extra non-selling	73.6	69.9	66.9	68.0	73.9

Table 3.17. Average Morale Scores by Age and Length of Service

Functional Group	Under 6 Months	6 Months– 1 Year	1–3 Years	3–5 Years	5 Years & Over
Under 20 years	74.7	75.4	72.3	70.8	—
21 to 25 years	75.0	73.8	72.3	71.2	71.6
26 to 35 years	77.9	74.8	74.7	72.6	74.5
36 to 45 years	77.9	76.8	76.6	76.1	77.2
Over 45 years	79.3	74.8	79.8	76.7	78.3

Table 3.18. Average Morale Scores by "Previous Experience"
Groups (Regular Small-Ticket Salespeople)

Previous Experience Group	Number of Cases	Average Score
"This is my first regular job."	175	74.9
"I have worked on other jobs but this is my first job in a store."	496	73.9
"I have worked in one or more other stores."	1,842	75.8

Table 3.19. Average Morale Scores by Previous Experience and
Length of Service

Previous Experience Group	Length of Sears Service		
	Under 1 Year	1–3 Years	3 Years & Over
"This is my first regular job."	77.9	75.7	76.1
"I have worked on other jobs but this is my first job in a store."	76.9	74.2	73.4
"I have worked in one or more other stores."	79.2	75.9	75.6

Note

This is a paper from the author's files, dated February 2, 1942. Excerpted
by permission of the publisher from "The More Things Change the More
They Stay the Same," *Journal of Management Inquiry* 1:1 (Mar. 1992): 14–
38. Copyright © 1992 by Sage Publications, Inc.

4

Industrial Organizations as Social Systems

An industrial organization is a social system. It is a complex of relationships that must be considered as a whole because each particular relationship is interdependent with every other relationship within the complex. Moreover, the industrial organization itself is part of a larger series of complexes representing the community, the industry, and the society, and is influenced by and influences all the others.

In part, the social system of a plant is formally organized. There is an established hierarchy of supervision. Systems and routines are prescribed governing the functional relations of various units. Policies and rules regulate many aspects of behavior. The formal organization is represented by the organization chart that outlines the relationships that are supposed to exist between individuals and groups.

The actual working organization of a plant, however, never conforms strictly to the organization chart. The formal organization fails to recognize many of the relationships that are vital to the functioning of the enterprise. The chart shows logical lines of vertical and horizontal coordination, but not actual patterns of human interaction in the performance of work. The informal organization expresses such patterns. It involves social codes, conventions, and customary ways of responding to situations that are prerequisites of effective group collaboration. The formal organization is chiefly concerned with serving the economic purposes of the enterprise; the informal organization not only reflects the actual pattern of working relationships but serves also to protect and further the interests of individuals and groups within the enterprise. This is not to say that the formal and informal organizations are necessarily in conflict. Informal organization is a necessary condition for effective collaboration, without which the economic aims of the enterprise could not be realized. If the formal and informal organizations are in reasonable harmony, each helps facilitate the functioning of the other. If they are in conflict, discord and trouble inevitably follow.

The benefits created and distributed by the enterprise to its members, in important part through the operation of the informal organization, satisfy a wide range of needs. These include not only the economic but those that can be broadly classed as social. Each individual makes somewhat different demands on the organization, reflecting background, personal capacity, and other factors. But the organization is more than a collection of individuals with individual demands. Satisfactions, however varied, are achieved largely through collaboration with others. Patterns of relations are established to govern behavior, and these patterns, together with the ideas and objects symbolizing them, constitute the informal organization.

Individuals and groups within the plant act in certain prescribed ways toward each other. The same individual acts differently toward his partner at the bench, his foreman, the plant protection man at the gate, the superintendent, and the general manager. His behavior differs also in talking with his fellow worker in the presence of the foreman or with his foreman in the presence of the superintendent. He acts in one way toward representatives of the office and in another toward members of other production departments. In each case, the behavior is responsive primarily to the relationships and only secondarily to the persons involved. Promote the fellow worker to foreman; he remains the same person, but the relationship has changed and behavior changes accordingly.

Division of labor and specialization of function create social stratification. A process of evaluation is constantly at work by means of which status values are assigned to individuals and groups performing various types of work, and people performing given tasks are assigned specific places on the prestige scale. Each job becomes a carrier of social value.

Relative status values are determined not only on the basis of job but also in accordance with a variety of other factors. Sex, nationality, age, seniority—practically any element of similarity or difference—can become the basis for the assignment of differential values. These values are often expressed symbolically. Common laborers wear overalls, machinists wear smocks, the foreman wears a vest and tie but no coat, the superintendent wears a coat. If the general manager has a carpet in his office, carpets become a symbol of superordination. If bench workers have rest periods and foremen do not, rest periods become a symbol of *subordination*. The range of symbolical objects is wide. A thorough study of the symbol system of a particular enterprise would be instructive—and in some ways amusing.

Management frequently fails to recognize the significance, sometimes even the existence, of this symbol system. Manifestations of employee concern with such matters are likely to be looked upon as "illogical" and "silly." Managers all too often fail to recognize that they have their own system of symbols with whose preservation they are just as concerned as their employees are with theirs. Symbols are important to all members of an organization. The possession of certain symbols is the outward manifestation of status—frequently, in fact, an important factor in defining status. Any action of management that deprives employees of their symbols or adulterates their value is a direct threat to their status and is bound to create attitudes of resistance and antagonism. The violence of response varies, of course, with the importance of the particular symbol; frequently, seemingly inconsequential things acquire an amazingly high symbolic value.

Any action perceived as a threat to status will be regarded by the employees affected as unfair and unjust. The threat may be real or imaginary, but the results are the same. Management may unintentionally alter an established social equilibrium and in so doing disturb the means by which the status of employees is defined. Technical changes may have demoralizing effects because they deprive groups of employees of certain of the symbols that define their status.

The concept of social (read organizational) distance is a valuable aid in understanding organizational behavior. Each employee and each group has a particular place in the social system. Employees are uncomfortable if for any reason there is confusion as to the status of an individual, because unless status is known others may not know how to act toward him. A significant characteristic of military systems is the precise and explicit manner in which social distance is defined and the unmistakable means by which status is identified.

One great difficulty in industrial organization, which is not present in military organization, is the fact that scales of value are never completely accepted by all groups in the plant. Shop employees resent the higher earnings of those in the office; women resent the disabilities imposed on the basis of sex. In some cases more than one system of values may be operative. Sears stores, for example, periodically select a "most valuable employee." Selections are made by management on the basis of its own scale of values. A number of employees who have been accorded this honor have confessed privately that the chief result of their award of this distinction was to estrange them from their fellows. In these cases, employees had a somewhat different scale of values from that held by management.

Working conditions, wages, selection methods, and other elements of industrial relations cannot be treated in isolation. Their significance can be assessed only in terms of the pattern of relationships in which they occur. The meaning of any object or event is determined chiefly by the social environment within which it occurs. A reconsideration of industrial relations from this general point of view is urgently needed. The "scientific management" approach—"finding the one best way"—has all but exhausted its potentialities. A fresh start must be made, a start emphasizing the functional unity of the entire industrial enterprise and the interrelatedness and interdependence of all its parts.

A beginning has been made along this line, but thus far only a beginning. The most important work to date has been the "Hawthorne Experiments" at the Western Electric Company. Somewhat less ambitious but nevertheless significant has been the program of research in organization structure and employee attitudes and morale conducted in recent years by Sears, Roebuck and Co.

The factual findings of the Sears studies strongly support the thesis that an industrial establishment is a social system in every true sense of the term, and that the parts of the system are interrelated and interdependent. Compensation cannot be considered an independent variable, any more than hours of work, working conditions, quality of supervision, or any other element of the employment circumstances can be so considered. All elements must be viewed as intimately related to all other elements; no change can be made in any one without affecting all the others and modifying the whole.

Each element must be considered a carrier of social value. Patterns of relationships tend strongly toward stereotypes, and these tend to be identified largely by symbols. The symbol system is constructed chiefly on the basis of the physical and ideological environment existing in the plant. Methods of compensation, work surroundings, hours of work, and behavior of supervisors are important primarily in terms of the social values ascribed to them and only secondarily in their own right.

Thus far, only the barest beginnings have been made in the direction of studying industrial organizations as social systems, but these beginnings are promising. This concept should open up a whole new field of thought in management theory and contribute significantly to the solution of many of the problems vexing modern industry.

Note

Unpublished manuscript, August 1943, author's files.

5

Development of the Organization Survey Program

At the last meeting, Dr. Carl Rogers [psychologist, well-known for his work in the field of nondirective counseling] discussed problems of individual maladjustment. This evening, I would like to discuss problems of group maladjustment, particularly those involving lack of effective integration within the workforce and failures or breakdowns in cooperation.

In our approach to these problems, we are in close agreement with Dr. Rogers on fundamentals. One of the basic findings of his research is that "within each individual there exist forces of growth, tendencies toward maturity, and capacities for dealing with life and life situations that are far stronger than are customarily realized. . . . These forces can be relied upon as constructive forces." This finding might be paraphrased to state a basic finding of our research at Sears: "Within each organization there exist forces of growth, tendencies toward maturity, and capacities for dealing with problems that are far stronger than are customarily realized. These forces can be relied upon as constructive forces."

Obviously, this analogy cannot be pushed too far because the social group is not nearly as well integrated an entity as the human personality. Nevertheless, stable groups are far more able to deal with their own problems than has been generally recognized. Just as Dr. Rogers has devoted himself to developing methods for releasing the constructive forces within the individual personality, our work at Sears might be characterized as directed toward releasing the constructive forces within the groups comprising our organization.

Despite this basic agreement in approach, the program at Sears has proceeded in a somewhat different direction. We fully recognize the importance of individual maladjustment and appreciate the value of individual therapy. However, we feel that many difficulties that apparently involve individual maladjustment actually arise from factors in the work situation and strains in group relationships within the organization structure. Problems of this type can be dealt with more directly and more adequately by means other than individual counseling. This point is illustrated by the question raised at the last meeting regarding widespread dissatisfactions of white collar workers over status, pay, and opportunities for advancement. No amount of individual counseling can effectively relieve "personal maladjustments" of this type. Any adequate solution must involve changes in thinking and practice at the managerial level and not merely among the workers.

In other words, many of industry's most serious problems are inherent in the structure of relationships within the organization and not in the individuals who comprise the organization. Such problems can be handled best by tackling the organization itself and, specifically, by working directly with those in positions to make organization changes, the executives. Nondirective counseling is only one method for accomplishing desirable changes in the thinking and actions of the managerial staff. A more direct method is an educative process that gives that staff better information and more adequate understanding. At the root of both approaches is the belief that individuals are basically flexible and that, given an opportunity to understand, they will be willing and anxious to adapt themselves and to change, and the better the understanding the more likely the adaptation.

Development of Method

Several years ago, Sears engaged an outside agency to conduct surveys of employee attitudes to determine the level of morale in its retail stores, warehouses, mail order plants, and wholly owned factories and to identify factors tending to undermine good personnel relations. Over a three-year period, more than 36,000 employees were surveyed by means of questionnaires answered anonymously. These surveys were of great value because they provided the company with specific information with which to correct a number of problems. In particular, they were a useful means for emphasizing to store managers and other executives the importance of morale to successful operations and the necessity for constant attention to problems at the work level.

These surveys, however, proved to have serious limitations. They had been undertaken with the simple, straightforward purpose of identifying sources of employee dissatisfaction on the assumption that by eliminating the apparent causes of unrest we could effect an improvement in morale. Aside from certain fairly obvious matters, we found that correction of difficulties identified by the questionnaire did not always bring about improvement in the way employees felt about their jobs and the company. A number of rather surprising facts developed from the surveys. For example, some highly paid employee classifications had lower morale than much lower-paid classifications. There were substantial differences in general levels of morale between different areas of the country and between cities of different size and demography— differences that had little relation to internal factors within the organization.

It became apparent from these and other findings that employee attitudes were not a matter of simple cause-and-effect relationships but rather a complex phenomenon involving a wide variety of interdependent factors. It was equally apparent that many common-sense explanations of employee motivation and behavior did not fit the facts developed by the surveys. As a result, we gradually grew aware of the need for a more adequate conceptual framework capable of offering more workable explanations and providing more reliable predictability.

Because our most puzzling data were in the area of group relations, it seemed wise that we consult and work with sociologists and social anthropologists. We were operating under a lucky star, because about the time we had come to this point in our thinking the Committee on Human Relations in Industry was created at the University of Chicago. This committee, representing various branches of the social sciences but leaning strongly toward social anthropology, has supplied the broader and more adequate conceptual framework we were looking for.

The committee has brought important assets to the task of studying problems of employee relations. These include extensive training in the various disciplines of the social sciences, as well as a broad background of field research in community and industry. One of the committee's principal assets has been the personality and skill of its members. Dr. Burleigh Gardner, executive director of the committee, has shown a unique ability in dealing with people from top management down to rank and file workers—an ability to deal with them on their level, to talk practical sense in their language, and at the same time maintain scientific detachment. Professor Lloyd Warner, chairman of the committee, has likewise provided a breadth of understanding and a depth of insight that have made substantial contributions to the entire program.

A Particular Project

One of the projects undertaken by Dr. Gardner and his staff merits note for purposes of this discussion. This project involves one of the largest and most critically important departments in the parent organization. The officers of the company had been concerned for some time by conditions in that department. There were many complaints from employees and employee turnover, including that of supervisors and executives, was unduly high. Other departments were critical of the services being rendered, and costs of operation were out of line.

Using a modification of the nondirective technique, Dr. Gardner and a member of his staff interviewed all executives and supervisors in the department. The interviews were relaxed, with enough time spent with all individuals to allow them to outline freely their conception of the problems of the department as well as the particular difficulties with which each of them was faced. Interviews started at the top and gradually moved down; several sessions were held with each person, developing more and more facts and greater wealth of significant detail.

Before long, definite signs of improvement began to appear. Employee complaints virtually stopped. Turnover dropped sharply. Output picked up and service was greatly improved. Not until much later was any formal report submitted, and that report contained only rather general findings and a set of suggestions and recommendations that for the most part had already been acted upon. The report when it was submitted was something of an anticlimax because by that time the problems of the department largely disappeared.

By using nondirective interviewing techniques, responsible executives both in and immediately above the department had an opportunity, possibly for the first time, to talk through their problems as they saw them. There are many things about a job an executive cannot discuss with a spouse or others outside the company because of their lack of knowledge of the details involved. People often feel that really bothersome matters cannot be discussed with their superiors for fear of raising doubts about their competence for the job. Even greater circumspection must be observed in discussing things with subordinates. All in all, the opportunities for really free and open discussion of ticklish subjects are scarce in most business situations.

Yet exactly this kind of opportunity was provided through the skillful use of the nondirective interview. Each person had an opportunity to talk out his or her problems freely and, in many cases, to think them through in sufficient detail to see without further help the kind of action on their part necessary to correct the situation. Often during the course of the interviews, people would come to the conclusion that certain things should be done, and then go ahead and do them. Frequently there was no need to wait for the approval of a superior, and many problems were corrected while the study was in progress. That is why significant signs of improvement began to appear before the survey was half complete.

It should be emphasized that these improvements were largely the result of the resources of the department itself. In some cases Dr. Gardner made suggestions based on his broad experience and his analysis of this particular organization. However, his chief contribution to the corrective process lay in liberating and focusing the creative abilities of the people in the department.

Combination of Questionnaires and Interviews

This corrective process has been repeated many times in other units of the company. There is no doubt as to its effectiveness or its usefulness in a wide variety of problem situations. Nevertheless, in this form the method is difficult to apply on any broad scope in an organization as widely scattered as Sears. There are not many people sufficiently skilled in this type of work. Knowledge of interviewing is not enough. Actually, the interviews are only partially "nondirective," and for effective results the interviewer must be thoroughly trained in the broader fields of human relations and have had experience in analyzing organizational problems. There are not many such people available.

In an effort to overcome this difficulty and to make the surveys more widely useful within the organization, the company in cooperation with the Committee on Human Relations and Social Research, Inc., developed a new type of survey based on a combination of questionnaires and personal interviews. For this purpose, we designed a special type of questionnaire, one that does not ask a great many detailed and specific questions but is limited to broad, general questions that will give some indication of the general level of morale within the unit being surveyed. The function of the questionnaire is chiefly to "take the temperature" of the unit, to determine whether problems exist and, if so, discover their general nature and location. If problems are indicated an interview team is sent in to secure more detailed information on the factors responsible and to work with the managerial staff in developing effective solutions.

The Corrective Process

The process by which problems are corrected lies at the heart of the program. Briefly, the objective is to give the executive a better understanding of the way his or her organization functions, the various influences at work in the particular situation, and the way these influences affect the attitudes and behavior of employees. At the same time, an effort is made to provide executives a more effective way of looking at their organizations and the problems found. With a clearer picture of the organization and a more systematic way of thinking about it, they are in a better position to take constructive action directed at the roots of the problems and not at superficial symptoms.

The emphasis is constantly on helping executives and their staffs solve their own problems. There is no effort to supply answers. Help is given in a permissive, noncritical way. The interviewing team is not sent in to put the executive on the spot. The team functions without disciplinary authority, but rather as an aid to help managers build more effective organizations.

A corollary of this principle is that problems are dealt with at the lowest possible level—that is, at the lowest point in the organization where, on specific questions, effective action can be taken. In retail stores for example, only certain problems need be handled at the store manager level; in many cases, problems can be dealt with by working with people down the line without bringing the manager into the picture at all. To have an effective organization, we must have people at each level who are able to deal with problems that arise at that level. The surveys are designed to strengthen each level and not merely the top. A determined effort is made to assure the entire organization that the survey will be helpful. It is carefully explained that the team has not come in to judge the people in the organization or to report the shortcomings of individuals to their superiors. A relationship of confidence is carefully established and rigorously observed.

Conclusion

The object of these procedures and the entire survey program is not so much to correct immediate difficulties as to develop the kind of organizations that can solve their own problems. A survey should leave an organization stronger and more self-reliant than it was before.

It is a basic tenet of our top management that this kind of organization is best achieved by improving managerial and supervisory skills. Skillful executives understand their organizations and are able to anticipate and avoid difficulties. They have the knowledge to recognize and the ability to reduce the seriousness of difficulties that cannot be avoided. Above all, they have the capacity to build effective participation and teamwork, to develop adaptiveness and the willingness to learn and change, and to generate enthusiasm for the job and for the organization.

By and large, we have been remarkably fortunate in having this kind of people in responsible positions in our company. The survey program, however, has proved a useful means for further improving managerial skills and for strengthening those points where strengthening may be needed. We feel, we think with justice, that the program is making an important contribution not only to improved personnel relations but to the continued success and prosperity of the company.

Note

From the transcript of session 11, Executive Seminar Series in Industrial Relations, Industrial Relations Center, University of Chicago, April 1, 1947.

6

The Organization Survey Program

The officers and senior executives of Sears, Roebuck are deeply concerned with the need to maintain sound and mutually satisfactory employee relations, not as a means of "keeping out of trouble," but because they recognize that high morale is an indispensable element of effective organization.

In our efforts to maintain high levels of morale, we have tried to avoid the pitfalls of oversimplification. We know that employee attitudes are products of complex patterns of influences, not all of which arise in the work situation itself. The company's position and reputation in the community plays an important role in determining employee attitudes. General company policies, local management practices, quality of leadership and supervision, opportunities for advancement, rates and methods of compensation, caliber of training, physical conditions of work—these and many other factors combine to influence the character of employee attitudes. In our general personnel program we have tried to give balanced attention to these various interrelated and interdependent elements of good personnel relations.

Organization surveys are an important component of our corporate personnel program. We employ the more comprehensive term *"organization* survey" rather than the generally accepted "morale (or attitude) survey." We use this terminology because the surveys have as their scope the functioning of the unit as a whole and the entire pattern of formal and informal relationships that comprise the local organization.

Our effort is not merely to determine the general level of employee morale but to analyze strains and cleavages within the organization that may impede its proper functioning. Determining the level of morale is useful chiefly as a means for helping diagnose organizational problems; it is not an end in itself.

The Two Survey Methods

In our survey work, we use two primary methods for securing the information we need: questionnaires and interviews. We have learned from experience that each of these methods, used by itself, has both strengths and weaknesses.

The questionnaire has the great advantage of anonymity, speed of coverage, and economy. Questionnaire results can be quantified, permitting direct comparisons between units and various employee classifications. However, questionnaire results are difficult to interpret except on a rather superficial level and offer few clues to the kind of remedial action that will be most effective in dealing with particular problems. Employee interviews do not suffer from these weaknesses. Their chief advantage is that they yield a kind of specific information that can provide the basis for effective remedial action. As a survey technique, however, interviewing has the disadvantages of slowness, expense, and the necessity of using specially trained interviewers who are not easy to find.

We have had extensive experience with both questionnaire and interview techniques. Before the war, we retained a New York firm specializing in employee attitude research to conduct questionnaire surveys that covered more than 36,000 employees. Since the war, in cooperation with the Committee on Human Relations in Industry of the University of Chicago and Social Research, Inc., an offshoot of that committee, we have used interviews as a means of studying a wide variety of problem situations. Out of this experience we have developed what we consider an effective combination of questionnaires and interviews that capitalizes on the advantages and minimizes the disadvantages of each method.

The Questionnaire

After extensive experimentation, we settled on a simplified type of questionnaire. Instead of questions about specific situations, the questionnaire asks broad, general questions covering employee attitudes in seven key areas of the working environment:
1. The company in general
2. The local organization and its management
3. The employee's department and its supervisor
4. The employee's immediate superior
5. Fellow employees
6. The job and working conditions
7. The personal side of the job

There are fifteen items in each category on which employees can express varying degrees of satisfaction or dissatisfaction. The items included are phrased in language used by employees themselves in interviews recorded in other studies, and provide an opportunity for them to express their feelings on all phases of their working lives.

So far as the questionnaire itself is concerned, we are not particularly concerned with responses to individual questions but rather with the general tendency of responses in each of the seven areas. In this respect, the questionnaire is patterned after the familiar "interest" or "personality" schedules used in psychological testing. The function of the questionnaires is not to develop detailed information but to serve as a diagnostic tool for determining the general "feeling tone" within the organizational unit and for identifying departments or categories of employees where problems exist. By this means we can survey a store or mail order plant and say in so many words, "Morale in this organization is generally good, but poor feelings are indicated among employees in departments X, Y, and Z." Or again, "Morale in department A is generally good, but negative feelings are directed toward the local organization and its management."

The Interview

By means of the questionnaires we are able to locate problem departments and identify the general nature of employee dissatisfactions. However, the questionnaires do not tell us *why* morale is low, although with experience those conducting the surveys are developing a remarkable ability to hazard shrewd conjectures. The real task of determining the "why" is the function of the interviewers. Because the questionnaire has already determined the general nature and location of problems, the interviewing team is able to concentrate its time and energies on the units most requiring assistance.

Our interviewers use a modification of the so-called nondirective interview used with such good effect in the famous Hawthorne Studies at the Western Electric Company. In this type of interview, the interviewer refrains from asking direct and specific questions but seeks to create an atmosphere in which employees feel free to talk and go into any matters they consider important. In such an atmosphere, the information obtained is more likely to be an accurate representation of what people believe. If specific questions were asked, employees would be more likely to talk about things the interviewer wants to know than about what is on their own minds. The object of the interview is to learn what problems people consider of most immediate concern, what they think about these problems, and how they feel about their jobs and the units where they work.

Information obtained in the interviews is never used in a way that will identify individual employees. They are assured that anything they say will be held in confidence, and that assurance is strictly adhered to. Employees seem to have no apprehension on this score because they talk freely in the interviews. Most people, in fact, seem eager to talk to make sure the survey team has a clear understanding of problems from their points of view.

Surveys are now usually conducted cooperatively by members of the Sears personnel staff and representatives of Social Research, Inc. At one time we believed that surveys should be conducted only by people from outside the company, but we have since experienced no difficulty in having members of our own staff take an active part in the work. Actually, many surveys are conducted by our staff working alone, with no impairment of results. The important requisites in survey work are the skill and integrity of the survey team, and so long as these are present it seems to make no difference whether the team is in the employ of the company or of an outside firm.

Since the purpose of the survey program is to assist in the development and maintenance of effective organizations, the survey is only half complete when the problem areas have been identified by means of the questionnaire and when the nature and origin of difficulties have been determined by means of the interviews. The survey is not complete until positive steps have been taken to correct the problems found. The process of correction lies at the heart of the program.

The Corrective Process

The survey begins with the local executive himself, say a store manager. The captain of the team sits down with the manager and, using a modification of nondirective interviewing techniques, gives him an opportunity to talk extensively about his organization and the problems he feels are of greatest moment. This step is important, because one of the crucial aspects of any organizational problem is the attitude of the responsible executive toward it. This initial interview also serves the purpose of providing a considerable amount of factual information to the survey team and of acquainting the manager with the objectives and methods of the survey. Similar interviews with similar purposes are then conducted with the local executive and supervisory staff, from the top down.

The corrective process actually begins with these initial interviews. Supervisors and executives are given an opportunity to talk out their problems freely and, in many cases, to think them through in sufficient detail to see, perhaps for the first time, how they can correct some elements of problem situations. Often during the course of the interview a person will come to the conclusion that certain things should be done and act at once. Thus, some difficulties are likely to be corrected while the survey is still in progress, sometimes before the survey proper actually gets under way. The corrective process is greatly accelerated, of course, as the results of the questionnaires and interviews build up a more complete picture of the operations of the unit, its organization, the problems and attitudes of its people, points of friction, and sources of difficulty.

When the survey team feels that it has the picture reasonably complete, it holds further discussions with the store manager. At this point the manager is frequently able to contribute additional elements to the picture, but the main purpose of these later discussions is to see that he becomes more fully aware of the nature of the problems in his store.

An effort is made to give the manager a new way of looking at his organization and how it runs. He is helped to understand the various influences at work in his particular situation and their effects on the attitudes and behavior of his people. By this means the manager benefits from the survey team's experience in similar situations and particularly from the team's broad training in principles of organization and human relations.

With a clearer picture of his organization and a better way of thinking about it, the manager is in a better position to take constructive action directed at the roots of problems rather than their superficial symptoms. The emphasis is constantly on helping the manager and his staff work out their own problems. They are most intimately familiar with the organization, and, above all, they are the people who will have to live with the results of whatever course of action is decided upon. It has been our experience that most executives and supervisors have within themselves the resources for dealing with their own problems. Simply stated, the function of the survey is to assist in liberating the creative resources of the executive and supervisory staff.

Developing Self-Reliance

The survey team works not only with the store manager but with the various key people on his staff. A basic principle of our survey work is that problems should be dealt with at the lowest level in the organization where, on a specific question, effective action can be taken. To have an effective store, plant, or parent department organization, we must have executives and supervisors at each level of that unit able to deal effectively with the problems of that level. The surveys are therefore designed to strengthen each level, not merely the top.

We have found that people may be handling difficult situations badly not through lack of ability or desire but because of conditions beyond their control, such as heavy pressure from superiors, conflicting demands, or faults in the structure or functioning of the organization. Blame and criticism in such circumstances can only accentuate the problem. A far better course is to assist in relieving pressure and conflict, to correct faults in the organization, and above all to strengthen the ability of individuals to deal with their own problems.

Implicit in this approach is the conviction that most of the problems we are dealing with are inherent in the structure of relationships within the organization, not in the individuals who comprise the organization. Such problems can best be handled by tackling the organization itself and, more specifically, by working with those in positions to take effective action, namely, the executives in charge. The objective of the program is not so much to correct immediate problems as to assist in developing the kind of organization that can solve its problems from this time forward. A survey has failed in its primary purpose unless it makes the particular store, plant, or department stronger and more self-reliant than it was before.

Considerable flexibility and informality are characteristic of our survey methods. Certain basic principles, however, are carefully observed. One of the most important of these is that information secured in confidence is held in confidence and never disclosed in a form that can indicate its source or jeopardize the position of subordinates. A closely related principle is that the survey team is careful never to fix blame. The team does not judge the personnel of the organization or report the shortcomings of individuals to their superiors. Obviously, shortcomings are observed in the course of the surveys, but to the extent that individual weaknesses are involved it is the responsibility of local management, not the survey team, to deal with them.

General Survey Findings

While I cannot present in one-two-three order a list of requirements for maintaining a high level of cooperation and enthusiasm among employees, I can outline some of the conclusions of our research to date that suggest an approach others may find useful in considering their own organization's problems.

One conclusion of which we are very sure is that problems of personnel relations must not be oversimplified. We are not dealing here with simple cause-and-effect relationships. For example, if employees complain of poor lighting, poor ventilation, or inadequate restroom facilities, correction of these conditions may not lead to any improvement in morale because the complaints may be only symptoms of more basic difficulties that have little or nothing to do with the objects complained about. Unless these underlying problems are recognized and dealt with, no amount of tinkering with superficialities can do much good.

We are also sure that employee attitudes cannot be influenced effectively by direct frontal attack. We have not considered it worth our while to try to explain "management's point of view" to our employees, or to educate them on the "economic facts of life." Frankly, we are deeply skeptical of the utility of such an approach and strongly suspect that it creates more antagonism and mistrust than it wins converts. In our efforts to retain the loyalty and support of our employees we are dealing with a problem far too complex to be handled in terms of "winning friends and influencing people."

Rather than trying to teach employees the "economic facts of life," it would be better for *us in management* to keep in mind one of the basic "*social* facts of life," that attitudes are largely the product of experience. If the experience of workers on the job causes them to dislike and mistrust management, no amount of "education" will change their feelings or behavior.

Another common example of superficial thinking has been the tendency in recent years to ascribe much of the blame for poor employee relations to "inadequate supervision" and to attempt to improve matters through supervisory training. There is no question but that faulty supervision has harmful effects on employee morale and many supervisors could benefit from proper training. However,

I question both the justice and the efficacy of making the supervisor the whipping boy where poor employee relations exist.

In many cases supervisors are themselves victims of poor handling by their superiors or they may be caught in a network of management policies and practices that are largely responsible for their own negative attitudes and behavior. Many of the real causes of poor morale may be matters over which supervisors have little or no control. Any effort to bring pressure on them to change their behavior, without first dealing with the forces that are causing that behavior, is likely to backfire. This is even more likely to occur when, as frequently happens, training programs are installed at the lower supervisory levels without any corresponding attention to the need for improving the skills of executives higher up the line.

One of the primary objectives of our organization survey program is to help improve executive and supervisory skills at all levels of the organization. From this standpoint, the surveys are in effect an executive and supervisory training program. They have the great advantage of having as their subject matter the specific current problems of the organization itself rather than a set of principles or rules dreamed up by an "expert" in the personnel department or purchased ready-made on handy vest-pocket cards.

Note

Excerpted by permission of the publisher from *Personnel*, November 1949. ©1949 by the American Management Association, New York. All rights reserved.

7

Findings of the Survey Programs

There is clear evidence from our studies that Sears employees are generally well disposed toward the company. An analysis of the responses of some eleven thousand employees to one questionnaire revealed that 77 percent thought Sears was either "better than average" or "one of the very best" places to work and only 1.5 percent thought Sears "poorer than average." Some 82 percent said they would rather work for Sears than almost any other company of which they knew. Our interviews have yielded similar results, emphasizing the high regard most people seem to have for the company.

Nevertheless, we are keenly conscious that many problems exist and that morale varies widely among various units of the organization. For example, the lowest unit surveyed had a "morale score" (using an arbitrary scale of 0 to 100) more than 50 points below the highest, with other units scattered between these two extremes. We have therefore made an effort to gain a better understanding of the factors that account for such differences.

The most important conclusion to which we have come is that there is no simple explanation for any given state of employee morale. Rather, our studies indicate the existence of a highly complex set of interdependent factors that combine in subtle and obscure ways to produce a particular level of employee satisfaction or dissatisfaction. Whether high or low, this level of satisfaction, in turn, seems to reinforce many of the factors producing it, thus setting in motion a kind of circular reaction that tends to keep good morale good and poor morale poor. It is for this reason that management, despite sincere and vigorous efforts, often finds it difficult to bring about perceptible improvements in problem situations.

Wages, Hours, and Working Conditions

Our studies indicate that many of the factors considered of primary importance by management often play relatively minor roles.

Analysis of the eleven thousand responses noted above showed that pay ranked in eighth place among the elements related to high morale. Interestingly enough, this eighth-place item related to *pay in comparison with other jobs in the same unit;* rates of pay as such ranked in fourteenth place. Hours of work, in twenty-first place, fared still more poorly as an influence on employee attitudes.

This is not to say that hours of work, rates of pay, and proper job differentials are not important. Wherever management is guilty of any serious shortcomings in these matters, they loom up much more importantly in employee thinking. The point is, these things in themselves are not enough; they are only the beginning. If the only basis management can conceive for employee loyalty and co-operation is the pay envelope and the short workweek, there can never be enough money or short enough hours to do the job. Management must have a firmer basis than this on which to build effective working relationships.

The role played by conditions of work is likewise misunderstood. Good equipment and pleasant surroundings can never of themselves develop high morale; their *absence,* however, can be a source of real difficulty. If employees are discontented with any phase of their relations with management, they are likely to seize upon and magnify any imperfections in their physical environment. They can tolerate situations they know are difficult for management to correct, but where annoyances appear unnecessary, employees are likely to interpret the condition as evidence of management's lack of concern for them as people. It is against this attitude that employees rebel. The poor working conditions are taken as evidence of the attitude and a convenient target against which to direct complaints.

Employee Benefits

The importance of management's attitude toward its employees is likewise demonstrated in the matter of employee benefits. Sears, Roebuck and Co. has a very broad and substantial program in this respect. [It should be noted that in 1950 when this paper was written employee benefits were usually provided at the initiative of employers and had not yet become a standard part of the employment package and a routine subject of collective bargaining.]

This framework of benefits has had a definite influence on employee attitudes. The influence, however, has been more indirect than direct. Important as the economic aspects of the benefits may be, their chief significance as regards employee morale is the fact that they are tangible evidence to the organization of management's concern for the welfare of its employees. This is not to minimize the economic aspects of the benefits, particularly profit sharing; they are effective as symbols chiefly because they *are* substantial and because, as such, they demonstrate the reality and sincerity of management's concern. If they were less substantial, their value as symbols and as an earnest of management's attitude would be diminished. Nevertheless, our studies show clearly that employees respond primarily to the evidence of management's concern and only secondarily to the economic values as such.

This point can be illustrated, albeit in rather general terms, by the experience of certain other companies with whom we have had an opportunity to become acquainted. Several of these in recent years have established various kinds of benefit plans, some of which provide substantial cash values. In those cases where the company already enjoyed good morale, the benefit plans were well received because they were perceived as an additional expression of a management attitude to which the employees were accustomed and in which they had confidence. In those cases where morale was poor, however, the introduction of a new benefit plan was often greeted with suspicion and distrust.

The important point in both types of circumstances is management's attitude toward its people. Is this attitude one of respect for those in the organization and genuine concern for their welfare, which they can see expressed in other phases of their working lives and in their routine contacts with those at higher levels in the organization? Identical benefit plans installed in companies with and without that attitude are likely to have precisely opposite effects.

The Special Role of Profit Sharing

What has been said above applies with special force to the Sears profit sharing plan. This plan, in continuous operation since 1916, is open to all employees with a year or more of service. Each member of the plan deposits 5 percent of his earnings in the profit sharing fund. At the end of the year the company contributes to the fund between 5 percent and 9 percent (determined according to a fixed scale) of its net profits before taxes and dividends. These contributions are credited to the accounts of employees on a dual basis of length of service and amount of individual deposit.

Sums credited to members are carried partially in cash or its equivalent but are chiefly invested in company stock, with dividends earned credited to the employees' accounts. The plan has been unusually successful and has been the means for enabling employees who make a career at Sears to build up substantial equities by the time of their retirement. Of special significance for present purposes is the fact that the profit sharing fund now [1950] holds in trust for its members approximately 19 percent of the company's outstanding capital stock, thus making Sears employees as a group by far the largest stockholders in the company.

Over the years the profit sharing plan has gradually assumed a role that transcends its function as tangible evidence of management's concern for the welfare of its employees. In a sense, profit sharing has become a "unifying principle" that serves as a symbol around which the entire organization revolves. Because of the magnitude of its holdings, there is a tangible community of interest between stockholders and employees. The making of profits for absentee stockholders has never been a rallying point around which the enthusiastic support of employees could be organized. However, where employees and stockholders tend more and more to become the same people, profitability of operations—with all that it implies—becomes a rallying point of dramatic consequence.

Here again, the influence on employee attitudes is primarily symbolic rather than direct. The actual holdings of individual employees are not nearly so important as the fact that the huge holdings of the profit sharing fund symbolize to them that they and the company are one, that they are in effect "working for themselves." In employee conversations one frequently hears the phrase, "Well, that's good for profit sharing." It would be rare indeed, over the length and breadth of American business, ever to hear the phrase, spoken by an employee, "Well, that's good for the stockholders"— and have the words be otherwise than a complaint.

Quality of Supervision

It has become quite the fashion in management circles to ascribe much of the blame for poor employee relations on "inadequate supervision" and to attempt to improve matters through supervisory training. There is no question but that faulty supervision has harmful effects on employee morale and that many supervisors could benefit from proper training. However, our studies have led us to question both the justice and the utility of making supervisors the scapegoats and blaming them when relationships with employees leave something to be desired.

In many cases the supervisors themselves are victims of poor handling by their own superiors, or they may be caught in a network of management policies and practices that are largely responsible for their own attitudes and behavior. Many of the real causes of poor morale may be matters over which supervisors have little or no control. Any effort to bring pressure on them to change behavior, without first dealing with the forces that are shaping that behavior, is likely to backfire. This is even more likely to occur when, as frequently happens, training programs are installed at the lower supervisory levels without any corresponding attention to the need of improving the skills of executives higher up the line.

The type of supervision prevailing in any organization is likely to follow closely the pattern set by those in the top levels of management. If higher executives tend to maintain friendly, easy, comfortable relations with those who report to them directly, these individuals in turn will tend to maintain similar relations with their own subordinates, down through all levels of the organization. This repetition of a pattern set by the top is a reflection of the tendency of executives as a group to copy, consciously or unconsciously, the traits and methods of their superiors.

Promotion from Within

For this reason, the type of leadership prevailing at the top is likely to be perpetuated for considerable periods of time. This tendency is particularly strong when, through a policy of promotion from within, future executives are molded early to an established pattern.

Where this pattern is one of good leadership skills, promotion from within can make a further important contribution to good employee relations. Executives who rise from the ranks are likely to have a better appreciation of the employee's point of view. Promotion from within tends to increase the respect and confidence of employees for their superiors because of their knowledge that those in higher positions really know their jobs and "won their spurs" in free and open competition. Furthermore, they are "all in the same family" and "all speak the same language" because, in a sense, they "all grew up together" as part of the same organization. There thus tends to be a higher sense of the "we" feeling than is likely to be the case otherwise.

As with most sound management policies, promotion from within serves two sets of needs, those of management and those of employees. The management needs, of course, are for qualified people to all responsible executive positions. The employee needs are two-fold: (1) the need of those with ability to find opportunity to develop and exercise that ability, and (2) the need of *all* employees to feel that they are part of an organization in which ability is recognized and rewarded. This latter need is an outgrowth of one of the most deeply rooted sentiments of the American democratic tradition, the American ideal of freedom of opportunity, with ability finding its own level and people advancing as far as their capacity and ambition will carry them.

In any organization where these sentiments do not find expression, people are likely to be deeply resentful toward the management which, by its policies and performance, runs contrary to a cherished ideal of what is right and proper. It is not necessary that all employees advance; many are not particularly interested in or qualified for advancement. All that is necessary is that opportunities be available to those who have both the necessary ambition and the ability. If this condition is met, the entire organization, including those content to find their niche at lower levels, is likely to be satisfied. If it is not met, the entire organization, those with ability and ambition as well as those without, is likely to be restive, discontented, and distrustful of management.

Size of Organization

The evidence of our surveys demonstrates that there probably is no more important influence on attitudes and morale than sheer size of organization (not necessarily size of the total company but rather size of the individual operating branch). Our studies show clearly the tendency of morale to decline sharply with increasing size, even under the same personnel and management policies.

The reason for higher morale in smaller units is fairly clear. Employees have a much better opportunity to know each other, so that cooperation between individuals and departments can develop on a more personal, informal basis and not be so largely dependent on impersonal systems and administrative controls. Employees can see much more readily where they themselves "fit" into the organization and the significance of their jobs in the whole scheme of things. Individual jobs and departmental functions are not so minutely subdivided, so that jobs have more meaning and importance and employees have a greater opportunity to use and develop more of their potential capacity.

In smaller organizations supervisors and executives are in frequent personal contact with employees, so that to the rank and file they appear as flesh-and-blood people who can be liked or disliked for their own sakes and not judged largely on the impersonal results of their administrative actions or on the basis of myths about "those guys in the front office." In a large organization such myths are often the chief means by which rank-and-file employees arrive at their feelings toward those in higher levels of management. Unfortunately, these myths often present badly distorted images of the individuals in question, distortions that could be readily corrected if the organization were small enough to provide an opportunity for more frequent face-to-face contact.

A further important advantage of smaller organizations lies in the fact that this closer, more frequent, more personal contact between executives and the rank and file makes possible a better understanding of each other's problems and points of view and greatly facilitates the adjustment of difficulties likely to arise in any working environment. In larger and more complex organizations such adjustments are often difficult and cumbersome to deal with because a larger number of people in different departments and at different levels must be consulted. The result is not only that action tends to be delayed, but the action taken may not really compose the difficulty or eliminate the grievance because the person making the controlling decision may be so far removed from the scene that he or she receives a garbled version of the problem, and the decision made may be wide of the mark so far as the real issue is concerned.

Administrative Decentralization

To an important degree, these are disadvantages inherent in large organizations, and they account directly or indirectly for much of the general deterioration of management-employee relations that has accompanied the rise of great corporations in our economic and social system. However, this situation is by no means wholly beyond management's control. In fact, our studies strongly suggest that through effective administrative decentralization it is possible to preserve the special economic advantages of large size without losing the special human advantages of small size.

This point is illustrated by the experience of a number of companies, of which Sears may serve as an example. Sears is generally regarded as a huge concern, and so it is viewed as a totality. But actually Sears is a combination of many units, most of which are physically and administratively separated and relatively small by contemporary standards. If Sears business were concentrated administratively and physically under one roof, rather than being scattered as it is over hundreds of separate entities, the morale of Sears employees would be much below the level at which it is today. Our studies suggest that the important factor here is not so much geographical dispersion as administrative decentralization, although the geographical factor is not without significance.

The Sears system is highly decentralized, and the local manager has authority and responsibility within himself for the day-to-day decisions that are of greatest moment in employee relations. He is subject only to a general framework of company policies; within that framework he has wide leeway for handling on the spot practically all problems that may arise. For this reason, he finds it easier to win the respect of his employees; he is in a position to exercise a kind of effective leadership that would be impossible for an executive whose own higher management allows him only a narrow leeway of judgment and discretion.

Thus, the local unit has sufficient autonomy to provide for itself and its employees most of the advantages of a small organization. The situation would be quite otherwise if management responsibility were highly centralized, if the local unit were operated as a kind of "dangling department" of a much larger entity. In such circumstances, there would be all the disadvantages of a larger organization, *plus* the complications of geographical distance and a much higher degree of impersonality between management and employees.

The point to be stressed is *administrative decentralization*, the placing of authority and responsibility as close as possible to the scene of action and permitting a wide range of discretion to those at each level of the system. Many organizations assume that they have such decentralization. There is a difference, however, between the form and the fact of decentralization. The mere issuance of an official policy or the redrawing of an organization chart cannot bring about decentralization if higher executives persist in reviewing (let along making) decisions that could be made further down the line, or if they set up rigid controls that allow too little leeway for those at the scene of operations. The essence of decentralization is an *attitude of mind*, a willingness on the part of those at higher levels of authority to permit their subordinates an adequately broad range of discretion.

This being the case, effective decentralization by no means depends on geographical dispersion; there are no compelling reasons why its essential features cannot be applied in substantial measure within a large organization operating at a single location. If this is to be done, however, it must be done on a basis of breaking down the large organization into a series of smaller ones and providing the smaller units sufficient administrative autonomy to permit them to function as integrated and meaningful entities.

Structure of Organization

At Sears we have found it expedient to enforce decentralization not merely through policy directives but more particularly through the design of the organization itself. Top management has sought to set up an organization structure that makes it difficult for executives to operate on any other basis than fairly extensive delegation of authority and responsibility.

This organization structure may be characterized as "broad" or "flat" in contrast to the more "vertical" or "tall" structures in which there are many layers of supervision between top and bottom. The extent to which Sears has gone in this respect may be indicated by the fact that only four levels of supervision intervene between the president of the company and the salespeople in the stores, a difficult achievement in an organization of well over 100,000 employees in the retail division alone.

To establish this kind of organization the company has gone directly counter to one of the favorite tenets of modern management theory, the so-called span of control, which holds that the number of subordinate executives or supervisors reporting to a single individual should be severely limited to enable that individual to exercise the detailed direction and control generally considered necessary. In an organization with as few supervisory levels as Sears, it is obvious that most key executives have so many subordinates reporting to them that they simply cannot exercise too close supervision over their activities. This has proved an effective means for assuring substantial internal managerial decentralization.

Personal Qualities

A significant feature of the "flat" type of organization structure is the high premium it places on the proper selection, training, and placement of key personnel; to work successfully, such an organization depends in large measure on the quality of executive competence at all strategic points. While important in all types of organizations, the quality of executive personnel is particularly vital in the "flat" structure because there are fewer levels of supervision and therefore less direction and control, thus increasing higher management's dependence on the skill and initiative of those further down the line.

In this type of organization structure, individual executives are thrown largely on their own, to sink or swim on the basis of their individual abilities. They cannot rely to more than a limited extent on those above them; and these superiors, by the same token, cannot too severely restrict, through detailed supervision and control, their subordinate's growth and development.

Not all individuals can function effectively in this type of system; it requires a very large measure of self-reliance, self-confidence, and personal capacity. The system tends to weed out those who lack these qualities in adequate degree. Those who are able to adapt to this type of organization, however, are likely to be not only better merchants and executives but also the kinds of people who can build and maintain teamwork and cooperation and high levels of employee morale, not so much because they consciously attempt to do so as because these results are a natural by-product of their ways of working and a reflection of their personalities.

On the other hand, in organizations characterized by many levels of supervision and by elaborate systems of control, not only has the individual little opportunity to develop the capacities of self-reliance and initiative, but the system tends to weed out those who do. Furthermore, our studies strongly suggest that those who survive in such an organization are often likely, by virtue of the very qualities that enabled them to survive, to have personalities and ways of working that do not foster employee teamwork and cooperation.

An organization with few layers of supervision and a minimum of formal controls places a premium on ability to stimulate and lead. The driver type executive, who functions through maintaining constant pressure and whose chief sanction is fear, cannot operate so effectively in such an organization. Under truly decentralized management, an executive accomplishes results and moves to higher levels of responsibility chiefly to the extent that he or she is able to secure the willing, enthusiastic support of colleagues and subordinates; they do not have the "tools," with which a more centralized system would to some extent provide them, to accomplish results in any other manner. The outcome is not only higher levels of accomplishment but, at the same time, more satisfying kinds of supervision and higher levels of employee morale.

Conclusion

Our studies suggest that the problem of employee morale is far more complex than is customarily appreciated. There are no simple cause-and-effect relationships, and often the influences of primary importance are subtle and obscure. Nevertheless, it is clear that the quality of personnel relations prevailing in any organization is not a matter of chance. The following points in particular merit the special attention of management:

1. One of the great advantages of the simple and relatively informal organization structure is that such a structure not only permits but enforces a maximum of informal, face-to-face relationships and keeps impersonal, "institutionalized" relationships at a minimum. This type of structure likewise provides a higher degree of freedom on the job, utilizes a larger measure of the individual's capacities, requires the exercise of personal judgment and initiative, and encourages the development of native abilities.

2. Such a structure requires an unusually high order of administrative ability if it is to operate successfully. In essence the structure requires a democratic type of leadership, which calls for higher administrative competence than the authoritarian variety.

3. Basic to all other factors is the attitude of top management itself toward the people who comprise its organization. The nature of this attitude will largely determine the structure of the organization and the quality of relationships that prevails within the structure.

4. High employee morale is a by-product of sound organization. It is not a result that can be achieved by and for itself; above all, it is not a result of "being nice to people" or plying them with favors. Nor is high morale something to be achieved at the expense of good operating results. The same policies, attitudes, and practices that are best calculated to produce good operating results over the long run are precisely the policies, attitudes, and practices that produce high levels of employee morale.

5. Good morale and good results are not mutually exclusive. They are two aspects of the same things: sound organization and capable leadership.

Note

Excerpted by permission of the publisher from "Factors Influencing Employee Morale," *Harvard Business Review* 28:1 (Jan. 1950). Copyright © 1950 by the President and Fellows of Harvard College. All rights reserved.

8

Toward a Typology of Organizational Malfunction

One line of thought on which we are working is the possibility of developing a typology of the malfunctioning of an organization that can be useful in studying social groups much as the typologies used by psychiatrists are useful in studying the malfunctioning of personality. This possibility was first suggested by the frequency with which questionnaire scores plotted on percentile charts tended to form themselves into patterns with which we began to grow familiar. Our interviewing, likewise, attested that certain types of problems tend to occur in fairly well-organized syndromes. For instance, we have found that certain kinds of difficulties typically follow changes in key management staff. We can usually predict not only the difficulties likely to occur but the sequence in which they are likely to appear.

A typology of the malfunctioning of organization would be useful not only for scientific purposes but for administrative purposes as well, for with it could be developed a symptomatology by which problem situations could be diagnosed and acted upon more rapidly and with greater confidence. Our survey program is primarily an administrative device. Useful as it has been for this purpose, it has certain unwieldy features because sometimes it has to go a rather long way around to reach a fairly simple conclusion. For administrative purposes, we would be better off if we had a group of people (preferably the administrators themselves) skilled at recognizing and diagnosing symptoms and dealing with the problems thus identified according to the therapy found useful for that particular difficulty.

It would be even more useful to be able to predict with reasonable accuracy the probable consequences of a given event or a given set of circumstances and to set in motion early a series of moves designed to minimize adverse possibilities. We are able to do precisely this in several problem areas (for instance, changes of key executives), and our success in these encourages us in our efforts to broaden the range of areas for which we can make reasonably reliable predictions.

As to our survey program as a whole, as things stand now we are somewhat in the position the medical profession would be in if the physician had to give a basic metabolism to determine whether a patient had a cold in the head. To continue the analogy, if we had a workable symptomatology (even a tentative one), we could recognize the head cold and treat it accordingly. On the other hand, if the symptoms in the case indicated a more dangerous or more complicated disability, we could always apply our equivalent of the basic metabolism or such other procedure as the circumstances might require.

Any typology of malfunctioning would have to be related, of course, to the underlying dynamic system and not merely to the symptoms. All of our research testifies to the frequency with which the identical symptom can arise from entirely different factors. In one context, complaints over wages can be a danger signal; in another, merely an indication of the normal desire of everyone to be making more than they are. Sometimes, complaints over wages can really be complaints over wages; but they may be verbalizations of resentments that grow out of situations that have little to do with wages. Because of the unreliability of symptoms taken in isolation, we have found it more and more useful to think in terms of syndromes. The fact that our questionnaire is so constructed as to yield results in the form of profiles has greatly aided this purpose.

The psychiatrists have found the concept of *integration* a useful one around which to organize their ideas about personality and its disorders. We think a similar concept, related to group phenomena, could form the basis for a useful typology of the malfunctioning of organization. Certainly, the degree of integration (internal and external) of any organization relates very directly to the underlying dynamic factors at work. One type of failure of integration leads to one type of difficulty that is different from that likely to arise from another type of failure. Moreover, the methods for dealing with the two sets of circumstances are likely to differ, although many of the symptoms may appear identical.

Note

Excerpted by permission of the publisher from "Organization Structure and Employee Morale," *American Sociological Review* 15 (Apr. 1950).

9

Industry as a Social Science Laboratory

The study of management-employee relations offers especially attractive possibilities for fostering the integration of a number of discrete social science disciplines. The problems of management-employee relations are among the most important facing our society, but because they manifest themselves within the confines of particular enterprises and industries they can be comprehended and worked with both in detail and in whole. Management-employee relationships represent a practical unit of study on which can be brought to bear the special concepts and insights of the several disciplines, not in isolation but in fruitful and meaningful integration.

The study of management-employee relations has a further (though as yet little realized) advantage for purposes of encouraging closer integration. This advantage arises out of the special role of the executive in the business organization and the necessity for his dealing with situations as a whole. The executive may utilize the findings and recommendations of experts, whether social scientists or otherwise, but his decisions and actions must be in terms of the special circumstances and requirements of the total situation with which he is dealing. He is forced to integrate, for to proceed otherwise would be to court disaster.

In a certain sense, business managers may be described as "practicing social scientists." They deal every day with the same raw materials as their academic counterparts. They may not always proceed in the same orderly and deliberate fashion or with the same regard for the niceties of scientific method, but many of them have remarkably clear insights and useful hypotheses that are more than mere rules of thumb. These insights and hypotheses, based as they are on experience in dealing with whole situations, can offer stimulating and fruitful leads to the scientist. Unfortunately, they have

been largely ignored by specialists insulated in their own precon-
ceptions and prone to discount heavily anything that does not fit
easily into their established patterns of thinking.

If the social scientist can benefit from the knowledge and understanding of the executive, the executive can benefit equally from
the concepts and findings of the scientist. This benefit can consist
not only in helping the executive in a business sense by improving
his managerial and leadership skills, but more importantly by contributing to the betterment of the whole system of human relations
in an important segment of modern life. The business executive
occupies a strategic position in our society. He is able to exert tremendous influence for good or ill. In some cases the nature and direction of this influence are undoubtedly a reflection of the tem-
peramental characteristics of the individual, but in probably the
majority of cases the executive is actuated by a sincere desire to do
the best job he knows how to do. Under these circumstances, the
social scientists can make perhaps their most important contribution to the common good by communicating something of their
ideas and knowledge to those in positions to act upon them, the
business administrators.

The key, of course, is communication. If the social scientists are
to influence the course of events, effective communication must be
an essential part of their job. Unfortunately, in too many cases they
have forced their thinking into conceptual systems that, however
neat, are too far from the realities with which the administrator
deals for them to make much impression upon him.

One way of dealing with this problem of communication is
through the medium of the consultant, the go-between to the aca-
demicians and the businessmen, and the interpreter of each to the
other. Certainly there is a role for such individuals. As a condition
of their survival as consultants, they have had to learn to talk both
the businessman's and the scientist's language. As a result, they
have been able to translate many of the findings of scientific research to executives and many significant advances in business
practices have been forthcoming from their efforts.

On the other hand, while consultants can be extremely useful to
particular businesses, they cannot provide an adequate solution for
the *general* problem of communication, simply because there are
not enough good consultants.

If the problem is ever to be solved in any adequate fashion, it
must be in terms of the scientists as a group, particularly those specializing in the field of management-employee relations, dealing
more closely with actual work situations, working more intimate-

ly with management itself, profiting by the experience and insights of creative management leaders, and developing systems of concepts and modes of expression that are meaningful and useful to those who must deal with (and not merely think about) the actual problems of group behavior.

The work of neither the consultant nor the universities can ever be too effective unless it is integrated into the patterns of management thinking and action. For this purpose, the consultants are sometimes found wanting. Management can depend on their counsel and advice for temporary periods, but it cannot use them as a permanent crutch or as a substitute for its own understanding of its problems and its own skill in dealing with them. Unless the consultant is able to leave management better equipped to handle its present and future problems, there has been no communication, no learning, no permanent benefit.

I agree with those industrial psychologists who emphasize the importance of having well-adjusted personalities at all levels of the organization structure, and with the fact that the source of hostilities in the work place can often be found in the personality make-up of the dominant individual or group in top management. We need to know much more, however, about the way personality works its way down through an organization. For this purpose, concepts of personality by themselves are not enough. We need a better understanding, for example, of the way different personalities tend to set up different types of organization structures and the way in which the structure itself, as well as the top manager's methods of dealing with the people in the structure, influences the attitudes and behavior of people at all levels of the organization.

The danger of the primarily individualistic psychological (or psychiatric) approach is precisely its tendency to concentrate too exclusively on the individual, and its failure, in many cases, to conceive properly of the individual as a functioning member of an organization and as molded and influenced, to some considerable extent, by the pressures and the system of relationships prevailing within that organization. Such concepts, of course, are by no means lacking in the disciplines themselves, but those seeking to apply the disciplines to business situations are often likely to over-stress such matters as selection, training, and individual therapy. Granted, such matters are important, but they cannot stand alone. No amount of improved selection can be of much avail if the organization itself is wrong and if the newcomer is either shaped quickly into the standard mold or forced out.

Likewise, training in better methods of supervision is often a hopeless task, not so much because the individuals might not wish to improve their ways of working with people but because they themselves may be caught in a system that enforces behavior at variance with the principles being taught. So long as the system goes unchanged, no amount of "supervisory training" can be of much help. On the other hand, if the system itself is improved in such a manner as to tend to enforce desirable types of behavior, explicit training might be much less necessary.

Much the same thing can be said of behavior therapy, whether of the individual or group variety. In many cases such therapy is called for and can prove highly useful, but if the future course of labor-management relations depends on any widespread effort along these lines, we are lost indeed. There are not enough therapists among all the universities and consultants combined.

Modification of the situation in which the individual lives and works is widely practiced by clinical psychologists and psychiatrists in dealing with psychoneuroses. A particularly fruitful area for further research would seem to lie in more detailed and more probing studies of general and specific factors in the working situation likely either to encourage or inhibit psychoneurotic behavior, particularly among executive and supervisory personnel. On the basis of the findings of such studies, it should be possible to manipulate and modify patterns of working relationships and systems of organization and control in such a way as to reduce substantially the need for individual therapy. The great potential contributions of psychiatry and clinical psychology, it seems to me, are in the field of preventive rather than remedial action.

Our own experience at Sears, Roebuck indicates that attitude surveys offer a particularly useful and promising approach to the study of basic problems of management-employee relationships. Much of what industry has done along this line has been criticized by academics, but such surveys are at least evidence of management's interest in understanding employee thinking and reactions, an attitude on the part of executives that speaks well for their receptivity to ideas and their concern for doing a better job of personnel relations.

Furthermore, while much of industry's work in the area is on a fairly superficial level, this is by no means true in all cases. Some of the work now being carried on by business itself meets the most exacting scientific standards and is contributing in an important way to the growth of scientific knowledge. Significantly, this growth of knowledge is not being achieved at the expense of what the businessman would call "practical results."

In our own survey work, we have found it necessary not only to look at the existing context of attitudes and relationships, but to seek out the underlying factors at work in particular situations. Among factors we have identified as important are such things as the peculiarities of individual temperament, the general atmosphere and tradition of the organization, conditions imposed by the nature of the work and the technical processes employed, the character of the organization structure, the system of controls utilized by management, and so on. These are matters that exert a profound influence on the pattern and quality of interpersonal relations, and unless they are understood it is impossible to understand what is happening at the work place and why.

A further advantage of surveys is that they represent a general type of method with which management is already familiar, and their results, if skillfully handled, can be readily interpreted to management. They are a technique that can be of great value as a means for more adequate communication between the social scientist and the businessman. Business executives are very much aware of many of the problems with which they are faced and receptive to ideas and suggestions that will assist them toward a more effective handling of such problems. On the whole, I think the social scientists have been prone to underestimate management's interest and its willingness to cooperate. It will be necessary, however, that they, the scientists, learn to talk the businessman's language, that they evidence some understanding of his problems as he sees them, and that they develop concepts that make sense to management people in terms of their own experience. Such an approach can be rewarding alike to business, to labor-management relations, and to the social sciences.

Note

Excerpted by permission of the publisher from "Discussion," in *The Psychology of Labor-Management Relations*, ed. Arthur Kornhauser, 97–103 (Madison, Wis.: Industrial Relations Research Association, 1949).

Part 3

Structure and Performance

In 1952 Worthy began to draft in book-length form a comprehensive account of his thinking coming largely from his research and executive experience at Sears. This work was cut short by his being called to Washington in early 1953 to serve as Assistant Secretary of Commerce in the Eisenhower Administration. He did, however, complete drafts of nine chapters, three of which are included in this collection.

The first of these, "The Ambiguous Legacy of Frederick W. Taylor," sets the stage for Part 3 of this collection. As Worthy's thinking developed, he found himself in sharp disagreement with certain aspects of the ideas of Taylor and his followers in the "scientific management movement." He recognizes the contribution made by Taylor to the phenomenal increase in the productivity of American industry that had taken place in the half century preceding the time this paper was written, but points out that some aspects of Taylor's approach and methods have led to undue complexity in organization structures and left a deleterious imprint on the quality of human relationships within the enterprise; these negative consequences he attributes primarily to the social ambience of the time and to attributes of Taylor's temperament that profoundly influenced his work. The papers that follow examine from Worthy's own experience other and more effective ways of structuring organizations and fostering quality relationships within the industrial enterprise.

In "The Sears X-Y Study," Worthy anticipates Douglas McGregor by at least a decade in his perception of how different assumptions about employee behavior lead to different patterns of managing. His views are somewhat more comprehensive than McGregor's. The latter limits his analysis to psychological considerations in the relationships between managers and workers, while Worthy is concerned with the way management attitudes shape organization structure, departmental and job design, vertical and lateral communications, and coordination across functional lines. Worthy thus combines analyses of personality differences (psychology) and studies of organizational structure (sociology and anthropology).[1]

The basic conclusions of the X-Y study are confirmed by an analysis of the workings of another and quite different branch of Sears, reported here as "The Sears Central Merchandising Organization." In this chapter from the 1952–53 manuscript, Worthy explores the highly effective manner in which the characteristic "broad" or "flat" Sears organization functions to develop high levels of executive competence and superior economic performance.

In a previously unpublished paper, "Evolution of a Structure," written in 1956, Worthy considers the dynamics of organizational stability and change. Here he explores the early history of Sears and the way in which its relatively loose and informal structure with minimal bureaucracy permitted Sears to adapt easily to changing market conditions. He learned from his Sears studies, his government service, and his experience as a management consultant on leaving Sears in 1961 that while some degree of bureaucratization is a necessary feature of large organization, bureaucracies create vested interests that are resistant to change and the spirit of innovation. In "The Bureaucratic Dilemma," written many years later, he emphasizes the need of the organization for both stability and adaptability and the importance of maintaining a balance between the two.

In "The Behavioral Dimensions of Span of Management Theory," Worthy provides an insightful analysis of the concept viewed from a behavioral perspective. Here he lays to rest simplistic notions of the theory, showing how it must be related to a variety of factors including the nature of the work, discretion permitted employees, stability of operations, and availability of information.

Worthy had a long-standing interest in size of organization and its effects on human relations that started with his original 1942 analysis of employee survey data. In "The Critical Problem of Size," a paper presented at the annual meeting of the Industrial Relations Research Association in 1952, he explored in depth the way in which the disadvantages of size can be offset by breaking down large, monolithic organizations into smaller administrative units. This can be achieved, according to Worthy, through decentralization of management, but to be workable the smaller, decentralized units may not consist of single functions but must include all functions necessary to produce meaningful goods or services.

—David G. Moore

Note

1. The research on which Worthy's views in the X-Y study are based was conducted in 1949–50. An unpublished version of this study was summarized in William F. Whyte's *Modern Methods of Social Research*, published by the Office of Naval Research in 1952, and again in his 1957 book, *Man and Organization*. Worthy's use of "X" and "Y" to designate two different types of organization structure and McGregor's use on "Theory X" and "Theory Y" to designate two different types of personality appear to be purely coincidental.

10

The Ambiguous Legacy of Frederick W. Taylor

Frederick W. Taylor (1856–1915), the "Father of Scientific Management," left a lasting imprint on industrial society. Coming to maturity at the time large-scale industry was beginning to dominate the American and European economic scenes, Taylor was one of the earliest and most creative of those concerned with thinking through the problems of organizing and controlling the new processes of production. Taylor's early education was pointed toward a professional career. Poor eyesight, however, forced him to break off his schooling in 1874. In order to conserve his sight, he took employment as an apprentice pattern-maker and machinist and in 1878 entered the employ of the Midvale Steel Company of Philadelphia, where by diligent application he moved rapidly from laborer through a series of subordinate jobs to the position of foreman of the machine shop. As a workman and still more as a foreman, Taylor found the disorganization and confusion of the shop a source of irritation and concern. He was also struck by the extent to which employees had developed "soldiering" into a fine art, and above all by the complete lack of objective standards as to what should constitute either a fair day's work or a fair day's pay. "Throughout American industry," as one of his followers later wrote, "management's concept of a proper day's work was what a foreman could *drive* workers to do, and the workers' conception was how little they could do and hold their jobs."[1]

It was to this problem that Taylor addressed himself, and it was through his efforts to work out the ramifications of this problem that he gradually developed the concepts that were to form the basis of the movement to which was later applied the name "scientific management."

The Setting

It is significant that Taylor should have begun his work from this particular standpoint. The emerging factory system, of which the Midvale Steel Company was a typical example, was presenting entirely new problems of compensation. What precedent had the factory manager to go on in setting rates for his employees? Two systems of payment were in current vogue: "class rates" and "piece rates." Under the class rate system, all people doing roughly similar work were paid the same rate, regardless of their individual productivity. The piece rate system at least had the virtue of providing greater rewards for the industrious and conscientious and of penalizing the inept and slothful, but it suffered from special shortcomings of its own.

The idea of piece rates was a carry-over from the old putting-out system, where payment by the piece was the logical and perhaps the only practical method of compensation. But when piece rates were brought into the factory the results were quite different from what they were under the earlier form of economic organization. Under the putting-out system, workers had little incentive to soldier, but under the factory system it was often very much to the workers' interest to operate well under capacity for the purpose of holding up piece rates. Under the putting-out system the livelihood of workers and their families depended on their output and soldiering meant deprivation. Piece rates were relatively stable and a high output did not carry with it the danger of rate-cutting by the factor for whom the work was being done. Rates might vary from time to time as a result of changes in the market for the goods being manufactured or as a result of bargaining between the factor and the cottage workers, but they were not subject to the frequency of change that later became characteristic of the factory. One reason for this lay in the fact that so long as the work was performed in the workers' homes the piece rate concept did not include the element of time, as it later did in the factory when the number of pieces produced per hour became a matter of significance. Under the putting-out system, to the factor the number of pieces produced by any one worker in any given period of time was of little concern; the worker's time was his own and whether he chose to work long hours or short was his business. Furthermore, the members of the worker's family typically joined in the work, so that the total output of the family unit was a function not only of the skill but of the numbers of its members, plus their diligence and persistence.

But when the work was brought into the factory the number of pieces produced by each worker during a given period of time became of great importance. For one thing, the worker was occupying valuable space and using expensive tools and equipment—no longer his own space and his own tools and equipment but those of his employer—and the worker who did not make good use of his employer's facilities was a liability to his employer. But the employer also found himself concerned with the high rates of output of the more efficient and more diligent producers. Implicit in all systems of factory wage payment is the concept, arising essentially out of ideas of social class, that a certain range of income is appropriate to persons of a given status in the community. Variations of earnings *within* this range are considered normal, but when any worker or, more seriously, group of workers begins to exceed the top of the range, management is likely to feel that something is wrong. Intimately related to the idea of a "going range" of wages is the idea of the "labor market" and the idea that no more need be paid for a given type or skill of labor than is necessary to secure the needed supply. When any group of workers persistently exceed, through their piece rate earnings, the amount deemed necessary to attract the number and kind of labor necessary for the work at hand, management is likely to feel that piece rates are too high and cut them accordingly.

Whatever the dynamics and whatever the rationale by which management justified its actions, the fact remains that in a great many cases piece rates were cut as output improved to the point where workers came to accept as logical and inevitable that earnings above a certain point would inevitably result in a cut in rates. This way of thinking has become firmly embedded in labor tradition and, despite strenuous efforts on the part of management to eradicate it, remains so today. While the persistence of the tradition is certainly due in part to legitimate fears based on management's own mistakes, it is also due in part to the idea, shared by *both* labor and management, that earnings within a given range are appropriate to persons of given skill and status. The individual worker, whatever the extent of his "economic" needs, is not likely to be too strongly motivated to exceed the range he conceives as appropriate for himself and others like him. Even if he could do so with ease, he is not likely to be too strongly impelled to break through the top of the range, particularly when to do so will bring down on him the ill will of his fellows and carry with it the danger of a cut in rates that will require greater physical effort merely to maintain a level of income he already enjoys.

For these various reasons, the dynamics of piece rates under the putting-out and factory systems were different. There was, furthermore, a difference between setting rates for *whole products* where the products themselves have a market value (as under the putting-out system) and setting rates for *processes*, which while they go together to produce whole products are themselves beyond the reach of the "objective determinations" of the market. In the latter case, the setting of rates becomes a matter of administrative decision and more subject to question because made by persons whose motives, so far as workers were concerned, were often suspect.

A Fair Day's Pay for a Fair Day's Work

Taylor resolved to change all this. There was no reason, it seemed to him, why a fair day's work and a fair day's pay on any job could not be objectively determined, why they could not be removed from the realm of conflict and resolved in terms of "scientific fact." In this feeling, Taylor was in tune with his times, for it was a period of naive faith (it seems to us now) in the certainties of science. Here lay the answer to all problems; matters that had theretofore been the subject of controversy could be readily resolved once the "facts" were ascertained and the "law" established. And if the proper scientific methods had been employed, the conclusions based on them would be recognized as just by all parties. The methods of science were to usher in a new era of industrial peace. The substitution of scientific knowledge for opinion, of facts for guesswork, would not only solve the technical problems of production but eliminate human conflict as well. "Scientific management will mean, for the employers and the workmen who adopt it . . . the elimination of almost all causes for dispute and disagreement between them."[2]

Throughout Taylor's writings runs a theme of concern for the welfare of the worker. He saw the interests of management and labor in fundamental harmony. As he pointed out on more than one occasion, most people "believe that the fundamental interests of employees and employers are necessarily antagonistic. Scientific management, on the contrary, has for its very foundation the firm conviction that the true interests of the two are one and the same; that prosperity for the employer cannot exist through a long term of years unless it is accompanied by prosperity for the employee, and *vice versa*; and that it is possible to give the workman what he wants—high wages—and the employer what he wants—a low labor cost for his manufactures."[3] The clue to the problem lay in the application of scientific methods to the problems of organizing work, setting tasks, and devising incentives that would liberally reward extra effort and sharply penalize slothfulness or failure to follow approved methods.

It became the constant aim of Taylor's life "to find some rule, or law, that would enable a foreman to know in advance how much work a man who was well suited to his job ought to do in a day." In the case of physically strenuous jobs, this involved the study of "the tiring effect of heavy labor upon a first-class man." His early work in this field at the Midvale Steel Company was patterned after two classes of experiments that had previously been made: "one by physiologists who were studying the endurance of the human animal, and the other by engineers who wished to determine what fraction of a horse-power a man was able to exert, that is, how many foot pounds of work a man could do in a day." Taylor emphasized that in these experiments he and his colleagues "were not trying to find the maximum work that a man could do on a short spurt or for a few days." On the contrary, the endeavor was to learn what really constituted a full day's work for a first-class man; the best day's work that a man could properly do, year in and year out, and still thrive under.[4]

Through these and similar investigations at Midvale, and later at the Bethlehem Steel Company and elsewhere, Taylor sought to establish for a wide variety of jobs what a man could and ought to be expected to do. For the achievement of the tasks thus "scientifically determined," Taylor insisted that "it is not only right and just that the workmen should be paid a very material increase in their wages (say from 30 to 60 percent higher wages than other workmen of their kind are receiving in establishments around them), but it is a fact that they cannot be made to cooperate in this way for the best interest of their employers without being paid an extra price."[5] Taylor's "differential piece rate system," that paid a high rate for tasks successfully completed but a low rate otherwise, was devised to help carry this thinking into practice.

Whether or not the worker achieved the required task depended not only on his own efforts but on a variety of factors over which he had little or no control. For Taylor's system to work properly it was essential that the worker himself be placed on jobs he was qualified to do, that he be instructed in the right methods of doing the job, that he have the right tools and equipment, that his machine be in good repair, and above all, that the flow of work be properly planned and scheduled. If failure to achieve a task was to be penalized so severely, management had a prime responsibility to see that no shortcomings on its part hampered the worker's effort. Thus Taylor's initial and relatively restricted objective of defining a fair day's work soon broadened into the study of all phases of production and organization, mechanical and human.

His work in thinking through the problems of technical organization produced remarkably fruitful results. These included improvement of machinery and tools, rearrangement of equipment to facilitate flow of work, improvement of material handling, standardization of raw materials, detailed analysis of production processes to eliminate unnecessary effort, and development of new and better methods of record-keeping and control. Above all, he emphasized the importance of properly planning the entire production process to the end that raw materials and semi-finished parts should move through the shop by the shortest possible routes and on schedules that would insure the precise coming together, at every stage of production, of the necessary materials, tools, machines, and workmen. As a result of these efforts, Taylor went a long way toward bringing production out of the confusion in which he found it, and in doing so laid the foundations for a truly phenomenal increase in the productivity of American industry.

Unfortunately, in the course of making these improvements, Taylor set the course of management thinking along lines that have had injurious consequences for the patterns of working relationships within the enterprise. This was largely a corollary of his efforts to apply to the problems of human organization the same concepts and methods he found so successful when applied to the problems of technical organization.

Designing the Machine

Taylor was an engineer. He sought quite explicitly to set up organizations in the same manner he might design a machine. And he visualized the role of people within the organization the way he visualized the component parts of a machine. Harlow S. Persons, one of his chief followers, summarized the approach:

> That the direction of the operations of a plant is analogous to the direction 'of the operations of a complicated and delicately adjusted machine' was early a favorite concept of the management movement. . . .

> It was the practical assumption of earlier American industry . . . that the individual is the determining factor in management. But the new

interest in predetermination and control led to increasing recognition that the non-human portion of a managerial situation embraces a larger number of inflexible, unyielding factors than does the human portion; that humans may by selection and training be adapted to the situation more easily than the situation can by change be adapted to humans.[6]

It was inevitable, perhaps, that the engineer played so dominant a role in the new industrialism. The entrepreneur had learned to rely on him heavily in carrying out his plans. The engineer was indispensable in building the railroads, the bridges, the factories, the machines—the visible elements of the new economic organization being put together by the entrepreneur. It was natural that the entrepreneur also look to the engineer to work out problems of internal organization, of work flow and work processes, of division of labor within the plant, for these were "details" largely beyond the range of interest of the entrepreneur concerned with putting together the major elements of the emerging industrial pattern. For their part, the engineers found it necessary to interest themselves in problems of organization and management: they had invented and designed the new production machinery and they soon found that their machines would work but poorly unless properly served by the human components of the organization. It is no accident, therefore, that the engineers should be the first occupational group in our society to actively interest itself in problems of management per se, nor that the American Society of Mechanical Engineers should become the principal forum of the scientific management movement.

The New Division of Labor

There had been a marked trend toward occupational specialization since well before Taylor's time. Taylor and his followers greatly accelerated the trend. What had theretofore been a more or less haphazard, unplanned, spontaneous development, they made explicit, conscious, and purposeful. A net result of their efforts was to give great impetus to the growth of specialization and in so doing to revolutionize the organization of industry.

Prior to Taylor's time, the basis of industrial organization was primarily the major processes involved in producing the product. In the handicraft shops, most experienced workers could and sometimes did produce entire products—shoes, clothing, wagons, furniture, and so on. In larger establishments there was a certain amount of departmentalization, usually based on process (foundry, machine shop, etc.), but here again most experienced workers could perform most or all of the operations involved in that particular process. The new basis of organization introduced by Taylor and elaborated by his successors was the specific operation. The unit of work was no longer the product or the process but each particular task. The final product or the total process was the result of many such tasks, each performed by different workers no one of whom could produce the completed product on his own. And essential as each particular task might be to the overall result, no task was significant in and for itself but only in its relation to all the other tasks. The individual employee was no longer the productive unit; in a real sense, only the plant or the department was productive.

Under the influence of scientific management, the process of specialization proceeded along four major lines:

1. Breaking down of tasks into ever smaller components;

2. Appropriation (Taylor's term) by management of various skills and responsibilities that had traditionally been reserved to workers;

3. Increasing specialization within management itself;

4. Extension of the principle of specialization to whole departments and subdepartments by grouping kindred activities together as specialized organizational entities.

These four lines of development are closely interrelated, but each exhibits special characteristics and has had special consequences of its own.

Specialization of Work

The most familiar aspect of the total process is that related to the increasing specialization of the worker himself. It was the constant effort of the scientific managers—chiefly through detailed job study and time and motion analysis—to break jobs down into increasingly smaller parcels. Operations were studied in minute detail, surplus or unnecessary elements lopped off, and the essential remaining tasks broken down into elementary components. The aim was to reduce as many jobs as possible to a few simple, repetitive motions, each specifically defined and prescribed. By this means it was sought to make possible the use of people of lesser skill and to shorten training time, increase output, and lower costs.

Appropriation of Worker Skills

The second major line along which the process of specialization developed under Taylor's leadership was a sweeping re-division of labor as between workers and management, with the end result of management appropriating to itself many of the skills and responsibilities formerly exercised by the workers.

It was a cornerstone of Taylor's system that the worker was to be given specific, detailed instructions as to exactly what to do and how to do it. A consequence of this was a drastic re-division of duties between management and workers in which the creative, thinking parts of work were reserved to management. Taylor was quite explicit in this: "As far as possible, the workmen, as well as the gang bosses and foremen, should be entirely relieved of the work of planning, and of all work which is more or less clerical [read "thinking"] in its nature. All possible brain work should be removed from the shop and centered in the planning and laying out department leaving for the foremen and gang bosses work strictly executive in its nature."[7]

To accomplish this, Taylor set as one of the aims of scientific management "the deliberate gathering in on the part of those on management's side of all the great masses of traditional knowledge, which in the past has been in the heads of the workmen, and in the physical skill and knack of the workmen, which he has acquired through years of experience."[8] In all of this, Taylor expressed not only his drive to control all elements of the working situation; he also revealed a fundamental attitude toward workers that was characteristic of his own work and that of his followers: "in almost all the mechanic arts the science which underlies each workman's act is so great and amounts to so much that the workman who is best suited actually to do the work is incapable (either through lack of education or through insufficient mental capacity) of understanding this science. This is announced as a general principle."[9] And

I can say, without the slightest hesitation, that the science of handling pig-iron is so great that the man who is physically able to handle pig-iron and is sufficiently phlegmatic and stupid to choose this for his occupation is rarely able to comprehend the science of handling pig-iron; and this inability of the man who is fit to do the work to understand the science of doing his work becomes more and more evident as the work becomes more complicated, all the way up the scale. I assert, without the slightest hesitation, that the high class mechanic has a far smaller chance of ever thoroughly understanding the science of his work than the pig-iron handler has of understanding the science of his work, and I am going to try to prove to your satisfaction, gentlemen, that the law is almost universal—not entirely so but nearly so—that the man who is fit to work at any particular trade is unable to understand the science of that trade without the kindly help and cooperation of men of a totally different type of education, men whose education is not necessarily higher, but a different type from his own.[10]

This, then, was the second major line along which specialization developed under Taylor's influence: not only was the physical content of each operation broken down into its elementary components and each assigned to a different worker; insofar as possible all thinking and planning were lopped off and transferred to management. Jobs that were already becoming machine-like through progressive physical simplification became even more so through the deliberate effort to minimize the essentially human characteristics of workers that most significantly differentiate them from machines.

Specialization of Management

The principle of specialization was not confined to workers at the machine or bench but was extended to management as well. This was the third major aspect of the specialization process.

By his sweeping re-division of labor as between workers and management, Taylor vastly increased the duties and responsibilities of management. For example, in the case of a machine shop organized on the principles of scientific management, Taylor estimated that there should be about one man in management for every three workers: "this immense share of the work—one third—has been deliberately taken out of the workman's hands and handed over to those on the management's side."[11]

This increased burden on management was so great that a considerable further division of labor within management became essential. Just as Taylor sought to simplify operators' jobs so that they could be performed by less-skilled people, he sought to break management down into its component parts so that they too would be within the capacities of those available for managerial assignments. Taylor was appalled, for example at the range of aptitudes required to supervise a work force; his biographer, Frank Copley, wrote:

> Planning requires a studious mind with both analytical and synthetical power, or power of constructive imagination. Preparation requires a mind of the ingenious, inventive, resourceful type. Scheduling, essentially the making of a timetable for dispatching, calls for a mind of the distinctly clerical type; orderly, with a fine sense of sequence, and fond of routine. The productionist should be aggressive, driving, persistent; able to control men, to direct, guide, and lead them. The inspector must have an investigating mind; patient, exact, precise, and painstaking.

> A mind capable of performing only one of these five functions is an elementary one. As it is capable of performing two or more, it is com-

plex. Commonly you find men capable of only one; frequently of two; occasionally of three; rarely of four; hardly ever of all five.[12]

Through what he called "functional management," Taylor sought to provide that "each man from the assistant superintendent down shall have as few functions as possible to perform. If practicable the work of each man in the management should be confined to the performance of a single leading function."[13]

It was Taylor's thought that each of these specialized people in management should exercise direct supervision over the work force with respect to his particular specialty. However, this proved cumbersome because workers received orders and instructions, frequently conflicting, from too many people. Those coming after Taylor preserved the idea of specialization within management but developed the "line and staff" concept whereby direct supervision of workers was reserved to the line and the various specializations organized into staffs advisory or supplementary to the line. Thus the principle of managerial specialization was consolidated.

Departmental Specialization

Specialization within the ranks of management led directly to the fourth aspect of specialization as developed under scientific management: the grouping of related functions, activities, and processes into specialized departments. The same logic that encouraged the specialization of individuals, whether workers or management, also encouraged departmental specialization. One scientific manager writing well after Taylor's time but accurately expressing the trend, enunciated the principle in this manner: "The functions of, or operations performed by, any business or group within business should be so separated, segregated and grouped that attainment of efficiency from repetitive experience may result and that full advantage may be obtained from special human aptitudes, abilities, and educational specializations, and from the intensive application of human effort to a single problem."[14]

Through the application of this principle, to which we may apply Taylor's term, "functionalization," various activities within organizations were grouped together not in terms of the purposes they were intended to serve but in terms of their technical similarity to each other. Throughout, the theory was that this practice would permit better supervision, make possible smoother scheduling, increase flexibility, smooth out peaks and valleys in workload, and generally improve efficiency. However this may be, the net result of functionalization was to round out and complete the four-fold process of work specialization that is perhaps the chief distinguishing characteristic of the scientific management movement.

Positive and Negative Consequences

The specialization of work encouraged by the scientific management movement had both positive and negative consequences for the development of modern industrial society.

The significant feature of the four-fold process of specialization—particularly that related to the breaking down of individual tasks into component parts—was not so much the fact that it made possible the use of "cheaper men" (Taylor's phrase), nor even the fact that it represented, as has often been alleged, a wholesale "de-skilling" of work. Workers who were already skilled—and thereby relatively high-priced—were not, by and large, forced back to the ranks of the semiskilled and the unskilled. For the most part, they probably moved into supervisory and management positions where their ability and experience, above all their knowledge of what production actually required, were urgently needed. On the other hand, many newcomers to industrial life—immigrants, migrants from the farms, and so on—who were without skill and who otherwise would have been condemned to a life of common labor, had an opportunity to move into at least semiskilled work. Taylor's claim on this point has been justified by the facts of industrial history:

> The laborer who before was unable to do anything beyond, perhaps, shoveling and wheeling dirt from place to place, or carrying the work from one place to another in the shop, is in many cases taught to do the more elementary machinist's work, accompanied by the agreeable surroundings and the interesting variety and higher wages which go with the machinist's trade. The cheap machinist or helper, who before was able to run perhaps merely a drill press, is taught to do the more interesting and higher priced lathe and planer work, while the higher skilled and more intelligent machinists become functional foremen and teachers.[15]

The output of American industry could not have grown to the extent it has grown during the past seventy-five years if it had had to depend on the relatively small numbers of skilled men available or the number who could have been trained in the complex skills of the well-rounded artisan. Means had to be found for simplifying jobs to the point where they could be learned quickly and with relative ease.

There are other grounds, however, on which the system of work specialization fostered by scientific management is open to serious and legitimate attack. These fall into three major categories:

1. Failure to make full and proper use of industry's human resources;

2. Relieving workers of initiative and responsibility, and denying them an opportunity to participate in the management of their jobs;

3. Creating needlessly complex organizational structures that greatly increased the problems of coordination and control.

The principle of analyzing operations to determine their elemental components was tremendously fruitful and constructive in itself. But it does not necessarily follow that after operations have thus been broken down the various components should be assigned to different people working in series, each performing an elementary, repetitive task. Peter Drucker has put his finger on the fallacy:

> The job, any job, gains tremendously in productivity and efficiency if analyzed according to "industrial engineering" principles. But at the same time it will be performed most efficiently and most productively if a number of different motions are recombined into a configuration of motions. We do not, as yet, know what configurations are the most efficient or the most productive ones. We only know that wherever we have been forced, especially during the last war, to set up a job as a configuration of elementary motions, with each motion an elementary and repetitive one, but with the total job representing a series of motions rather than one, we have obtained a very substantial, not to say tremendous improvement in productivity and efficiency, and increasing decline in fatigue, rejection rates and faulty work—in other words, improvements in productivity and efficiency that may well be comparable to those we obtained from the first application of the original "industrial engineering" concept.[16]

Unfortunately, Taylor and his followers who originated and developed the "industrial engineering" concept failed to see the distinction Drucker makes. They proceeded on the assumption that individual workers should be assigned to the smallest possible components into which operations could be divided. Such an assumption was logical where the elements of an operation could be simplified to the point where they could be performed by machines. They failed, however, because of their mechanistic bias, to appreciate that there are fundamental differences between organizing machines and organizing people. Implicitly, in fact, the scientific managers from Taylor down to the present have viewed the worker as a sort of "imperfect machine tool" (Drucker's phrase) that would be most productive if confined to a simple, repetitive task.

By this approach, scientific management has failed to utilize properly the greatest resource at its command: the complex and multiple capacities of people. On the contrary, it has attempted to abstract out only those parts of the abilities of workers that happened to fit into the technical needs of the organizations they were building, and has deliberately sought to utilize as narrow a range of ability as ingenuity could devise.

Unfortunately, the gains achieved by this process were grossly wasteful of human potentials because it deprived large portions of the working population of any real sense of doing useful, significant work. In a very great many cases tasks have been broken down into such simple elements that they no longer have meaning in themselves for those who perform them. Many workers have no chance to do a whole job or to make anything they can identify as their own; frequently they have only a vague idea of what the end-product of their labors is, let alone any feeling of personal accomplishment with respect to it.

Because of the extent to which job specialization has been carried, it is often difficult for the worker to see his place in the scheme of things, to appreciate the importance of his contribution to the total process. Too often, the individual job is like the isolated piece of a jig-saw puzzle: essential to the completed picture but meaningless by itself. And because there are so many "pieces," many of those at the work level have only a hazy notion of the total pattern.

This difficulty is greatly increased when not only individual jobs but the work of entire departments is specialized. The functional type of organization brings together in one place large numbers of people who are not only on approximately the same job level but who are performing approximately similar tasks. People in such departments work at specialized operations that have meaning to management because they are a necessary part of the total process. But the worker often cannot see that total process; in many cases, he sees only the small and likely in its own right uninteresting part to which he and his fellows are assigned. In a real sense, under these circumstances, the job loses its meaning for the worker—the meaning, that is, in all terms except the pay envelope.

Another serious consequence of functionalization, particularly when carried to the extremes it is often carried, is its tendency to enforce the conception of people as *means* rather than *ends* in themselves. On the one hand, the tendency toward over-function-alization arises from this type of conception; on the other hand, it makes difficult dealing with people otherwise than as means. Individual activities no longer have meaning or importance in themselves, and those who do the work have no value except as means for helping to accomplish the broader tasks to which the whole organization is devoted.

Over-functionalization makes more general and more acute one of the common errors of our times, the error of dealing with people by categories rather than as individuals. People are categorized by status and function rather than reasonably well-rounded persons; they become "hands," not "people." Despite the frequent protestations of today's management about the importance of the individual, over-functionalization makes it difficult and often impossible actually to think of people as individuals, much less deal with them on individual terms. The attempt to use people as *means* rather than *ends* has alienated them from unity with management in the productive process. Their own labor becomes to them likewise a means, something alien to their real purposes and interests, something through which to procure the good things of life rather than a good in itself; something to be given sparingly, as a cost.

Sense of Responsibility

This deprivation has been aggravated by the extent to which initiative and responsibility have been transferred from workers to management. In part, this was an inevitable consequence of destroying the meaning of work itself. Because jobs had little meaning for their own sake, workers were likely to have little feeling of responsibility for them, except insofar as they were impelled by fear of punishment or hope of reward.

But to this natural result of breaking jobs down into simple, repetitive movements and further obscuring their relation to the whole by means of the functional type of organization structure, was added another and more potent influence: the transfer of initiative and responsibility from workers to management. This was one of the deliberate aims of Taylor's policy, part of the "sweeping re-division of labor" previously noted. Taylor conceived it as management's task to determine not only *what* should be done but *how* it should be done, down to small details. "Each man," as Taylor said, "must learn how to give up his own particular way of doing things, adapt his methods to the many new standards, and grow accustomed to receiving and obeying directions covering details, large and small, which in the past have been left to his individual judgment."[17] As Taylor's biographer noted, his "action in seeking to find out what his men ought to be able to do with their equipment and materials included, as a necessary consequence, the *prescribing* of what they should do, or the assignment to them of tasks carefully measured in accordance with the knowledge he developed."[18]

Workers were excluded from the exercise of initiative; theirs was a purely passive part. "Under this new type of management there is hardly a single act or piece of work done by any workman in the shop which is not preceded and followed by some act on the part of one of the men in the management. All day long every workman's acts are dovetailed in between corresponding acts of the management."[19] Thus, those on management's side were constantly initiating action on the workers, with little room for worker initiative.

Taylor emphasized the importance, under his system, of "the intimate cooperation of the management with the workmen, so that together they do the work in accordance with the scientific laws which have been developed, instead of leaving the solution of each problem in the hands of the individual workman."[20] But as workers were excluded from the determination and interpretation of these "laws," this kind of cooperation consisted simply of "you do what I tell you to do"; it was not cooperation that was called for but docility. The workers' part was conceived as purely passive. They were expected to accept without question the directions from their "betters." As Taylor himself often admonished them: "You are not supposed to think. There are other people paid for thinking around here."[21]

Here, again, Taylor revealed his basic attitude toward workers. He frequently refers to them as children. For instance, he calls attention to "the analogy that functional foremanship bears to the management of a large, up-to-date school."[22] And again: "All of us are grown-up children, and it is equally true that the average workman will work with the greatest satisfaction, both to himself and to his employer, when he is given each day a definite task which he is to perform in a given time."[23] Looking on workers as children, to be enticed by rewards and threatened by punishments, it was natural that Taylor had difficulty seeing them as self-reliant adults interested in taking an adult attitude toward their work and capable of making an adult contribution to it.

From time to time the question of what we now call "worker participation" seemed to bother Taylor and his followers, but they seldom did much about it other than affirm its importance and their concern for promoting it. Taylor once stated: "we ask our workman before he starts kicking, 'try the methods and improvements which we give you; we know at least what we have believed to be a good method for you to follow; and then after you have tried our way if you think of an implement or method better than ours, for God's sake come and tell us about it and then we will make an experiment to prove whether your method or ours is best. . . . And if [your method] proves to be better, what I advocate every time is, not only that the new methods shall be adopted, but that the man who made the suggestion be paid a big price for having improved on the old standard.'"[24]

This was hardly the way, however, to encourage workers to think constructively about their jobs, to exclude them from the initial process of analysis and decision and require them to make a case for their ideas before a judge and jury already committed to an established course of action. As a matter of fact, Taylor's approach put a premium on *not* using ideas and suggestions from workers, as witness this illuminating statement by Henry L. Gantt, perhaps the most influential of all of Taylor's followers: "It is the duty of the investigator to develop methods and set tasks, and unless the methods developed by him are pretty generally a great deal better than those suggested by the workmen, he is not retained in the position."[25] Under these circumstances, it would be the rare methods man indeed who could afford to permit, much less encourage, independent thinking on the part of workers.

Management today is seriously concerned with the apathy of workers, their lack of concern for efficiency, their disinterest in finding new and better ways of doing their jobs. Much of the difficulty lies in the fact that industry, following Taylor's principles, has systematically deprived workers of real and effective participation in industry. Their jobs have made too few demands on their higher faculties, they have had too little opportunity to think, to take initiative, to make their own contribution to the improvement of their jobs. Industry is reaping what it has sown, for without participation there can be neither initiative nor responsibility.

Coordination and Control

By minutely subdividing operations, by separating the "thinking" parts of work from the "doing," by increasing specialization within management itself, and by grouping activities on the basis of specialized functions, scientific management greatly complicated the problems of coordination and control. This was the third major weakness of the system of specialization developed under Taylor's influence.

The individual, whether worker or manager, was no longer "productive" in himself; his work was useful only as it dovetailed with the work of many other people, many of whom he never saw and about whose work he knew little. Likewise, the specialized department was not "productive" in itself but only as its activities were integrated into the overall pattern. Great effort was required to synthesize these diverse activities into an operating, productive whole. The integration had to be deliberate and conscious, imposed from the top down, because the organization had been so fragmented that it had little internal cohesion and little capacity for spontaneous cooperation. Hence the necessity for elaborate systems of controls, for strings, as it were, converging at a central point from which the activities of each segment of the organization, and to a considerable extent each individual, could be manipulated.

Here again the analogy of the machine is obvious—and perfectly conscious in Taylor's mind. Integration was conceived as a mechanical process to be achieved by mechanical means. The organization was set up like a machine and it had to be operated like a machine. But because its components were human rather than mechanical the task of controlling and directing it was highly complicated and taxed the ingenuity of the scientific managers. The elaborate contrivances of the modern industrial organization, the masses of paperwork and red tape, the layers on layers of supervision are evidence of the difficulty of controlling human organizations in terms of mechanistic principles.

Modern industry requires intimate cooperation, a fact often noted by Taylor. What he overlooked was that cooperation must be between *real people*, not between abstract functions. But "real people" were lost in the intricacies of his system. As he himself was fond of saying: "In the past the man has been first; in the future the system must be first."[26] By his reliance on mechanical forms of integration he stultified the natural tendencies of people working together to achieve a more organic form of integration, thus increasing still further his dependence on mechanical contrivances.

Modern industry is committed to, indeed based on, extensive division of labor, and was so committed well before Taylor's time. But the special type of division of labor, the four-fold process of specialization previously analyzed made the task of integration, the task of management, more difficult than it need have been.

Because Taylor conceived the task of management as largely that of designing and operating a system, he required a different kind of manager than industry had known before. He himself has given this colorful, rather idealized sketch of his conception of the traditional "old style" manager:

> It was not enough for a manager of men to be able, competent, and well-trained. It was also necessary for him to secure and control his men through his attractive and masterful personality. Through all times and all ages the great personal leaders of men have had rare gifts which command at the same time *the admiration, the love, the respect, and the fear* of those under him. Men with this rare combination of qualities are born, not made. . . . The great captains of industry were usually physically large and powerful. They were big-hearted, kindly, humorous, lovable men, democratic, truly fond of their workmen, and yet courageous, brainy and shrewd; with not the slightest vestige of anything soft or sentimental about them. Ready at any minute to damn up and down hill the men who needed it, or to lay violent hands on any workmen who defied them, and throw them over the fence, they were men who would not hesitate to joke with the apprentice boy one minute and give him a spanking the next. Such men would be recognized in any age as real men, fit to be the leaders of other men.[27]

For this kind of leadership, which he considered too rare to count on, Taylor wished to substitute a more bloodless sort, one that relied on "science" and on "system" and kept human idiosyncrasies under decent control.

Broader Meanings and Implications

One aspect of Taylor's personality emerges with clarity from his writings: his virtual obsession to control the environment around him. This characteristic was expressed in everything he did: in his home life, his gardening, his golfing; even his afternoon stroll was not a casual affair but something to be carefully planned and rigidly followed. Nothing was left to chance if it could be avoided. Every personal action was thought through carefully, all contingencies considered, and steps taken to guard against extraneous developments. And when, despite all precautions, something did transpire to upset his plans he gave every evidence of internal distress that sometimes expressed itself in blazing anger and sometimes in black brooding.

Taylor's theories of management bear the unmistakable impress of this characteristic. His biographer states the relation between his

system and his temperament with clarity: "Just as he strove to intellectualize himself—that is, manage his whole life according to
reason, right arrangement, and systematic regulation—so he sought
to intellectualize industrial management. In each case the central
idea was the same—*control!* First we see the intellect using its powers of analysis, abstraction, and comparison for the setting up of
definite standards. No sooner is this done than all things seem to
conspire to break down the standards. And in one's power to resist
this conspiracy lies one's control."[28]

Reading Copley leaves the impression of a rigid, insecure personality, fearful of the unknown and the unforeseen, able to face the
world with reasonable equanimity only if everything possible has
been done to keep the world in its place and to guard against anything upsetting his careful, painstaking arrangements. Anything
that threatened his arrangements was a threat to him personally,
to be resisted with all the resources at his command. Taylor presented to the world a well-organized, well-adjusted front, but his
personal organization and adjustment consisted precisely in the
extent to which he had developed his skill of control.

Looking on the world in this way, distrusting it, fearful of anything he had not anticipated and planned for, it is clear why he left
so little room in his system for initiative and spontaneity on the
part of workers—or even, for that matter, on the part of those in
management. Initiative and spontaneity left too much to chance
and were hence intolerable. The only way to organize the work of a
plant was to set it up like a machine: restrict the roles of its human
components so that insofar as possible they too were machine-like
and predictable, performing their allotted functions in a prescribed
manner and on a meticulous schedule that would mesh the entire
machine into a smoothly operating whole.

Obsession for Control

The obsession for control that was so marked in Taylor gave the
scientific management movement a most peculiar twist. The implications of this were apparent in Taylor's writings and became
even more clear in the work of his followers. It was all very well,
these men found, to organize the work of the shop, but no sooner
was everything under control there than influences from outside
the shop, from other segments of the enterprise (for example, sales,
finance), began to infringe upon and upset their neatly contrived
arrangements. Thus the scientific managers soon became con-

cerned with the need to extend their control to the entire enterprise. But this, too, proved insufficient because it became apparent that there were external pressures on the enterprise itself and that until these were properly organized and controlled, scientific management could not come into its own.

There was a fairly general tendency among scientific managers to move from planning and control within the individual plant to thinking in terms of a "planned society." As one of them put it, "Taylor's revolution in mental attitude, to be effective, cannot stop short of the organized community."[29] Henry L. Gantt railed against "commercial men" and financiers and demanded that the control of industry—all industry—be turned over to the engineers, who alone knew how to run "the huge and delicate apparatus." "Most assuredly," he asserted, "finance and industry must be socialized somehow." He was in favor of an organization "similar to the cartel system" wherein prices would be fixed by committees of producers, distributors, and consumers; reason, planning, and control were to replace the chaotic market processes he saw about him.[30]

In 1916 Gantt proposed a fantastic organization, called "The New Machine," which was to be "a conspiracy [sic!] of men of science, engineers, chemists, land and sea tamers and general masters of arts and materials—a fellowship at deadly enmity with all parasites and pretenders—held together in their war against humbugs by their common love of what is really so and by their common scorn of purse-lipped, pious altruisms."[31] The aim of the "New Machine" was apparently a form of corporate state whose economic system would have consisted largely of public service corporations—managed, of course, by engineers trained in the skills of scientific management.

Some years later Rexford Guy Tugwell, who was deeply influenced by the literature of scientific management, concluded that in order to realize the full potentialities of machine production management must be extended to social management. One of the leading contemporary exponents of scientific management, Lyndal Urwick, in 1933 advocated establishing in each industry a council representing producers, distributors, and consumers, and in each locality a regional council to handle problems of a regional nature. He carried the concept over into the field of international economic activity and proposed an economic general staff for each nation that would integrate national economic affairs with those of every other nation.[32]

Scientific management has been taken up enthusiastically in

Europe, where it has had perhaps an even wider vogue than in this country. But it is in Soviet Russia that scientific management has had its fullest flowering. Lenin looked on the Taylor system as the "last word in capitalism" and encouraged its "systematic trial and adoption" in Russia as a means for accelerating industrial production. And from Lenin forward Russia's planning has been characterized as "an attempt to do on a national scale what scientific management was doing within the individual plant."[33] The author of this statement, a contemporary [1952] student of scientific management, makes the following illuminating statement:

> Another feature of the Russian situation that is different from that in American management is that scientific management (rationalization) has become a mass movement. In most of the other countries, and particularly in the United States, it has been a matter determined by individual plant managements. Progress has been made in a more or less informal or hit-or-miss fashion, with plants gradually adopting such techniques as the management may be familiar with or which may appear to be applicable. As a result, the extension of techniques and principles has been very irregular and not widely understood. Certainly they are not now fully employed nor fully understood in Russia, but the development of a national program along these lines gives promise of effecting some startling results.[34]

Note the suggestion of envy at the lack of equal authority in this country to extend the scope of scientific management. Note, too, the implied deprecation of a system that allows each individual management to choose which if any elements of scientific management it will adopt. "Just think," he seems to say, "what startling results we could have in *this* country if only the scientific managers had authority to require operating management to see the light and follow their better principles."

The scientific manager's obsession for control springs from failure to recognize or appreciate the value of spontaneity, either in everyday work or in economic processes. It is an easy step from distrust of spontaneity in the workplace to distrust of spontaneity in the marketplace. Hence the need for *planning*. And hence the machine as the model for human organization. For the machine has no will of its own. Its parts have no urge to independent action. Thinking, direction—even purpose—must be provided from outside or above. To those who have inherited Taylor's point of view "human nature" is something annoying, unavoidable perhaps, but regrettably so, and to be kept in bounds so far as possible.

Herein lies Taylor's basic error and the essential flaw of the scientific management movement: failure to appreciate and utilize the multifaceted potentialities of the human beings who staff the workforce.

Postscript

The foregoing paper was written in 1952–53. From the perspective of forty years later, I want to add this brief note.

Nothing in this paper is intended to question the importance of Frederick Taylor's work. He laid the foundations for the phenomenal increase in the productivity of workers and industry during the past century, not only in this country but in the other industrial and industrializing countries of the world. In the last decades of the nineteenth century, there simply were not enough skilled and semi-skilled workers to meet the pressing needs of the burgeoning industrial system. The principles laid down by Taylor greatly facilitated the conversion of a very large population of industrially unskilled immigrants from abroad and migrants from American farms into skilled and semiskilled workers, substantially improving their standards of living and creating a more broadly distributed prosperity than history had ever known.

These were truly magnificent achievements, but they were realized at great and unnecessary human cost. Any assessment of Taylor's role in the development of modern management must consider both the debit and the credit sides of the ledger.

Notes

Unpublished manuscript, 1952–53, author's files.

1. Harlow S. Person, "The Origin and Nature of Scientific Management," in H. S. Person, ed., *Scientific Management in American Industry* (New York: Harper & Bros., 1929), 2.
2. Frederick W. Taylor, *The Principles of Scientific Management* (New York: Harper & Bros., 1947), 142.
3. Ibid., 10.
4. Ibid., 53–55.
5. Quoted in Frank Barkley Copley, *Frederick W. Taylor: Father of Scientific Management*, 2 vols. (New York: Harper & Bros., 1923), 2:159.
6. Harlow S. Person, "The New Attitude toward Management," in *Scientific Management in American Industry*, 27.
7. Taylor, *Scientific Management*, 98–99.
8. Quoted in Copley, *Frederick W. Taylor* 1:13.

9. Taylor, *Scientific Management*, 41.

10. Frederick W. Taylor, *Testimony before the Special House Committee* (New York: Harper & Row, 1947), 49.

11. Ibid., 44.

12. Copley, *Frederick W. Taylor* 1:299.

13. Frederick W. Taylor, *Shop Management* (New York: Harper & Row, 1947), 99.

14. Thomas R. Jones, "Theories and Types of Organization," in *Production Executives Series No. 83* (New York: American Management Association, 1929), 29.

15. Quoted in Copley, *Frederick W. Taylor* 1:326.

16. Peter F. Drucker, address before the Society for the Advancement of Management, New York, April 20, 1950. In this address and elsewhere Drucker gives numerous examples of the application of this principle of recombining elementary tasks. See particularly his "The Way to Industrial Peace," *Harper's*, November 1946; "The Human Factor in Mass Production," American Management Association, *Production Series No. 175* (New York, 1947); and *The New Society* (New York: Harper & Bros., 1950), 171–73.

17. Taylor, *Shop Management*, 133.

18. Copley, *Frederick W. Taylor* 1:219.

19. Taylor, *Testimony*, 44–45.

20. Taylor, *Scientific Management*, 115.

21. Copley, *Frederick W. Taylor* 1:189.

22. Taylor, *Shop Management*, 109.

23. Taylor, *Principles of Scientific Management*, 120.

24. Taylor, *Testimony*, 199–200.

25. H. L. Gantt, *Work, Wages, and Profits* (New York: The Engineering Magazine Company, 1913), 159.

26. Taylor, *Scientific Management*, 7.

27. Quoted in Copley, *Frederick W. Taylor* 1:152.

28. Ibid., 350.

29. Robert Bruere, "Industrial Relations," in *Scientific Management in American Industry*, 464.

30. Leon Pratt Alford, *Henry Lawrence Gantt* (New York: American Society of Mechanical Engineers, 1934), 273, 265, 298.

31. Ibid., 265. See 264–77 for an account of "The New Machine."

32. Lyndal Urwick, *Management of Tomorrow* (London: Nisbet & Co., 1933), 135.

33. George Filipetti, *Industrial Management in Transition* (Chicago: Richard D. Irwin, 1949), 9.

34. Ibid., 202–3.

11

The Sears X-Y Study

In the aftermath of a sharp but temporary downturn of sales in 1949, the national personnel department of Sears, Roebuck undertook a study of how representative store managers were coping with the problems of falling sales and profits and what could be learned from their experience. One of the specific problems the study addressed was that of payroll expense. Of special concern was the tendency observed in some stores to increase the number of persons in staff and supervisory positions.

In order to secure factual information on this question, two groups of midsize stores were selected for study. They were carefully chosen for comparability in all respects but one. They were of similar size, carried the same lines of merchandise, and were located in communities of comparable size and demography. In number of employees they ranged from a low of 96 to a high of 113. They differed in only one important respect: structure of organization.

Because in Sears terminology all stores in both groups were "B" stores, for purposes of the study one group was labeled "X" and the other "Y." Stores in the X group had a simple type of organization structure with a minimum number of staff and supervisory employees. There was a store manager at the top, a single assistant manager, and approximately thirty (actual range: twenty-seven to thirty-two) heads of selling departments ("division managers" in Sears parlance). There were, in addition, the usual non-selling or "service" activities such as shipping and receiving, customer service, maintenance, and unit control (the auditing and credit functions reported up separate lines of authority independent of the store managers).

All division managers (heads of selling departments) reported directly to the store manager, with the assistant manager typically responsible for the non-selling activities. The manager and his assistant usually worked as what might be called a "management team." There was a sharp difference in status between the two but generally speaking the latter functioned as alter ego of the former. There was always a division of responsibility between them, but the term "management team" best describes their relationship and the entity to which the (approximately) thirty selling division managers and the four or five people heading the non-selling activities reported; this, in other words, was a very broad span of control.

Stores in the "Y" group had more limited spans of control with an intervening level of supervision between the heads of the selling departments and the "management team." Instead of reporting directly to the top, the thirty-odd division managers were divided between two merchandise managers, one for soft lines and the other for hard lines. In these stores, the assistant store manager typically served as "operating assistant" to the store manager, responsible for the non-selling functions and for administering in a "staff" capacity the operating controls (payroll and so on) for the entire store, selling as well as non-selling.

In separating out these two groups of stores for purposes of study, the investigators had been prepared to find differences between them, but not for the range of differences discovered. As anticipated, there was a difference in payrolls as a percentage of sales, in favor of the more simply organized stores in the X group. This difference was not as great as might have been expected because the added cost of the two merchandise managers was offset to some extent by lower rates of pay at the division manager level.

The more interesting difference was that the X stores tended to be superior to the Y in sales and profit performance. Beyond this, employee morale, particularly at the division manager level, was generally higher in the X group, and a review of the records of the two groups of stores going back over a period of several years disclosed that more people had been promoted out of the X stores to positions of higher responsibility in the company than had been promoted out of the Y stores. In summary, on all these points—payroll expense, sales and profit results, caliber of key personnel, employee morale, and executive development—the X group out-performed the Y group.

In reviewing the data, the reasons for this superiority seemed clear. For one thing, in the X-type store the manager and his assistant, the "management team," were spread very thin. They had reporting to them thirty-odd selling department heads and the amount of time they could devote to any one of them was small, at least on average. Under these circumstances, the best way for store managers to accomplish their jobs was to have highly qualified people as division managers. The best way for them to do a successful hardware business, for example, was to make sure they had as managers of that division the best hardware merchants they could develop or find, and so on through the other divisions. Precisely because they themselves were spread so thin, these store managers and their assistants had strong incentive to seek out people of initiative and ability, people who could take responsibility, who could be trusted to use good judgment, who could move ahead on their own without having to clear everything in advance. By and large, the division managers in the X stores measured up fairly well to these specifications, and their results showed it.

The situation was different in the Y-type stores. Here, people at the merchandise manager and operating assistant level tended to be of quite high caliber, but those at the division manager level often compared less well with their opposite numbers in the X group. Store managers with merchandise managers tended to look to these aides for results and were not under the same kind of compelling pressure to build up high levels of competence at the division manager level. In an X store, if there were problems, say, of building volume in hardware the store manager looked to his hardware division manager; in a Y store, he looked to his hard lines merchandise manager. The difference in the caliber of division manager personnel in the two groups of stores was thus a direct consequence of imperatives arising from the organization structure within which they were working.

But the explanation for the differences in caliber did not stop here. Not only were the managers of the more simply organized stores under strong compulsion to develop or recruit high caliber talent, but that talent, once in place, was exposed to a kind of experience that tended to enhance their capabilities further. Because the store manager and his assistant were spread so thin (one cannot help but continue to use this phrase) the amount of detailed supervision they could give to each division was limited. The division managers were forced to assume responsibility; they could not constantly run to their superiors for approval but had to make their own decisions and stand or fall by the results. If, for example, the hardware division manager had a $10,000 open-to-buy for a particular period, the division manager had to decide how much of that total to spend on builder's hardware, how much on power tools, how much on garden equipment, how much on nuts and bolts, and so on. Overall guidance would be given, buying plans would be reviewed by the store manager or his assistant, and one of them would sign purchase orders and requisitions; but because these executives were also reviewing the buying plans and authorizing the purchases of twenty-nine or so other heads of divisions, the amount of detailed checking was necessarily limited. For practical purposes, the division manager had to make most of the decisions. He or she had to take a chance, had to make a commitment, had to live with mistakes.

The division manager's task in the Y-type store was less demanding. Here, too, the hardware division manager might have a $10,000 open-to-buy. Here too that person would draw up a buying plan, investing so much in this line of merchandise and so much in that. But the plan had to be submitted to the hard lines merchandise manager for approval, and this individual, because *he* would be the one the store manager held responsible, would review the plan in close detail, make numerous changes as his judgment dictated, and the final plan would be his and not the division manager's.

Observation of the way that the two types of stores worked indicated that one of the disadvantages of the more complex organization was that it safeguarded people too closely against making mistakes. Because of the closeness with which they were supervised, it was difficult for these division managers to get far off base or to stay off base very long. But precisely for this reason they were deprived of one of their most fruitful means of learning.

For people learn as much, sometimes more, from their mistakes as from their successes. Perhaps this is at the root of some of the problems of modern industrial organization: that people have been so hemmed in by supervision and controls that they have too little opportunity to move ahead on their own—which, if the opportunity is real and not fictitious, always carries with it the danger, even the probability, of making mistakes—and are thereby deprived of an important means for growth and development. It is just barely possible that a child could be so protected that it would never be in danger of being run over by a car, or of falling out of a tree and breaking its leg, or of drowning in the lake, or of meeting any of the other disasters, fatal or otherwise, to which childhood is subject. Perhaps a child *could* be protected to this extent, but if it were it would never grow up; it would never be more than a weak and worrisome thing, hardly a real person, and certainly not a strong, self-reliant individual capable of being entrusted with adult responsibilities. If children are to grow into competent, self-respecting, self-reliant adults, they have to have room to grow, which means room to fail as well as succeed. So too for the development of adults into increasingly competent managers.

In any event, much of the superiority of division manager personnel found in the stores with the simpler type of organization seemed attributable to the fact that the nature of the structure tended to force them to accept responsibility, to exercise initiative, to develop self-reliance, and to learn from experience.

Note has already been taken of the larger number of promotable people originating in the X stores and of the fact that this appeared to be due to the greater necessity in these stores for picking high-grade division manager talent to start with and the more stimulating quality of experience gained in the more simply organized stores. Beyond these factors were differences in the style of leadership prevailing in the two types of stores. Because managers who worked directly with the heads of their divisions rather than through an intervening level of management did not have time to supervise in detail, their leadership tended to be largely in terms of setting goals, leaving to their division managers much of the task of working out how the goals were to be met. In the more hierarchical stores, the manager generally not only set the objectives for the divisions but with the aid of two merchandise managers worked out in some detail the means by which they were to be achieved, and the completed "package" was then handed down to the division managers. Much more than in the X stores, division managers in the Y stores were in the position of carrying out plans that they had little part in making and striving for goals they had no part in setting. Leadership in the simpler structures might be characterized as "goal oriented" and in the more complex structures as "method oriented." It would be equally valid to characterize them as "people oriented" and "system oriented."

In the X stores management perforce, by the very nature of the structure, had to concern itself primarily with *people*. Store problems had to be looked on as problems of people and not problems of things. If the performance of a division was unsatisfactory, the way to improve it was to strengthen the management of the division, by special training or otherwise, for only thus could the improvement be permanent.

This technique of management involved not only selecting highly qualified people in the first place; it also involved working with people as their individual needs required to bring them up to levels of competence where they could be entrusted with larger measures of personal responsibility. This type of store management did not involve blind delegation. Managers had to have a sure idea as to which individuals could move ahead largely on their own and which required help.

In the X stores a considerable part of the time of the manager and the assistant was devoted to the newer division managers or to those whose performance was not up to par or who otherwise needed help. The emphasis was on developing individual competence, bringing people along to the point where they could run their divisions with a minimum of direction and supervision. In the Y stores, on the other hand, the emphasis was on the manager and the immediate assistants doing the thinking and planning and depending on close supervision and administrative controls to insure proper execution at the division manager level. The intervening layer of supervision, moreover, tended to deprive the division managers of direct contact with the store manager, which in the X-type stores was an important factor in their development. Stores in the X group produced more astute and more skillful merchants than did those in the Y group, and the internal dynamics of the two groups largely explained the difference.

These contrasting dynamics not only had important influences on the growth of individuals; they also had significant consequences for the merchandising performance of the stores. The substantial delegation down to the division manager level characteristic of the X stores meant that detailed planning was done closer to the scene of action by persons in intimate contact with the merchandise and the market, and in consequence the plans tended to be better plans. In the Y stores, real delegation did not extend beyond the two merchandise managers, and detailed planning was done largely by people a step removed from direct customer contact. Plans developed at this higher level tended to have less of the flexibility characteristic of those developed at the division manager level, and less capacity for changing as conditions changed, for capitalizing on unexpected opportunities, and for sidestepping unforeseen difficulties. One of the great advantages of the X-type structure lay in the fact that it had more centers of initiative and decision making; the structure was more freely articulated and in consequence had greater adaptivity, and undoubtedly in the long run greater survival power.

The findings of the study thus were fairly clear; equally clear, apparently, was the indicated course of action. If the differences between the two groups of stores were related so directly to differences in organization structure, the logical move would seem to be to convert the Y stores to the X-type structure and all would be well. But before making any such recommendation, those conducting the study thought it wise to make a further check. Representative stores in the two groups were revisited, and this time attention was focused on the personalities and ways of behaving of the store managers themselves. Valuable information was also provided by the field representatives of the personnel department, who spent much of their time in the stores and knew the store managers well. The results of this supplemental investigation caused the members of the survey staff to proceed cautiously in making any recommendation for sweeping organizational changes.

Although each store manager was very much an individual with personal characteristics uniquely his own, managers of the two types of stores grouped themselves roughly into two fairly distinct personality types. The differences between them were most apparent in their general attitudes toward the people in their organizations, as revealed in the way they talked about them and in their behavior in face-to-face relationships.

Managers of the X stores typically took a great deal of pride in their employees. Walking through the store with a visitor from the home office they were likely to pause frequently to introduce the visitor to division managers, salespeople, and others, often making some complementary comment about their performance or the condition of their division, or relating some recent incident of merit. These store managers took special pride in their promotable younger people. They would recount their history, their special qualifications, what was being done to further their training, and how soon they would be ready for more responsibility. These managers were not indiscriminate in their pride or their praise. They held people to high standards and were critical of those who failed to measure up. They were usually good judges of people, able to evaluate their strengths and weaknesses and to deal with them accordingly. In part, perhaps because of their skill on this score, they usually *did* have people in whom they could take pride. It was this orientation that generally characterized the attitudes of the X-type managers in their relations with the people in their organizations.

Managers of the Y stores tended to be somewhat different. They had less of the warm, outgoing orientation that was so pronounced in the X managers. They were rather distrustful of people, and at some time during the store visit were likely to make comments to some such effect as "It's hard to get good people these days"; or, "they've been spoiled by the government or the unions"; or, "there's something wrong with the educational system"; or, "people just don't believe in doing a fair day's work anymore"; or, "young people have lost their ambition, you don't see many of them these days who are willing to *work* to get ahead the way we had to do." These managers often seemed to expect the worst of their people, and they often found their fears justified. They felt that people had to be watched, that their work had to be checked closely—otherwise, no telling what might happen.

This sketch of the two types of managers has been deliberately overdrawn to emphasize their differing orientations. But there was a definite difference in their general outlook on life and in their general attitudes toward people, and *this difference reflected itself in the kinds of organizations they set up and the ways they related themselves to the people in them.*

Sears as a company was administered at this time with a high degree of decentralization. The individual store manager had vested in himself a wide degree of latitude and discretion, and this extended, within limits, to the manner in which he set up his organization. As the two groups of stores were studied further it became clear that the two different types of managers tended to set up the kinds of organizations with which they could work most comfortably.

The Y managers tended to have less confidence in their people and to feel that their employees had to be closely supervised, that someone (that is, themselves and their key staffs) had to do the "real thinking," and that detailed controls had to be set up to make sure that those further down the line followed through. These managers had simply tried to create the kind of organization that would accomplish precisely this.

The X managers, on the other hand, tended to have more confidence in the capacities of their people to work out their own problems, and they had enough skill in evaluating them to be rather sure in their judgments as to those in whom they could place confidence and how far. They relinquished none of their responsibility for guidance and direction or for final results, but they sought to capitalize on the initiative and good sense of their subordinates rather than try to do all the "real thinking" for them. Their primary method of solving problems was to work with the people involved, to the end of handling not only the immediate problem but of strengthening the ability of their subordinates to deal with other problems in the future. To this end they liked to work directly with their division managers rather than through an intermediate staff that they were likely to feel would only get in the way. In other words, the X managers no less than the Y managers had tended to set up the kind of organization with which they could work most comfortably.

Viewed in this light the task of changing organization structures loomed as by no means the simple matter it had first appeared. With all the apparent superiority of the X-type structure, there was a very real question of how effectively the Y-type manager could function in it.

This doubt was reinforced in the years that followed by observing what often happened following store manager changes. It was not uncommon for a store manager transferred from a Y-type store to one already set up on an X basis to begin reconstituting the organization along lines more nearly approximating the structure he was used to. These changes were usually not begun immediately nor, once begun, accomplished quickly; the movement was gradual but its direction unmistakable. Always, of course, the changes were quite "logical"—inventory problems, the need for building up, say, the soft line divisions, the shortage of high caliber people for division manager jobs, and so on. Whatever the justification, over time the organization structure of the manager's new store tended to become not too different from that of the one he had left.

The reverse process was equally pronounced. An X-type manager transferred to a Y-type store was likely before too long to report to his zone office that as he had become familiar with his new store he found he had one more merchandise manager than he needed. Sometime later he might report that as soon as he could make certain moves to strengthen some of his division managers he would probably have a second merchandise manager available for transfer. Here, too, the end result was likely to be conversion of the organization of the manager's new store to correspond more closely with that of his old.

The task of changing organization structures thus appeared as considerably more complex than issuing directives and redrawing organization charts. For Sears' purposes, the results of the study were inconclusive. It appeared unwise to try to change organization structures arbitrarily, without regard for the styles and personalities of incumbent managers. On the other hand, it was obvious that personality changes of any magnitude are extremely difficult to bring about and likely to require the equivalent of psychoanalysis or religious conversion—both well beyond normal administrative capabilities. The chief lesson that Sears drew from the study was recognition of the importance of selecting people for key positions who exhibited X rather than Y characteristics. This was a lesson well worth learning.

Note

This paper is from a previously unpublished manuscript written in 1952–53. Excerpted by permission of the publisher from "The More Things Change the More They Stay the Same," *Journal of Management Inquiry* 1:1 (Mar. 1992): 14–38. Copyright © 1992 by Sage Publications, Inc.

12

The Sears Central
Merchandising Organization

The functions of the parent organization of Sears, Roebuck may be divided into two broad categories: "administrative" and "merchandising." The administrative functions are headed, respectively, by a controller, a treasurer, a secretary, and vice presidents for operating, factory management, personnel, and public relations. The merchandising functions are headed by a merchandising vice president. The company's retail stores and mail order plants are organized into five geographical territories, each headed by a territorial vice president. All of the foregoing report to the president.

The primary function of the merchandising organization is procurement of the merchandise sold through the company's retail stores and mail order plants, to the total amount of about five billion dollars in 1952. Closely related to this "buying" function is the provision of overall guidance and direction to the sales promotional activities of the field. Buying is the only function in the Sears organization that is centralized; all others are decentralized to the maximum degree, most of them down to the individual store or mail order plant, and in many cases down to individual departments *within* the stores and plants. Buying, on the contrary, is centralized wholly within the parent organization. Only in this way is it possible to capitalize on the advantages of large-scale purchasing, long-range merchandise planning, and the consistent development of merchandise sources.

Buying activities are divided among forty buying departments, each headed by a supervisor (note title), a senior executive who reports directly to the merchandising vice president. Reporting to the same officer are an assistant on buying, a retail merchandise manager, a mail order merchandise manager, and a merchandise controller. These latter four individuals serve in a "staff" capacity to the merchandising vice president and in no way compromise his "line" relationship with the supervisors of the forty buying departments. The merchandising vice president and the four staff activities reporting to him comprise the "general merchandise office."

The organization of each buying department parallels that of the general merchandise office. Reporting to each supervisor is a retail merchandise manager, a mail order merchandise manager, a controller, and from five to twenty buyers depending on the volume and complexity of the line. There are a total of about four hundred buyers at the present time, plus about one hundred assistant buyers, most of whom are in training for buying assignments. As in the case of the parallel functions in the general merchandise office, the retail and mail order sales managers and the controller serve the supervisors and the buyers in a staff capacity without in any way compromising the supervisors' line relationship with the buyers. Each of these staff people maintains close functional liaison with the parallel functions at the general merchandise office level: retail sales managers with the retail merchandise office, mail order sales managers with the mail order merchandise office, and controllers with the merchandise control office. The assistant on buying in the general merchandise office, in addition to serving the vice president in a staff capacity, assists the buyers and supervisors in various ways, particularly with respect to long-range planning and development.

In addition to the general merchandise office proper there is also a factory management department headed by its own vice president. Factories fall into two general categories: wholly owned and affiliated, the latter being merchandise sources in which the company has a minority ownership interest. Where a buying department does business with a wholly owned or affiliated factory, close liaison is maintained between the buyer and/or supervisor and the factory management department.

The "staff" functions of the general merchandise office in some cases comprise fairly sizable organizations in themselves. Reporting to the retail merchandise manager are four staff assistants who aid in maintaining liaison with the retail sales managers of the various buying departments. Also reporting to this executive are a national retail advertising manager responsible for overall sales promotional plans and advertising services to the stores, a national display manager responsible for display services to the stores, and a director of sales training responsible for training support for the sales promotional program.

Reporting to the mail order merchandise manager are a series of departments responsible for the planning of mail order sales promotional activities and preparation and distribution of catalogs. Reporting to the assistant on buying are the merchandise testing and development laboratories, the merchandise shopping and comparison department, and an economist. The staff of the merchandise control manager includes a number of specialized assistants who maintain liaison with the various buying departments and otherwise assist in the performance of the overall control function. All of these staff activities serve two primary purposes: advising the merchandising vice president and providing specialized services to the buying departments. These services are of three general kinds: overall coordination of sales promotional activities to assure maximum selling impact, liaison with the field, and the provision of various kinds of technical assistance (for example, merchandise testing and development).

Despite its seeming complexity, the structure of the parent merchandising organization is essentially quite simple. It is built around the forty buying departments, each of which is responsible for its own merchandising results. Four basic functions are represented in each buying department: buying per se, and the staff functions of retail sales management, mail order sales management, and merchandise control. Each of these functions is likewise represented in the general merchandise office, whence various essential services are available as needed to the individual buying departments.

It should be further noted that whereas *buying* for the entire U.S. portion of the Sears system is centralized in the parent organization, *selling* is completely decentralized to the field. The buyers work out the merchandise structures of their lines, develop merchandise sources, and enter into master contracts with suppliers. Each buying department issues a merchandise list, which in effect is the "catalog" from which the individual stores order against the master contract entered into by the buyers. But the buyers have no authority to compel the stores to fulfill commitments they have made.

The retail sales manager in each buying department is the representative of the buyers to the retail stores in the field. In this capacity the sales manager works with the advertising, display, and sales training departments to assure proper support of the buyers' plans, and coordinates their plans with overall sales promotional strategy. For these purposes contact is maintained with the field to see that the potentialities of the line are understood, to develop and maintain enthusiasm for the line at the store level, and to assist in working out any problems that may arise from a store standpoint (for example, service of supply, mechanical service, sales training, and the like). An important part of this executive's work is counsel with the buyers on the needs of the stores, the sales prospects of the line, and other field matters on which the buyers need to be informed. The mail order sales managers provide similar services to the buyers in their departments for the mail order side of their business. The controller is the "figure man" who evaluates inventories and buying commitments in the light of sales trends, analyzes gross profit structures and the balance of sales as between various items in the line, and advises the buyers on the strategy and timing of their plans and on the sales and profit performance of their lines.

None of this in any way relieves the buyers of their responsibility for maintaining *personal* contact with the field, both retail and mail order. The greater portion of the buyer's time must necessarily be spent working with sources, hence the need for providing staff services of the types noted. But no amount of staff assistance can take the place of the buyer's intimate personal knowledge of conditions in the field.

If the basic unit of the parent merchandising organization is the buying department, the basic unit of the buying department is the individual buyer, the focal point around which all parent merchandising activities revolve. The buyer's is the irreducible, "nontransferable" responsibility for the performance of the line. While "selling" is technically a responsibility of the stores and mail order plants, the buyers are ultimately responsible for what happens to their lines in the field. This means not only that their buying and sales planning must be "right," but that they must gain the support of the field; if they fail to gain this support, no amount of "rightness" in their merchandise or plans will excuse the poor result.

Thus we have a picture of an intricate crisscrossing and interweaving of work patterns and relationships, with the buyers and the buying departments as the nuclei of activity.

There are several features of this parent buying organization worth noting. For one thing, it has a very broad span of control: forty buying departments, all reporting directly to the merchandising vice president. Status-wise, the supervisors of these departments are on a level equal to that of the heads of the four staff departments, and the latter in no way attenuate or compromise the "line" relationship between vice president and supervisor. This means that the amount of detailed supervision the merchandising vice president can provide the supervisors is small. They see him on special occasions when they feel it necessary to go to him for counsel on some matter of major importance or when they want him to be informed on some significant development. They see him, too, when he inquires about some matter of sufficient moment to require his personal attention, or when the performance of their department is not up to expectations; otherwise, they operate largely on their own, assuming personal responsibility for decisions often running into tens of millions of dollars.

Most of the individual buying departments are likewise characterized by broad spans of control, with sometimes as many as twenty buyers, plus the three functional staff executives reporting to a single supervisor. Here, too, the supervisor is spread very thin and must perforce delegate broad responsibilities to the buyers, many of whom make decisions involving millions of dollars on their own.

The structure of the parent merchandising organization as a whole and of the individual buying departments thus parallels the structure of the X-type stores discussed in the preceding chapter. The characteristics of the two structures are comparable. Both enforce a high degree of delegation of authority and responsibility, simply because those at higher levels are spread too thin to do otherwise. Both place a large premium on having outstandingly good people in key positions. Both heavily underscore the need for confidence in subordinates and the necessity of having the kind of people in whom confidence can be reposed; otherwise they cannot be trusted to make decisions on their own where mistakes in judgment could be brutally costly.

Both require people with large measures of independent initiative because no one higher up gives them detailed instructions. Both demand a type of leadership that is primarily "people-oriented" rather than "method-oriented" because in both cases problems manifest themselves primarily as problems of people rather than problems of things. Both require superiors skilled in evaluating people and sufficiently adept in administration not to get themselves involved in red tape or in anything but matters of the greatest importance; otherwise they will not have time for the really important things nor time to work with the people in their organization who really need their help.

In the case of the parent organization as well as the stores, the broad span of control rests on the assumption that the primary motive force of the organization lies in the initiative and drive and intelligence of the people in the organization; that it does not have to be imposed from the top down; and that the chief function of the leader is to channelize and direct and imaginatively utilize that force. Granted this approach, the broad span of control makes more sense than the narrow, provided it is buttressed by whatever steps are necessary to make sure the organization is staffed by the kind of people who can function in that kind of organization. If these conditions are met, the broad span of control should provide superior economic performance, for the energies of the organization infinitely exceed anything that can be imposed from the top. It should be more adaptive to changing conditions and have greater growth and survival power because there are more centers of decision making and these are closer to the scene of action. It should contribute to higher morale and greater personal satisfaction because people are working in a freer, more exhilarating environment. And it should provide both the stimulation and the opportunity for growth in greater measure. This is not an easy or comfortable kind of organization in which to work. But it "stretches" people, makes them call on potentials and develop capacities that might otherwise have lain dormant, makes them bigger, often, than first they knew.

Another striking characteristic of the parent merchandising organization is the large number of people who are involved in practically everything that happens, the freedom with which they move across departmental lines, and the manner in which they work together in coordinate rather than superior-subordinate relationships.

Even the simplest actions are likely to involve a number of people and several different departments. The introduction of a new item of merchandise, a power lawn mower, for example, will suggest something of the process. The buyer may have been working on this new item for several years, in cooperation with the source, the factory office, and the merchandise development laboratory. When it is finally ready for production, catalog copy and layout must be prepared (working with the catalog advertising department); it must be incorporated in the merchandise list that goes to the stores (working with the merchandise list department, which is part of the operating organization); because it is an important item with large volume potential, a strong sales promotion plan must be developed and properly integrated into the overall merchandising strategy, for which purposes the buyer works with the retail merchandise office and the national retail advertising and the national display departments; to make sure that salespeople understand the new item and know how to sell it intelligently, he works with the sales training department; because a special compensation plan may be necessary, he works with the compensation division of the parent personnel department; because it is a piece of mechanical merchandise for which repair parts must be stocked and repair services provided, he works with the national service department (part of the operating organization); because warehousing and transportation problems are involved, he works with the service of supply and the transportation departments (also units of the operating organization); because the source may have difficulty financing the large production anticipated, he may work with the controller's office and the factory department on an arrangement to compensate the source in advance of actual delivery of the merchandise.

This is a simplified description of what is likely to take place in introducing a new item of merchandise or in taking many other kinds of action. In many of these interdepartmental contacts the buyer is aided by the departmental supervisor, controller, and retail and mail order sales managers; in other necessary contacts, he works directly. In all cases contacts are made freely back and forth across departmental lines. Generally speaking, the heads of the various functions named—operating, advertising, personnel, auditing, and so on—do not involve themselves in the contacts made with or by their subordinates; unless the matter is of sufficient importance to require that they be consulted, the subordinates work things out for themselves.

The process of working things out is largely one of colleagues working together. The buyer or the retail sales manager cannot command the aid of the display people to design a new fixture, or the approval of a proposed incentive plan by the compensation specialist, or the service of a laboratory engineer in working out a problem in design or production. This does not mean that these or any other individuals may arbitrarily withhold cooperation or take arbitrary, uncompromising stands with respect to their particular areas of responsibility. Rather, it is expected that all people who may be involved in any specific matter will work together amicably and cooperatively, and that they will resolve conflicts and disagreements themselves without resort to higher authority. This means that all members of the system must depend for personal effectiveness on their ability to cooperate with others and to gain their cooperation in turn.

The former merchandising vice president, now vice chairman of the board, used to have a piece of advice he gave to all key people coming into his organization. It went something like this: "I shall hold you responsible for thus and so. Your standing and progress with the company will depend on how well you accomplish it. To do your job, you will have to work not only with the people in your own department but with a great many other people in other parent departments and in the field. *But you do not have one shred of authority to compel these people to work with you or to force them to accept your ideas.* If you have any disagreements with anyone I expect you to work things out between yourselves. I don't want you or anyone else coming to me to arbitrate disputes or to get me to use my influence to change somebody's mind. If you come to me for such a purpose I shall take it you don't have the ability this job requires. You've got to get results, but you've got to get them on the basis of the soundness of your plans and on your ability to get the full and voluntary support of everyone else, in whatever department they may be, who may be necessary to make your plans succeed." The present merchandising vice president, who was brought up under this system, is following a similar practice, a practice that sets the tone of the entire merchandising organization.

The people who may or should be involved in any particular matter will vary considerably according to the nature of the matter. A brief summary has been given of some of the contacts likely to occur in introducing a new item of merchandise. Other kinds of problems are likely to involve a different configuration of contacts: for example, improving a line of merchandise, or bolstering the sales of a line not moving according to expectations, or developing a new packaging program, or changing the balance of sales in a line, and so on. There is no manual that spells out who should be consulted on each kind of problem and what channels are to be followed in reaching any particular conclusion; these vary not only according to the nature of the problem but from time to time for even the same problem. This applies not only to securing necessary clearance and approvals; it also applies to seeking advice and counsel from anyone in the organization who might be able to help, such as someone in another department who had a similar problem at one time or another.

The actual patterns of interaction are so complex and so variable that not only can they not be charted or "manualized," but any attempt to do so would introduce rigidities that would be undesirable. As things are, each person is expected to *know* or to *find out* the right way to proceed in each situation and to whom to go for ideas or advice. The effectiveness of executives and specialists depends on their skill in knowing what to do and in finding their way around within the system. This puts a large premium not only on having the kind of people who can work easily and effectively without the guidance and support of clear-cut procedures; it also rewards stability, on having people who have been there long enough to know the ins and outs of the organization, on having a low rate of personnel turnover so that the number of new people "learning the ropes" at any one time will be small enough that the rest of the organization can give them the coaching they need. People acquire the kind of knowledge they must have to function effectively only by "growing into" the system; it cannot be acquired from formal instructions or official directives. This is one of the reasons "promotion from within" is so important at Sears.

People must be around long enough not only to "know the ropes" but to know the *people*. Actually, knowing the people is a large part of "knowing the ropes." This involves more than knowing who fits where in the formal structure. Knowing whom to see on certain things is often very much more than knowing who has what title or who occupies what position; the formal structure is too simple and too general to provide a sure guide in "finding one's way around." Above all, people accomplish their jobs through ability to cooperate with others and ability to win their cooperation in return. People must get to know others in the system as individuals and not simply as people performing particular activities.

The system closely approximates what Elton Mayo called an "informal organization." The "formal organization" is that described at the beginning of this chapter. The way work is actually accomplished is through an intimate, flexible, and ever-changing pattern of informal ad hoc relationships that crisscross back and forth across the lines of the formal organization without too much regard for the formal structure. One of the great virtues of this system lies in the fact that the formal organization does not interfere with getting the job done. Throughout, attention is focused on the real problems of buying and merchandising and on the real people who are dealing with these problems.

The way the system works comports closely with the realities of human nature. The organization is neither conceived or operated as a machine where relationships are abstract and impersonal; it is planned and functions as a system whose component parts are *real people* who can be relied upon to work out their own problems in cooperation with their fellows. There is an implicit assumption that, granted technical competence, men and women of good will and integrity can work together as a team, naturally and spontaneously, and that the results of that teamwork will be far superior to any patterning or directing that could be enforced from the top down.

If the parent merchandising organization were set up on a "functional" basis, many of the characteristics named would be lost. Strict adherence to the functional theory would suggest that the work of the retail sales managers be pulled into the retail merchandise office, the work of the mail order sales managers into the catalog advertising department, and the work of the controllers into the merchandise control office. In other words, the people performing these functions would be grouped together into functional departments rather than assigned, as they now are, to the individual buying departments.

On the surface there might seem to be a certain amount of logic in such a course; in fact, at some times in the past at least two of these functions, mail order sales management and merchandise control, were so "functionalized." It might be argued that combining people performing similar functions into specialized departments would promote greater efficiency in the performance of such functions. It might also be argued that by means of such a regrouping it would be possible to eliminate a number of jobs, as for example having one person handle the retail sales management of two or more smaller departments, each of which now has a retail sales manager of its own; similar economies might be possible with respect to the mail order sales management and merchandise control activities. It might be further argued that better supervision and coordination could be provided because those performing each function would be working directly for functional specialists rather than for buying department supervisors who, whatever their skill in buying, might be wanting in some of the functional skills. And because of this closer and more "professional" supervision, it might also be possible to use people of somewhat lower caliber and hence less costly and more readily available.

Such an organization might be possible but the arguments for it would be specious. For one thing, it would greatly complicate the formal organization structure and make far more difficult the informal collaboration within and across departmental lines that is so striking a feature of the present system. To take the place of that informal collaboration, it would be necessary to develop elaborate procedures and controls that would not only be less effective but probably so expensive as to offset any savings that had been anticipated; in other words, necessary integration of the system would have to be achieved largely by mechanical means.

This kind of organization would deprive the supervisors and buyers of much of the responsibility they now have because it would deny them direct access to and control over some of the functions that are necessary for achieving those results. Friction and conflict would develop between the buying departments and the functional departments that would require the frequent intervention of the merchandising vice president or of some additional staff specialists he might find it necessary to employ to assist him in "coordination." Thus, effective responsibility would move to a higher level in the organization and would probably come to rest ultimately with the merchandising vice president himself. The "administrative unit" would no longer be the individual buying department but the entire parent merchandising organization.

Because of this vastly greater degree of centralization, the merchandising vice president would probably have to shorten his span of control by interjecting a new level of supervision between himself and his supervisors, perhaps by dividing the buying departments into five or six groups, each heading up to a "group merchandise manager." Initiative likewise would move to higher levels. The organization would lose much of its present drive and spontaneity, much of its present resourcefulness and adaptiveness, and much of the stimulation it now provides for personal growth and development.

These are some of the consequences that might be anticipated from application of the theory of functional specialization to the parent merchandising organization. The superiority of the present system is clear, not only in "human" terms but in terms of productive performance as well.

It should be noted that in the system as it now stands the existence and importance of the various functions are recognized. But instead of separating these into specialized functional departments, they are kept closely integrated with, in fact incorporated into, the buying departments. Necessary overall "functional coordination" is adequately provided through the four functional assistants to the merchandising vice president: the assistant on buying, the retail and mail order merchandise managers, and the merchandise controller. But these executives and their staffs in no way undermine the integrity of the relationship between the supervisors and their functional aides.

In a complex organization certain activities must be separated out and assigned to functional specialists. The question is, where are these functional specialists to be placed in the organization structure? Are they to be grouped together into specialized functional departments, or are they to be assigned directly to the central activity it is their purpose to serve? In the case of the Sears parent merchandising organization, that central activity is the buying and distribution of merchandise. The functions are therefore grouped around that central activity. This is the only relationship that makes sense: function to merchandise. The relation of function to function is a meaningless abstraction—and horribly complicated in practice.

Note

This paper is from a previously unpublished manuscript written in 1952–53. Excerpted by permission of the publisher from "The More Things Change the More They Stay the Same," *Journal of Management Inquiry* 1:1 (Mar. 1992): 14–38. Copyright © 1992 by Sage Publications, Inc.

13

Evolution of a Structure

Some of the unique features of the Sears organization as we know it today [1956] originated early in the company's history. Most notably, these are simplicity of structure, strength of the line organization in relation to staff, and absence of extensive bureaucratic baggage.

From its earliest days, Sears has given wide latitude to its key people, and this latitude extends far down into the organization. It suited the purposes and personal inclinations of both Richard Sears, who founded the company, and Julius Rosenwald, who succeeded him, to surround themselves with aggressive, highly competent executives and to give them a very free rein, subject only to their working well together and producing results. The history of Sears from an organizational point of view is largely the history of the changing roles of this group of aggressive, capable, cooperative men in a loosely structured, highly personal organizational environment. [This paper was written in the mid-1950s. During the seventy years of the company's history to that time, there were few women in executive positions in Sears or other American business enterprises.]

Chief reliance has always been placed on individual judgment rather than on stated rules and procedures. Especially during the early, formative years of the company, the relationships between key men, and to a considerable extent the actual nature and content of their jobs, were left to work themselves out naturally rather than be forced into a preconceived organizational framework. Jobs were not fixed and duties precisely defined. The organization was sufficiently flexible to permit men to find their own level and scope in terms of their own abilities and drives. As a result, big men found themselves with big responsibilities and smaller men with smaller. Generally speaking, men gravitated to jobs, or created jobs, that were neither too big nor too small for their capacities, a disparity that would have been much more frequent if the effort had been made to fit them into neatly contrived organizational slots.

This kind of situation would have led to chaos if there had not been strong leadership at the top. But the company had that kind of leadership. It had in Julius Rosenwald, who joined the firm in 1895, a leadership that could capitalize on the relatively unfettered drive and initiative of its top people because it was strong enough to channel that drive and initiative to serving the company's needs rather than be dissipated in personal feuds and rivalries.

This tradition of finding good men and giving them a relatively free hand within a fluid, loosely structured organization was firmly established by Julius Rosenwald. It was continued and reinforced under General Robert E. Wood, who followed Rosenwald, and remains a striking feature of the post-Wood Sears under Theodore Houser.

Sears may not now have in full degree the freewheeling character it had in an earlier day; the organization in 1956 is much more elaborate and complex than it was in 1906 because the company itself is much larger than it was then and is engaged in a far wider range of activities. But the organizational spirit is much the same today as it was fifty years ago, and insofar as circumstances permit, key executives are given the kind of free rein, without undue organizational restrictions, that will permit them not only to find their own level but in the process keep the organization in a constant state of fluid adaptivity that keeps it young, vigorous, alert, and growing.

The organizational development of modern Sears can be traced from the year 1906, when the company moved to its present mail order and headquarters location on the west side of Chicago. By that time, the company was twenty years old. It had survived the hazards of its early years and developed a form of organization and a management team well-adapted to its needs and opportunities.

The entire business was handled from a single location, and the business itself was solely mail order. The organization was simple. It was built around three primary functions, merchandising, operating, and auditing/finance, each headed by a vice president. The merchandising function embraced responsibility for both the procurement and sale of goods, including planning and production of the catalog. The operating function was concerned with processing customer orders, receiving, storing, and shipping goods, and handling the large volume of customer correspondence associated with the mail order business. The auditing/finance function was conventional.

While these three functions were coequal in an organizational sense and closely interrelated in their activities, the merchandising function, quite naturally in a merchandising institution, was dominant. The work of merchandising was carried on by a group of department heads, each in charge of a given classification of goods. Julius Rosenwald frequently referred to this group as a "federation of merchants," suggesting the nature and spirit of the organizational arrangements. Merchandise department heads had almost unlimited authority within their respective product-line areas. They established quality standards and selling prices for their merchandise. They selected their sources of supply and dealt with them independently, using the two chief buying advantages Sears had in those days: volume purchasing and prompt payment of bills. In those cases where procurement problems made it necessary to buy or start factories, the factories were supervised and often largely run by the merchandise department heads themselves. Preparation of catalog copy and layouts was likewise the responsibility of the individual merchandise departments.

These department heads (called "supervisors") reported to the merchandising vice president and the general merchandise office. The latter, as the vice president's staff, concerned itself largely with overall inventory control and establishing the size and cost limits of the catalog. In keeping with the federation concept, the general merchandise office influenced and exercised authority over the individual merchandise departments only to the extent required to fulfill these two principal responsibilities. The primary role of the merchandising vice president was to provide overall leadership, to make sure that each department was headed by a competent man, and to hold each man accountable for satisfactory sales and profit results, leaving to the men themselves a very wide degree of latitude as to the manner of accomplishing those results.

Unlike the merchandising function, which was almost completely decentralized, the operating function was tightly centralized and closely controlled. This was essential in view of the nature of the work, which involved receiving and storing incoming goods, receiving and shipping customer orders, handling vast quantities of customer correspondence, and many related activities of comparable character. Highly rationalized systems, precise production routines, and tight time schedules were devised to regulate the flow of work, and close controls were established to insure their rigid observance.

In the substantial economies thus achieved, the operating function made a major contribution to lowering the costs of distribution for the public and to increasing the profitability of the company.

There were seeds of conflict in the working relationships between the merchandising and operating functions. There was considerable overlap between them because both functions were involved with the same merchandise: one with buying it and promoting its sale, the other with handling it and dealing with the customer. Moreover, there were aggressive, purposeful men in both functions who were not easily walked over. Conflicts did arise, but they were settled directly and usually on the spot by discussions between those immediately concerned and without recourse to higher authority. No decrees were issued outlining the boundaries between functions. Instead, there was a process of gradual adjustment and accommodation between the men themselves in terms of the concrete problems at issue. And because the focus was on what was necessary to get the job done rather than on some abstract principle of who should do what, the job was not only done better but the organization was able to adapt and change as the jobs themselves changed with continued company growth.

As this brief sketch indicates, during the early years of the present century the structure of the Sears organization was relatively simple. It was divided into three primary functions with a straight-line flow of authority and responsibility and great reliance on informal, personalized cooperation across organizational lines, a process facilitated by the fact that organizational boundaries were few and loosely drawn. There was little in the way of staff organization to complicate either the straight-line or the interfunctional relationships.

That this organization was well suited to the needs of the time is attested by the business success the company enjoyed during those years. That it was well suited to cope with new problems is attested by the relative ease with which it adapted to the very great changes of the years following 1906, with constantly improving business success. Some of these changes were the result of internal pressures; others, of changes and new opportunities in the national economy, including those arising from the First World War. In either case, the adaptivity of the organization and of the people in it proved to be one of the company's major assets.

In the course of adapting to these changes, the modest-sized, relatively simple organization of fifty years ago gradually evolved into the large-scale, relatively complex organization we know today. Between 1906 and 1956, the Sears organization has changed substantially, to all outward appearances. But in its most essential characteristic it has remained very much the same. *This characteristic is reliance on the judgment and initiative of able people working within a fluid framework of organization.* It is this characteristic that is important, not the details of successive stages in the evolution of formal organizational structure.

After the organization had achieved a relatively stable form in the early years of the century, the first major new development that challenged its powers of adaptation was the opening of branch mail order plants. The first two of these were in Dallas and Seattle, both opened in 1910. The purpose of the branches was to improve service and reduce transportation costs for regions most remote from Chicago. The opening of branches introduced problems of administration with which management had no previous experience and which required extensive changes in organizational relationships.

These changes were largely in the operating end of the business; the merchandising function was affected only incidentally. As previously noted, the operating function was highly centralized. This arrangement had worked well as long as all operations activities were under one roof. But when these—the receipt, storage, and shipment of merchandise; the processing of customer orders; and the handling of customer correspondence—came to be performed not only in Chicago but in Dallas and Seattle as well, an entirely new set of administrative circumstances was created.

Initially, an effort was made to control the activities of the new branch plants as closely from central headquarters as the activities of individual operating departments in the Chicago plant had theretofore been controlled from the same point. But this effort soon ran into difficulties. Increasingly, executives in the branch plants began to question the workability of referring all but the most routine decisions to Chicago. They were closer to the customers and closer to the problems; they had a more intimate knowledge of local circumstances than those in Chicago could possibly have. Difficulties that could have been handled expeditiously on the spot, if they had the authority to do so, had to be referred to Chicago, with consequent delays and the ever present danger that decisions made without feel for the local situation were often not good decisions. And the sheer volume of paperwork incidental to referring so many things to Chicago and providing Chicago with the necessary data for exercising detailed control of outlying local operations placed a heavy burden on the organization and threatened to negate the economies the outlying plants were designed to achieve.

Very soon, therefore, following the opening of the first branch plants, processes were set in motion to transfer greater and greater authority and responsibility to local managements. The opening of the Philadelphia plant in 1920 hastened completion of a trend toward operating decentralization that was already well advanced by that time. For whereas the Dallas and Seattle plants were essentially field stations for storing and shipping merchandise, the Philadelphia plant had its own edition of the catalog carrying types of merchandise specifically adapted to the needs and characteristics of the northeastern section of the country. Problems of inventory control, reordering of stocks, and disposal of slow-moving merchandise were even less susceptible to geographically centralized control than storing merchandise, processing orders, and handling correspondence. The trend toward decentralization was also greatly strengthened by the fact that Lessing Rosenwald, son of the president, was placed in charge of the Philadelphia plant and in a position to argue the case for decentralization with somewhat greater force than his counterparts in the other plants.

The net result of this trend, begun in 1910 and essentially completed about twelve years later, was the effective decentralization of all branch plant activities. These plants patterned their organizations and procedures on those of the Chicago plant, with suitable adaptations for their smaller size and local circumstances. They looked to Chicago for advice and assistance on special problems, but to all intents and purposes by the early twenties they were independent entities with a high degree of local autonomy in the day-to-day conduct of their business.

This change was accompanied by a gradual shift in the relations between the home operating office and the branch plants. Originally, this had been a direct line relationship. But as time went on, the operating office began more and more to assume the kind of functions now known as staff and to remove itself from the chain of command. The operating office function as thus developed became in due course a key component of what came to be known as the parent organization.

By freeing the company in this manner from the straightjacket of rigidly centralized operations, the way was opened to successful further growth that could not have been accomplished under the original system. Sears now has eleven mail order plants strategically located in various parts of the country. With time and greater experience, the processes of decentralization are being carried further and further, not only with respect to operating activities but merchandising functions as well. It can be truly said that Sears mail order managers are today, and have been for many years, full-fledged members of the Sears "federation of merchants."

Note

Unpublished manuscript, 1956, author's files.

14

The Bureaucratic Dilemma

All organizations are inherently conservative because a degree of stability is a necessary condition of survival. Organizations are fragile. They can and do change, but too-rapid or too-drastic change can severely hamper their ability to function. At the same time, organizations *must* change if they are to survive. There are natural mechanisms in organizational processes that are resistant to change and therefore, within limits, have survival value. The danger is that these mechanisms, if not kept in check, will operate so effectively to prevent change that they themselves endanger the organization's capacity for long-term survival. The strength of change-resisting mechanisms varies directly with organizational size.

Perhaps the strongest of these mechanisms is the vested interest people in positions of authority and responsibility have in keeping things the way they are. These people have achieved their present positions through existing arrangements, and efforts to change those arrangements significantly are likely to be seen as threatening. Ambitious people on the way up appraise organizational realities as they are and chart their courses accordingly; they are likely to resist changing the shape of the playing field.

One way in which the mechanism of personal self-interest manifests itself is bureaucratization. The tendency toward bureaucracy found in virtually all organizations results in part from the efforts of people in key posts to build fiefdoms that will provide a measure of self-protection or a means for furthering personal ambitions; in either case, the resulting elaboration of structure introduces organizational rigidities that are resistant to change, including change initiated from above.

Because a primary purpose of bureaucracy is to resist change and reduce risk, the propensity to innovate and take risks varies inversely with degree of bureaucratization.

All organizations start life in an entrepreneurial mode because they are created to undertake something new—not necessarily new in the literal sense of never having been done before, but in the sense of being done for the first time by this particular organization. As the enterprise becomes established and begins to prosper and grow, bureaucratic tendencies begin to appear. Some degree of bureaucracy is inevitable simply because it is one aspect of complex organization: the increasingly segmented and specialized formal structure required by expanding scale of operation. Also, as noted, bureaucracy is one of the means by which an organization preserves the stability necessary to function and survive.

The problem is maintaining balance between the entrepreneurial spirit with which the enterprise was launched and the structure required for stability. Beyond the very smallest organizations, some specialization of function, and therefore protobureaucracy, is required to convert the entrepreneurial spirit into operating reality. But bureaucracy, whether proto or fully developed, tends to evolve a rationale and life of its own, and there is always the danger it will envelop and smother the entrepreneurial spirit. Unless controlled and kept in balance, stability mutates by imperceptible degrees into rigidity that in time comes to verge on immobility.

The propensity of bureaucracy to thrive is a universal characteristic. Specialists have a vested interest in their specialty, and their personal security and future prospects are closely tied to the status and strength of their particular function in the total organizational structure. In the minds of specialists, functional interests easily become identified with organizational interests, and enhancement of function is readily equated with serving organizational purposes.

These tendencies are greatly strengthened by the growth of professionalism in functional areas: accounting, advertising, marketing, personnel, and the like. Spurred by influential professional societies, loyalties to the profession develop that are not always fully congruent with loyalties to the company. Organized professions provide opportunities for career advancement along professional rather than corporate lines, which may at times tempt practitioners to pursue professional rather than corporate aims.

The heads of engineering, personnel, marketing, R&D, and their counterparts in other functional areas have no lack of good ideas (often coming to them through professional channels) as to ways their particular activities can be enhanced for the benefit of the enterprise. The more highly qualified they are in their specialties, the more and better ideas they are likely to have. These are likely to be good ideas, not frivolous. Improved selection and better training can undoubtedly help raise productivity. Additional market research staff could well improve marketing. A bigger R&D budget could in time produce significant product improvements.

The problem lies in the fact that there are no natural limitations on the growth of specialized functional staff. While the enterprise as a whole is subject to a market discipline—the revenues it generates must cover all costs and provide a reasonable profit—specialized functions within the enterprise are not directly subject to the market test. The personnel department does not produce revenue and there is no reliable, objective way to balance its costs against the benefits it produces. It must rely for its budget on its ability to influence the budget allocation process, and here the only limitation on functional ambition is the judgment, ultimately, of the CEO who must weigh competing claims and produce a total budget within the bounds of aggregate affordability.[1]

The processes here described have significant consequences, one of which is the gradual buildup of overhead costs and resultant drain on productivity. Another, with implications more subtle but equally grave, is a dampening of the spirit of innovation and risk taking that are essential to the health of the economic system. The strength of the dampening process varies directly with size and time: the larger and older the organization grows, the more entrenched and debilitating it becomes.

Note

From a memorandum in the author's files, dated December 1979 to William C. Norris, chairman and chief executive officer, Control Data Corporation.

1. See Peter F. Drucker, *Management: Tasks, Responsibilities, Practices* (New York: Harper & Row, 1973), 141–42.

15

The Behavioral Dimensions of Span of Management Theory

A span of management is not simply a mechanical arrangement for a certain number of people to report to a particular superior; it is a dynamic system of human and organizational relationships. Some of these are specific and subject to precise definition. Others are in varying degrees imprecise, intangible, and elusive but highly important, as they influence the way people behave within organizations and the effectiveness with which organizations function. In any set of organizational circumstances a variety of factors combine to determine the workable span of management. Some factors are in some degree subject to deliberate managerial control, and advantage should be taken of these to establish as wide spans of management as circumstances can be arranged to allow.

Factors That Determine the Span of Management

It has long been recognized that there is no universally applicable span of management.[1] Urwick's dictum that an individual superior cannot effectively direct the work of more than five or six subordinates whose work interlocks[2] has been superseded by recognition that a variety of factors, in addition to interdependence of tasks, goes into the determination of the optimum span of control. Factors that have been identified include:

—Limits on the range of permissible discretion on the part of subordinates (government functionaries cannot be permitted the latitude of individual judgment expected of management consultants).
—Limits on the acceptable range of variation in product (compo-

nents of space vehicles must be built to far closer tolerances than components of furniture and hence require closer and stricter supervision and control in their manufacture).

—Character of work (manufacturing generally requires closer supervision and shorter spans of management than retailing; patient care is largely the professional responsibility of individual practitioners subject to only the most general oversight.)

—Stability of operations (a work process that is well established and routinized requires less supervision than a new process or one susceptible to frequent change).

—Competence of superiors (other things equal, the more competent superior can direct the work of more subordinates than one who is less competent).

—Character of supervision imposed on superiors (superiors subject to detailed supervision from above are likely to set up shorter spans of management in order that, in the interests of their own survival, they can exercise detailed supervision on those below them).

—Skills of subordinates (a bimodal distribution probably exists here: unskilled work and highly skilled work tend to require less supervision than semiskilled work).

—Availability of information for decision making at various levels in the organization structure (effective decisions cannot be made at levels below which pertinent information is reasonably accessible).

These are some of the variables that influence determination of feasible spans of management. Others might be identified, but these are sufficient to demonstrate the necessity for a contingency approach to determining the optimum span in any particular organizational setting. Depending on the directions in which the variables lean—some may lean in one direction, others in another—a feasible span may be quite narrow in one case and very wide in another, and both work equally well.

Furthermore, the optimum is a range, not a point. Even if all variables could be identified and quantified, it is most unlikely that means could ever be found to determine precisely the *one* best span for any given set of conditions; rather, in any particular situation there is a range of feasible spans. That range will lie somewhere in a broader continuum from very narrow to very wide, and there probably will always be a lower and an upper limit to the workable range in a given set of circumstances.

Controlling the Variables

Some but not all of the variables significant to the span of management are susceptible in some degree to conscious managerial control. In general, there are great advantages to be realized in finding ways to operate effectively at the broadest feasible range.

The span of management is obviously related to the extent to which an organization is centralized or decentralized. Broad spans require greater decentralization of authority and responsibility than narrow spans. Herein lies the root advantage of broader spans of management: they tend to build better human organizations. If substantial delegations of authority and responsibility are to be made, there is a premium on having well-qualified subordinates; if delegations are limited, the importance of quality in subordinates is correspondingly less.

In studies made some years ago at Sears, Roebuck and Co. it was found that department managers in "flat" organizations tended to be more competent than those in otherwise similar but "tall" structures [see chapters 11 and 12 in this volume]. The flat Sears structures had very broad spans of management: thirty-odd department heads in medium-size retail stores reporting to single management teams consisting of a store manager and an assistant; forty heads of major buying departments reporting to a single merchandising vice-president. In both the retail store and the parent buying organization the key executives were spread very thin. The amount of time these executives could give to any of their large numbers of subordinates, or the amount of individual surveillance or support they could provide, was limited. To manage successfully the organizations for which they were responsible, they were compelled by the structure of the organizations they had created to staff their key positions with the ablest men and women they could find or develop. Neither the store manager nor the vice-president had the time to involve themselves in departmental details; in each instance, the key to successful performance lay in the competence of their department heads.

In retail stores of similar size but with "tall" organizational structures (that is, with an intervening level of supervision and correspondingly shorter spans of management), the store manager was less dependent on high competence at the department head level because of the closer direction, control, and support made possible by the intervening level of supervision.

Not only were executives who were operating in structures with broad spans of management compelled to recruit top quality personnel for their key posts, but that personnel once in place was exposed to an especially rich learning and development experience. To function effectively in such a structure, department heads had to learn to accept and handle more autonomy than their counterparts working under closer supervision. They had to make more decisions on their own; they could not constantly run to higher authority for help; they had to take greater personal responsibility for the performance of their units. If they made mistakes they could not blame someone else and had to rely more on their own resources to work their way out. If they were successful the success was their's and not someone else's. In either case, learning and growth were enhanced.

In neither the merchandising organization nor the flat store organization were authority and responsibility delegated carelessly. In both instances the senior executives displayed keen ability to evaluate people. They had good people judgment. They could select men and women with development potential, follow their progress, and sense with confidence when individuals were ready for more responsibility. They were able to bring people along as fast as individuals were ready, but not so fast as to exceed their still-growing capacities. Because they knew which of their subordinates could move ahead largely on their own, and because they were not burdened by details, they were able to give help to those subordinates who needed it and stay as close as necessary to them as long as circumstances required. Altogether, the structures with broad spans of management tended to recruit more competent personnel for key positions and to provide them with a richer, more stimulating learning environment in which the growth of individuals was enhanced.

These structures were not altogether comfortable or easy ones in which to work. They made great demands on people. They required that men and women take personal responsibility for themselves and their work. They provided support, but not nearly as much as that provided by spans of management where there was more structure on which to lean. Not everyone could be successful, much less happy, in such an organization, and those who could not adapt to it were likely to be weeded out fairly quickly.

This process of selectivity points to another characteristic of the more horizontal organization structure: in it, problems are more likely to be seen as problems of people rather than as problems of things. If improvement is needed in a department, the problem is likely to be perceived as one requiring working with the department manager, not just to correct the problem at hand but to strengthen the department manager's capacity to deal with this and with future problems as well. In fact, under these flat structures the greater part of the process of managing tends to be the development of people: setting goals for them, holding them to high standards of performance, encouraging them to assume larger measures of autonomy and responsibility, and giving them help as needed for individual growth. There is much to be said for a philosophy and practice that sees a large part of managing as a task of developing people rather than refining procedures.

Designing Managerial Jobs

Other things equal, shorter spans of management may well be more effective than longer for accomplishing a given set of results, economic or otherwise, within a short period of time. It may be more expeditious for higher authority to intervene directly to correct a departmental problem than to work with the department manager to improve his ability to handle problems on his own. Unfortunately, such a course is likely to require continuing intervention, whereas strengthening capacity to handle problems at the departmental level is more likely to enable higher management to stay freer of operating details and to concentrate on the kinds of problems with which only higher management can deal. This is an important advantage and well worth additional thought and effort to find means for broadening the span of management to the widest degree possible within workable range in particular sets of circumstances.

Not all variables bearing on placement of the range are susceptible to deliberate modification and control, but some of them are. Among these, preeminently, are the interrelatedness of organizational tasks and the selection of key personnel.

Urwick's definitive wording of the span of control concept reads: "No superior can supervise directly the work of more than five, or at most six subordinates *whose work interlocks*" (Urwick's italics). Quite clearly, this implies that broader spans of management are possible if the work of subordinates can be made *less* interlocking, *less* interdependent. In many organizations, the work of constituent units is more interlocked and interdependent than it needs to be. Classical organization theory encourages the grouping of similar tasks together on the theory that this makes supervision easier, improves worker skills, and increases overall productivity. But it also increases the interdependence of units organized in this fashion because none of them can operate except in close synchronization with the other specialized units; in other words, their work is closely interlocked and the viable span of management for their direction is correspondingly limited.

Rather than bringing like work together chiefly because it is like work, it often makes better sense to *group specialized activities around the purposes they are intended to serve.* The effort should be made to organize work into units that are as nearly autonomous as possible, so that those heading each unit will have control over the maximum feasible number of elements that go into the accomplishment of complete tasks or significant components of complete tasks. Considerable thought and experimentation have gone into job design for workers. Managers' work, no less than workers', needs to be meaningful, needs to be structured in holistic fashion. Managerial work needs to be designed not only with technical elements in mind; insofar as possible, technical elements should be clustered in meaningful configurations. Managers, like workers, need a sense of *accomplishing* something, not just *doing* something; their results need to be comprehensible and measurable in real units, not abstract processes. And they need the maximum feasible degree of control over the factors that enter into the accomplishment of meaningfully identifiable tasks.

This approach to organization can greatly enlarge the extent to which practical delegations of authority and responsibility can be made. Authority over and responsibility for more elements of a total task provide a richer working and growing experience. By this means managers do not merely become increasingly expert at particular specializations but gain more experience in managing, to their own benefit and that of the organization.

Study of the best ways to design jobs for managers is a singularly promising field of endeavor that should be explored more aggressively and imaginatively than it has to date. Broader spans of management are likely to be a by-product of the effort to develop more humane organizations.

Notes

Excerpted by permission of the publisher from "The Behaviorial Dimensions of 'Span of Management' Theory," in *The Evolving Science of Management: The Collected Papers of Harold Smiddy and Papers in His Honor,* ed. Melvin Zimet and Ronald G. Greenwood (New York: AMACON, a

1. For a concise history and a comprehensive bibliography of the span of management theory, see David D. Van Fleet and Arthur G. Bedeian, "A History of the Span of Management," *Academy of Management Review*, July 1977.

2. Lyndall Urwick, "Executive Decentralization and Functional Coordination," *Management Review* 24:1 (Dec. 1935): 356.

16

The Critical Problem of Size

An essential factor in organization structure is the size of the administrative unit. Studies of employee attitudes at Sears, Roebuck and Co. have demonstrated a clear-cut inverse relationship between the size of the unit and the level of employee morale: many factors are unquestionably at work, but by and large the smaller the unit the higher the morale, and vice versa.

In smaller organizations, necessary cooperation between individuals and departments is greatly facilitated by the fact that people know each other personally, whereas in larger organizations cooperation is much more dependent on impersonal administrative controls. In a large mail order plant, for example, those who do the detailed work of controlling an inventory of tens of thousands of items and those who actually handle the merchandise itself must work in close coordination with each other, but because of the large number of people in each group personal relations across divisional lines are few and necessary coordination between the separate but related functions must be accomplished through a complex system of procedures. In a small retail store, where there must likewise be coordination between the functions of inventory control and handling merchandise, the situation is quite different. Salespeople, office clerks, and employees in the receiving and shipping rooms know each other on a first-name basis and cooperation between them is a personal matter of associates working together. Cooperation develops spontaneously and not as a result of orders or of a system of formal procedures set up to establish coordination. An organization such as this operates primarily through the face-to-face relationships of its members and only secondarily through impersonal, institutionalized relationships.

In the smaller organization, employees see much more readily where they themselves "fit" and the significance of their jobs in the whole scheme of things. In fact, seeing where they fit is an important part of being able to cooperate. In large, complex organizations, cooperation must depend to a much greater extent on a status system (expressed in an appropriate system of status symbols) that denotes working relationships in more or less purely functional terms. In such organizations, personal interaction is much more segmental than in smaller, simpler structures where people know each other as individuals and where cooperation is more likely to involve larger portions of personalities. The record clerk in a mail order plant has difficulty seeing beyond her routine task of processing inventory control cards; stockmen and order fillers are a world apart. The clerk in the office of a small store can readily see the relationship between her work and that of other employees, and the manner in which all their efforts dovetail into the overall task of serving the customer. Each individual job takes on more meaning and importance precisely because it is subordinate to but a necessary part of a larger function, and because that relationship can be seen and appreciated by all members of the group.

One of the interesting and instructive contrasts in the Sears organization is that between the mail order plants and the catalog order offices. They are, respectively, the largest and the smallest units operated by the company, the former typically employing several thousand people and the latter often as few as five or six and usually not more than twelve or fifteen. An anecdote involving these two types of units will illustrate the manner in which work is likely to acquire greater personal significance in smaller organizations than in larger.

A few years ago a bad snow storm struck the upper Midwest two or three days before Christmas, badly snarling rail and truck deliveries. Afterwards, a number of customers of one order office took the trouble to write to company headquarters about how the women of that office had gone out of their way to make sure that merchandise was delivered in time for Christmas, often at considerable personal trouble and inconvenience. Although customers are supposed to pick up their merchandise at the order office, in some cases where the merchandise did not arrive until Christmas Eve, too late to be picked up, employees on their own volition delivered the merchandise themselves, in their own cars and over bad roads, because otherwise the children would not have had their presents on Christmas day.

These order office workers had written up the orders for this Christmas merchandise. In many cases they knew the customers and the children for whom the gifts were intended. They had processed the orders, forwarded them to the mail order plant, and punched up on any delays. When the merchandise arrived at their place of work, it meant something more to them than so many packages or so many dollars.

In the case of these order office employees there was a personal concern for the job, a personal desire to get the work done, that could not have been expected in the mail order plant—although the same customers, the same merchandise, and the identical orders might have been involved. This is not in any way to disparage the efforts or conscientiousness of mail order employees, but it would be hard to conceive the shipping clerks, for instance, in the distant mail order city going to the same trouble and personal inconvenience, well beyond the call of duty, to get the orders into the hands of customers in time for Christmas morning. To them, the merchandise was so many packages, so many pounds, so many hours of labor. Management, of course, was concerned with getting the merchandise back to the customers' homes promptly and within the limits of the standard operating schedule, but management's interest, too, was abstract. The merchandise was so many dollars, not a doll buggy or an electric train for a flesh and blood girl or boy anxiously awaiting Christmas morning, as it was to the order office employees. Jobs in smaller units, in other words, are likely to have greater personal significance than is often possible in larger units simply because their relationship to something that transcends the job itself in importance is much more readily apparent.

A further advantage of smaller organizations lies in the fact that closer contacts between the executives and rank and file tend to result in friendlier, easier relationships. To employees in such units, the "big boss" is not some remote, little-known, semimythical personage but a flesh and blood individual to be liked or disliked on a basis of personal acquaintance. This more frequent, more personal contact between executives and rank and file makes possible a much better understanding of each other's problems and points of view and greatly facilitates the adjustment of any difficulties that may arise.

In sum, the smaller organization represents a simpler social system than does the larger unit. There are fewer people, fewer levels in the organizational hierarchy, and a less minute subdivision of labor. It is easier for employees to adapt themselves to such a simpler system and find their place in it. Their work becomes more meaningful, both to them and to their associates, because each of them can readily see the relation and importance of their jobs to other functions and to the organization as a whole. The organization operates primarily through the face-to-face relationships of its members and only secondari_y through impersonal, institutionalized relationships. The closer relations between the individual employee and higher executives in such an environment is only one aspect, but an important one, of the relatively simple and better integrated social system of the smaller organization.

The problem of size goes far beyond any considerations of employee morale as such, important as these may be in terms of industrial stability and human satisfactions. The broader implications have been well-stated by Yale Brozen:

> Our present value system is anti-totalitarian. A continuation of technological change in the direction of more rapid growth in the efficiency of highly centralized, large organizations than in that of small and decentralized organizations may change this. . . .

> Technological change which brings giantism not only imperils democratic values; it also signs its own death warrant. Social structures which are rigid and in which men are not free inhibit progress. Change finds it much harder to get itself accepted in large organizations since more decisions are made by rule and less by re-evaluation of possibilities. . . .

> Technological change which tends to increase the scale of enterprise decreases the opportunity and likelihood of further change. If a nation is to maintain its avenues of expansion, it must develop the techniques appropriate to small-scale production.[1]

This, then, is the dilemma of modern industrial society: the tendency of technological change, on the one hand, to foster the growth of large organizations and, on the other, the human costs of such growth. But the dilemma may be more apparent than real, for in many cases there is no inherent reason why it may not be possible to break down the large organization into a series of smaller components, each of which can enjoy a greater measure of local autonomy and function as and exhibit many of the characteristics of small organizations. Effective internal decentralization within the framework of large organizations can make such organizations at once more efficient technically and more democratic socially. It should also make them more adaptive and give them greater survival power.

The breaking down of larger organizations into smaller units must be done in such a manner as to permit these smaller units to function as integrated and meaningful entities. The change, in Peter Drucker's phrase, must be constitutional, not mechanical; it must be in the structure of the enterprise, not merely in its procedures.[2] Where the technology of the enterprise permits, this will require extensive modification of the system of "functional organization," one of the central concepts of Frederick Taylor's theory of management and the basic idea on which much of modern management practice rests.

Essentially, functionalization is an extension of the principle of specialization. Just as particular activities have been broken down into simple components and each component assigned to a different person, so many operations (often after having been highly "simplified") have been separated out of the broader complex of activities of which they are a part and set up as specialized and semi-independent organizational entities. This procedure is justified as a means of speeding output through specialization, providing better supervision and control, and permitting the use of persons of lesser skill, either to achieve lower costs or to overcome shortages in the supply of skilled workers.

There may be a certain spurious efficiency in this kind of organization, but it is likely to have serious off-setting liabilities. We are here concerned with one of the consequences of functionalization that has been almost entirely overlooked: its effect of *increasing the size of the administrative unit and making effective managerial decentralization impossible beyond the point in the organization hierarchy at which the functional divisions begin.*

This fact can be illustrated by a hypothetical example. Assume an organization that performs three primary functions or operations, A, B, and C. (These might be any three processes likely to be found in any company; their actual nature is not important for purposes of this illustration.) Assume further that the volume of output requires three units each of A, B, and C. Under these circumstances, the organization could be set up in either of two ways:

1. It could be set up in three divisions, each function (A, B, and C) being represented in each division. Such an organization, for which the term "integrated" seems appropriate, might be diagrammed as in figure 16.1 ("S" representing first-line supervision and "M" representing general plant management).

2. On the other hand, the organization could be set up in three functional divisions, one division having all three A units, another all three B units, and the third all three C units. Such an organiza-

Figure 16.1

tion could be represented by figure 16.2 (again using "S" and "M" to designate the two levels of supervision and management).

This second alternative illustrates the functional type of organization. It is the norm of scientific management theory and typical of much modern organization practice in industry, government, and elsewhere. Whatever its advantages, real or apparent, it has the effect of expanding the size of the administrative unit.

Figure 16.2

In the integrated type of organization, illustrated by the first example given, the administrative unit is the division, because each division, comprising as it does all operations essential to the turning out of a completed product, can operate with a high degree of autonomy. The total organization is composed of three relatively independent divisions, any one of which could continue to function even if the others shut down (fig. 16.3).

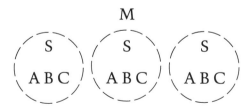

Figure 16.3

The situation is quite otherwise in the functional type of organization. Here no division can operate except in the closest coordination with both the others; any difficulty in one will have immediate repercussions in both the others, and if one breaks down the others must very soon come to a halt. In this case, *the administrative unit is no longer the division but must of necessity be the organization as a whole* (fig. 16.4). In the current example, this unit is by definition three times as large as that represented in figure 16.3 and to that extent far more subject to the difficulties inherent in larger size per se.

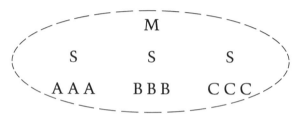

Figure 16.4

This point can be further illustrated by reference to the problem of delegation. In the integrated type of organization represented by figures 16.1 and 16.3, M, the plant manager, can delegate a very substantial measure of authority and responsibility to each of his three S's, because each S has under his direct supervision and control all the functions necessary to turn out a completed product. In the functional type of organization represented by figures 16.2 and 16.4, however, M can delegate only a limited amount of authority and responsibility. Each S supervises a single function and therefore controls only part of the total process. All significant decisions must be made by M, for only he holds within his hands all the elements that must be kept in proper balance. All he can delegate effectively are matters pertaining immediately and more or less exclusively to each of the individual functions, and in practice these may be largely routine.

People in management talk a great deal about the importance of delegation and are often critical of their subordinates for failing to exercise the responsibility supposedly delegated to them. But if an organization is set up along strictly functional lines, no amount of "supervisory training" can make it possible for people in the S position to exercise more than limited responsibility. Failure to assume delegated responsibility is no doubt often a matter of individual temperament, but in a very great many cases the structure of the organization makes significant delegation impossible regardless of how much management may wish to delegate and regardless of how willing and even anxious subordinates may be to accept larger measures of responsibility.

Such an organization, in fact, puts a premium on people in the S position who do not have too strong a drive in the direction of independent authority and responsibility, for any marked effort along these lines is likely to lead to conflict with the other S's and to create a critical situation that will require the intervention of M to restore the necessary balance and harmony within the organization. This suggests another weakness of this particular type of organization structure. Individuals with the capacity for independent action necessary to function properly in the M position are not likely to survive too long in the S position; they either learn to adapt themselves, and perhaps lose permanently the special capacities of independence that the M position requires, or they are likely to be forced out by the conflicts they create.

The difficulty the functional type of organization has in developing people for higher levels of responsibility is increased further by the kind and quality of experience those in the S position acquire. In the integrated type of organization represented in figures 16.1 and 16.3 each S performs many of the same functions and exercises much the same kind of responsibility and authority as M; each division, in effect, is a smaller version of the organization as a whole. Each S, therefore, acquires a kind of experience that will help prepare him for eventual advancement to the M position; an S, in fact, has an opportunity to practice at and gain skill in the M role. His level of responsibility is less than that of M but is not greatly different in kind. He can practice the M role without exposing the organization as a whole to unduly serious consequences in the case of mistakes made in the process of learning.

The situation is quite different in the case of the S's in the functional type of organization represented in figures 16.2 and 16.4. Here the S in charge of AAA becomes more and more skilled in the A function. He may know something about B and C. In fact, he may have had experience in running B and C (perhaps in the course of a "job rotation" program to "train" him for further advancement), but he does not see the organization as a whole and he does not gain the experience in coordination or the skill in *management* that his counterpart in the integrated organization acquires as a natural by-product of supervising ABC. Above all, each S in the integrated type of organization is likely to have delegated to him a much larger measure of real responsibility and authority than is possible in the functional type of organization. The opportunities for personal growth and development are therefore likely to be greater in the former than in the latter.

A further important consequence of the principle of functionalization is its tendency to extend and complicate the administrative hierarchy. This is because not only workers but supervisors as well must be more closely supervised and controlled to assure the necessary degree of coordination between the several functional divisions into which the organization has been split.

In the integrated type of organization (figures 16.1 and 16.3) coordination between various activities can be achieved on a fairly informal basis because of the more direct and more personal relations between the individuals performing the different specialized operations. But where the work of the organization has been broken down into a series of functional divisions (as in figures 16.2 and 16.4), cooperation can no longer be achieved with equal spontaneity. After all, the purpose of setting up functional divisions is to enable each to achieve a more efficient system. Each unit, therefore, tends to operate in terms of the logics of its own particular system. And because the technical requirements for efficiency are likely to be different for each function (else why set them up in different divisions?) the logics of each are likely to vary accordingly. And because each function is only part of the whole, the logics of each function will tend to differ from the logics of the whole. To the extent that these logics differ, and they often differ greatly, there is likely to be conflict or at least the potential for conflict.

In order to achieve the necessary degree of coordination and cooperation between administratively separated functions, management is forced to build up an elaborate hierarchy of supervisory levels. This brings into play the concept of the *span of control,* which holds that the number of subordinate executives reporting to a single superior should be severely limited to enable that individual to exercise the detailed direction and control the functional type of organization requires. If this limit is set at seven (as it is by a number of organization theorists, although generally in practice the number is somewhat larger), it can be readily seen that in an organization of any considerable size a great many supervisory levels will be necessary.

As the supervisory hierarchy becomes more and more extended, management finds it necessary to institute more and more formal controls. These may be of fairly wide variety and may be more or less complex, depending on the particular technologies involved. In the functional type of organization all of them are likely to be characterized by a considerable degree of abstractness. The effectiveness of the organization as a whole may be judged in terms of physical output, or volume of sales, or the P&L statement. But where the internal structure of the organization is broken down into a series of specialized divisions, there are no "natural" standards of performance and management is forced to exercise considerable ingenuity in inventing controls for administrative purposes. Unfortunately, contrived controls such as these are likely to be often become the source of conflict themselves. The individual supervisor or executive is under strong compulsion to operate in such a manner as to make a good showing in terms of the particular set of controls to which he is subject, and often he does so only at the expense of effective collaboration across divisional lines. This conflict is likely to be particularly acute when two closely related functions report up two different administrative lines and operate under two different systems of standards and controls.

The management of organizations that have been overfunctionalized to the extent characteristic of much of modern business imposes a severe burden on the top administrative group. Functions and activities have been so subdivided and specialized that no individual unit can operate except in closest coordination with others, and the system is likely to be so complex that this coordination cannot take place spontaneously. If it is to occur, it must be accomplished by means of specific administrative action from higher authority. In an organization of any size, this requires additional staff to assist the higher executives to carry the burden they are forced to assume. Growth of staff complicates the situation still further, because a consequence is likely to be the elaboration of formal controls to permit the staff to perform the functions and exercise the responsibilities that have been delegated to it or that it gradually assumes in an effort to strengthen its own position or extend its own authority.

An objective appraisal suggests that, to too large an extent, work processes have been analyzed from a strictly "rational" or mechanical point of view with too little attention to the human factors involved. As a result, functions have been separated out of their context and set up as semi-independent activities. Necessary collaboration and cooperation between units thus artificially separated becomes possible only through an elaborate system of controls and a complicated administrative hierarchy. Under these circumstances, management necessarily becomes more strongly centralized, despite the frequently expressed concern of business leaders over the need for greater delegation of authority and responsibility. Too often this is simply because the nature of the organization structure makes effective decentralization impossible.

Much of the vast scale of organization that is characteristic of modern industry, much of the tendency toward greater and greater centralization of authority and responsibility, much of the growing impersonality and abstractness of working relationships are a result not so much of economic and technical factors as of an unhappy and often unnecessary principle of organization. This is the principle of functualization, which was one of the cornerstones of Frederick Taylor's philosophy of "scientific management" and which, largely as a result of his influence and that of his followers, has been widely applied in modern organization practice.

I have tried to suggest that there is an alternative principle of organization, which we may call the integrative, and that by proper application of this principle it should be possible to preserve the economic and technical advantages of large-scale operation, which are often very great, and at the same time restore many of the essential human values that can be realized only within relatively small working groups. By this means we should be able to achieve the objective stated by Bertrand Russell when he wrote: "I do not mean that we should destroy those parts of modern organization upon which the very existence of large populations depends, but I do mean that organization should be much more flexible, more relieved by local autonomy, and less oppressive to the human spirit through its impersonal vastness, than it has become through its unbearably rapid growth and centralization, with which our ways of thought and feeling have been unable to keep pace."[3]

Notes

This paper was originally published under the title "Some Aspects of Organization Structure in Relation to Pressures on Company Decision-Making," in the Fifth Annual IRRA *Proceedings* (Madison, Wis.: Industrial Relations Research Association, 1952). Reprinted by permission of the publisher.

1. Yale Brozen, "The Social Impact of Technological Change," *Journal of Engineering Education* 41:3 (Nov. 1950): 151–53.

2. Peter F. Drucker, *The New Society* (New York: Harper & Bros., 1950), 268.

3. Bertrand Russell, *Authority and the Individual* (London: George Allen and Unwin Ltd., 1949), 62.

Part 4

Management Values

Concern for values is a leitmotif running through most of the things Worthy has written, as for example his report on the Sears X-Y Study in which the values of managers were found to be critical factors in the design of organization structures. Six of the papers included in this collection deal explicitly with values issues and are grouped together in Part 4.

"Democratic Principles in Business Management" contrasts the ideology of free enterprise with the dictatorial manner in which many business leaders manage their own companies. How can managers, he asks, equate the underlying values of the "free enterprise system" with the stifling bureaucracies that they have allowed to develop in their own businesses? He then goes on to show how mechanistic concepts that may be appropriate to organizing technological processes are not appropriate to organizing human beings. He calls attention to the basic rights of all humans and argues that these should be used as a frame of reference in managing any organization. It is interesting that Worthy's message in due course came to the attention of Sears' chief executive officer, General Robert E. Wood, who promptly pronounced it the "official philosophy of the company." His memorandum to all officers of the company, sending them a copy of Worthy's talk, is included as a preface to the paper.

Worthy sought to broaden executive understanding through better education at the university level. Sears' experience with the recruitment of executive trainees from colleges and universities raised grave doubts in his mind regarding the quality of education for business careers prevalent during the late 1940s when this memorandum was written. Of particular concern to him was the narrowness of business education at the university level that was then focused on middle-level occupational careers rather than the development of business leadership. In 1950, Sears' factory vice president, E. P. Brooks, left the company to become the founding dean of the Sloan School of Management at Massachusetts Institute of Technology. Brooks sent a copy of his plans for the school to General Wood, who sent a copy to Worthy for comment. Worthy responded with a memo outlining his ideas on the subject of education for business. Wood sent a copy of this memo to Brooks, who forwarded it to Alfred Sloan. Sloan was enthusiastic and declared, according to Brooks, "It should be the Bible of the School." Later, in 1954, when Worthy was on leave from Sears as Assistant Secretary of Commerce, he delivered the same memo as an address at the annual dinner of the School of Business at the University of Chicago and it was published in the School's *Journal of Business* in 1955. In this paper entitled "Education for Business Leadership," Worthy anticipates some of the primary themes in the Gordon and Howell and Pierson reports that were instrumental in reshaping business education in America during the 1960s. While considerable progress has since been made in business education, many of Worthy's observations are as relevant today as they were over forty years ago.

During the 1940s and 1950s numerous members of the academic community and others registered vigorous opposition to the human relations movement, seeing in it an effort to use scientific methods to manipulate and control the work force. The issue was addressed in comprehensive fashion by the Industrial Relations Research Association in its annual volume for 1956. Worthy was one of the editors of this volume and contributed a chapter entitled "Management's Approach to 'Human Relations.'" Here he argues that management's interest in improving the quality of management-employee relationships is "something less than a monstrous plot." He develops the thesis that "American management has shown a marked concern for good employee relations" because of certain unique elements in the nation's history and traditions—including chronic labor scarcity, the rise of the labor movement, desire at all levels to improve the American way of life, and egalitarianism and uneasiness about an excessive use of authority. He examines these historic elements in detail and argues that the human relations movement, far from being a management plot, is essentially a recent manifestation of concern for traditional American values.

Worthy was concerned about the tendency he found in certain quarters, including some within his own company, to see the human relations approach as a tactic for "keeping out the unions."

The Sears organization survey program was sometimes misapprehended on this score. By the late 1940s, his Sears responsibilities had broadened to include coordination of the work of the company's five territorial labor relations managers, who handled union matters in their respective territories. In connection with this responsibility, Worthy in 1952 addressed to his superior, Clarence B. Caldwell, vice president for personnel, a memorandum warning against this bastardization of the human relations approach and stressing that efforts to "build and maintain a sound and effective organization" are good in their own right whether employees join unions or not.

Throughout Worthy's writings and career runs the theme of confidence in others. This is especially marked in his attitudes toward workers of whom, in the absence of evidence to the contrary, he always seems to expect the best. In a recent Academy of Management paper, "Overachievement at Work," he gives formal expression to this philosophy and his conviction that "overachievement is a more natural form of human behavior at work than underachievement." Once again, he underscores the importance of management values and basic assumptions about employees.

In "A Working Philosophy of Personnel Management," Worthy's "farewell address" as president of the Industrial Relations Association of Chicago, he outlines his concept of the appropriate role of the personnel manager in the modern business organization, and challenges his colleagues to "aid in the task of working out, in practical and realistic terms, the means for making industrial society the good society"—an appropriate note on which to end this collection of Worthy's writings on management.

—David G. Moore

17

Democratic Principles in Business Management

To All Officers of the Company:

I am sending to you a copy of a remarkable address which James Worthy a member of our Personnel Department made on May 27th of this year. It came to my attention only a few days ago. I want every officer in the company to read this address carefully because it represents the official policy of this company to be translated into action all through the company in all layers of authority.

Worthy has put his finger on what I regard as the greatest weakness of large industrial organizations in this country. We complain about government in business, we stress the advantages of the free enterprise system, we complain about the totalitarian state but in our industrial organizations, in our striving for efficiency we have created more or less of a totalitarian organization in industry, particularly in large industry. The problem of retaining our efficiency and discipline in these large organizations and yet allowing our people to express themselves, to exercise initiative and to have some voice in the affairs of the organization is the greatest problem for large industrial organizations to solve.

I would like the officers of the company to read every word of this speech and then pass it on to his personnel people, to the store managers, the plant managers and the factory managers and try to see that the principles set forth are put into practice.

R. E. Wood

October 14, 1948

The address to which General Wood refers was delivered before the Industrial Management Institute of Lake Forest College, May 27, 1948. The text of the address follows:

My text this evening is an excerpt from an editorial that appeared in *Fortune* magazine for January 1948: "the record of 1947 suggests that, given proper understanding of their own system, the American people might enter into a period of economic development making all previous standards as obsolete as the Model T Ford. In any case, it is time for a wholesale revaluation of values. For years many Americans and most Europeans have looked on socialism and planning as the wave of the future. Today it is possible to assert that American democratic capitalism is in fact the great forward experiment of our time, that while promising no cheap utopia it is itself utopian."[1]

The editorial goes on to question how well Americans really understand their system, which it defines as one "wherein the 'hidden hand' of prices, costs, and profits does most of the job of allocating the country's resources and energies while government provides the indispensable framework for the release of private initiative."

The problems posed by this editorial deal largely with technical questions of fiscal policy and political questions of government control of business activity. The real problem, it seems to me, is much broader than this. Certainly, fiscal and political questions are important and must be dealt with intelligently. But in our concern for these matters, it is vital that we do not neglect the equally important questions of the internal organization and management of business itself.

We hear a great deal, nowadays, about "Free Enterprise" and the "American Way of Life." The *Fortune* editorial is one of the more recent and more intelligent expressions of these ideas—and ideals. Without doubt, one of the most remarkable facts of world history has been the achievements of democratic capitalism during the past 150 years, particularly in America. Without doubt, too, the basis of these achievements has been largely the release of creative, productive energies made possible by the freer political and economic institutions that have been characteristic of American society. Those facts are widely recognized, and the defense of the "free enterprise system" is almost always couched in terms of its achievements and the self-evident advantages of free economic processes as opposed to stifling bureaucratic controls.

One of the acute ironies of our time is that those who see most clearly the virtues of free enterprise, those who are quickest to leap to its defense, are too often those who fail to see the full implications of the system they are so anxious to preserve. It is easy for us in business to see the stifling effects of too much government control; what we often fail to see is that the essential principles we advocate for government apply equally to the internal organization and management of our own businesses, and the violation of these principles produces within business itself the same stifling results, the same frustration of spontaneous productive energy, that their violation in the larger field of government policy produces within the general economic system.

I would like to lay down this thesis: that the essential principles of free enterprise apply not only in the politico-economic sphere but equally in the internal affairs of business enterprise itself. These principles must be adapted to this specialized field of action; obviously, they cannot be applied literally. Perhaps the greatest challenge of modern times is for creative business leadership that can develop within industry itself the methods of democratic organization and control that were worked out for the political state during the past three hundred years.

The essence of "free enterprise" is a system of economic and political organization that taps *spontaneously* the creative and productive resources of its citizens. Under conditions of small-scale enterprise, the "hidden hand" of prices, costs, and profits was a reasonably adequate means for accomplishing this spontaneous release of energy and for channeling it in socially desirable directions. Unfortunately, this "hidden hand" is quite inadequate for tapping any high percentage of the productive energies of a nation when the greater number of its workers are no longer independent enterprisers but employees of larger corporate entities and are not directly subject to the stimulus and control of the economic processes of the market.

Business management must develop within its own organization structure a system of incentives and control that will be as effective in releasing and directing the productive energies of individuals and groups as the "hidden hand" of prices, costs, and profits has been in releasing and directing the efforts of corporate enterprises.

One thing is clear at the outset: the method of prices, costs, and profits can be literally applied to only a very limited extent *within* business organizations with any effective results. Perhaps the most ambitious effort in this direction to date has been the wide extension of incentive compensation. While this effort has achieved a certain amount of success, it has fallen short of accomplishing any significant overall increase in worker productivity, and even such increases as it has achieved have often been accompanied by new and unforeseen complications that have made the system something less than an unmixed blessing.

The chief weakness of financial incentives within business is that they represent an attempt to appeal to workers primarily in economic terms and by the use of concepts that are meaningful to the businessman because they reflect his ways of thinking but that have little significance to workers who are accustomed to acting in accordance with a somewhat different scale of values. The experience of business with incentive methods of compensation makes it evident that management must develop more effective means than have thus far been developed for releasing and directing the productive energies of those who comprise business organizations.

The problem with which we are dealing here is one of *efficiency*, the efficient utilization of resources, both human and material. The efficiency of an engine is measured by the ratio of energy output to the potential energy contained in the fuel it consumes. In the same way, the efficiency of an economic system must be measured by the ratio of productive results to potential productive energies. In these terms our economic system, for all its undoubted achievements, is operating at a level of efficiency with which we should be thoroughly dissatisfied.

One of the serious stumbling blocks to effective human organization is a deep-seated attitude of mind characteristic of our times. The physical scientist and the engineer have exercised a profound influence not only on outward aspects of modern life but on our inward thought processes as well. Among other things, they have strongly influenced our thinking about problems of organization and human relations. The transference of their mode of thought to a field for which it was never designed has badly distorted our apprehension of our problems and seriously misdirected our efforts to deal with them.

If we consider closely our generally accepted theories of organization, we cannot help but note a curious parallel to the machine. Our ideal of an effective organization is a "smoothly running machine," an organization in which all parts operate with a minimum of friction and a maximum economy of effort. Each component is carefully designed for its particular task, and the whole responds readily to the touch of the operator's hand.

Our phraseology employs mechanical images. Organization charts are called "blue prints." A common argument for the use of psychological tests cites the care with which machines are selected to insure their suitability for the task at hand and urges that people be selected and placed with comparable measures of their abilities and capacities. "Management engineering" and "human engineering" have become recognized and respected terms. All our thinking about organization displays a strongly mechanical turn of mind.

I submit that the nature of human organization cannot be properly apprehended in terms of mechanistic concepts. The machine and its component parts have only one purpose, that for which the engineer designed them. The purpose of a human organization, whether business or otherwise, can only be defined in terms of the people in it, because unlike the component parts of a machine the people who comprise a human organization are something more than parts of that organization. They are flesh and blood men and women, with sentiments, ambitions, and needs of their own that range far beyond the confines of the organization of which they may be a part, and the extent to which they serve the needs of the organization willingly and enthusiastically depends on the extent to which the organization serves their needs as sentient, aspiring human beings.

Viewed in these terms, the problems of economic organization and administration have a close parallel to problems of political organization and administration. In politics, we are all familiar with the ideas of the democratic and the authoritarian state. Despite our unshakable faith in the superiority of democracy as a form of civil government, a great many managements apply essentially authoritarian principles in the administration of their business affairs, under the mistaken notion that business and political life are two different orders of things. Actually, the two institutions, business and government, are closely similar in their most essential aspect: the fact that both are organizations of human beings and that both depend, in the long run, on the creative intelligence and effort and on the voluntary support and acceptance of the people who comprise them.

One of the great paradoxes of our society is that we have failed to apply to the internal affairs of our businesses the principles we all recognize, when applied to political organization, as largely responsible for the tremendous growth in national wealth and the superb social progress our nation has enjoyed.

Many businesses resemble the authoritarian state in the sense that all direction, all thinking, all authority flows from the top down, with little flow in the other direction. While the top man may delegate certain parts of his responsibility and authority, the delegation is largely in terms of those at lower levels simply implementing someone else's orders. While the overall directive may be broken down into a series of parts and parceled out to different people, and while these people may be expected to show initiative, drive, and judgment in executing their work, their activity is essentially that of carrying out an order.

To make such an organization work, management is forced to set up a rigorous system of controls to see that things get done and to insure that people do not make too many mistakes in carrying out their orders. Minimal reliance is placed on the people in the organization, and the system depends primarily on the initiative and judgment of those at the top.

A corollary to this tendency is the elaboration of staff organizations: if the exercise of judgment and skill are largely reserved to higher levels, these people, because they lack direct contact with the scene of action, must be assisted by specialized advisory staffs. The result is a further extension of the system of controls through the efforts of the staff departments, as well as a considerable complication of the organization structure, thus leading to the necessity for more controls to hold the whole organization together and make it work. At the same time, because of the necessity for operating the controls and because people at each successive level must be closely supervised and directed in their work, the supervisory hierarchy becomes more and more extended.

What are some of the implications of this situation in terms of the people in the organization? Staff specialists are prone to believe that line supervisors can't be trusted to use good judgment consistently—and by "good judgment" they are likely to mean what they would do under particular circumstances. Therefore, they feel impelled to establish precise rules to govern every contingency, or to appropriate broad areas of responsibility from line supervision and vest them in their own departments—all for the purpose of guarding against the possibility of supervisors or line executives making mistakes.

Certainly, subordinates must be given direction and work within a framework of policy, but the tendency has been to substitute systems of bureaucratic control for the good judgment that should arise from the subordinate's more intimate knowledge of immediate circumstances. Even more serious is the effect of such controls in undermining the initiative and judgment of supervisors so that

ultimately their judgment really can't be trusted because they have
never had an opportunity to use it.

What is the effect of this bureaucratic system of supervision and
control on rank and file workers? I need only note the frequent and
bitter complaints of management itself over the apathy of employees, their lack of initiative, their want of interest in the affairs and
problems of the enterprise, their all-too-frequent antagonism to
management. Rather than blame this state of affairs on agitators,
or on faults in the educational system, or on errors in family methods of raising children, many managements need only look within
their own organizations.

In effect, all many organizations demand of their lower-level
employees is their animal energies, their muscle power. They have
gone to great lengths—through too-close supervision, through time
and motion studies, through breaking jobs down into their simplest
possible elements—to take all judgment from the operator, to relieve him of all initiative, to reduce his work to the lowest possible
repetitive mechanical level. These efforts are usually justified in
terms of the supposedly greater efficiency that can come from
shorter training time, ability to use less skilled people, and greater
proficiency that can come from repetition of simple movements
and operations. Granted all this, but how much does industry lose
in depriving the worker of creative relation to his job? I hazard the
guess that industry has lost far more than it has gained.

One supremely important result of this process has been to destroy the meaning of the job for the worker—the meaning, that is,
in all terms except the pay envelope. It has had the equally important effect of seriously undermining the confidence of workers in
management, and because they are restless and discontented they
are easily subject to strong leadership that may arise in opposition
to management. Their jobs have made so few demands on their
higher faculties, they have had so little opportunity to think, to
take initiative, to make their own contribution to the improvement
of their jobs, that when aggressive anti-management leadership ar-
rives, promising workers a kind of freedom that management has
not provided, they readily respond. Without question, one of the
great appeals of unions is the promise of giving workers a more effective voice in matters that affect their jobs, a promise that workers can stand up and be men, not just draft animals or machines.

A further serious consequence of the authoritarian system of administration is its tendency to inhibit the adaptiveness and problem-solving ability of the organization. Because judgment and ini-

tiative flow from the top down and because of elaborate systems of supervision and control, those at the lower levels gradually lose their ability to solve the problems that confront them and their capacity to adapt to new situations. The processes of adaptation and problem solving thus tend to move to higher levels in the organization. As problems become more complex, often because they have not been properly solved, corrective action must be taken at higher and higher levels and eventually must be dealt with at the top of the management hierarchy.

This upward movement does not stop even at the top of the organization. In many cases it tends to move right out of the organization itself to the level of the trade association or its equivalent, and from there often keeps right on moving until it comes to rest at the governmental level. This upward movement of the problem-solving process is a significant characteristic of management today. It is particularly apparent in the field of collective bargaining, where the president of the United States is sometimes forced to intervene personally in disputes between workers and employers. Because problems have not been handled effectively at their point of origin, usually at the lower levels of individual companies, they have moved higher and higher and have become more and more complex until they can be dealt with only at the highest levels of the national government.

Management, of course, is bitterly resentful of this gradual encroachment of government into business affairs. But management itself must bear much of the responsibility for this tendency because by its policies and methods of administration it has stifled the adaptiveness and problem-solving ability of its own organization, and because it has created within itself an internal system of bureaucratic control that is fully as deadly for productive efficiency as governmental bureaucracies.

We in management are greatly concerned about the preservation of "free enterprise" and the "American Way of Life." In a real sense, much of our problem is this: we cannot preserve "free enterprise" as an economic system unless we adapt its fundamentals to the internal operation and management of our own businesses. We cannot preserve "free enterprise" in the market place unless we strengthen it in the work place, unless we extend to our business structures the democratic ideals we take for granted in our political structures.

Obviously, this is no easy task. Political institutions cannot be taken over intact by business. Business cannot be run by the ballot box or by a Congress. These were inventions to solve the problem of effective participation by the citizenry in the affairs of their governments. We must develop other inventions, adapted to the special circumstances of business that will give to employees at all levels of our economic organizations a greater sense of personal participation, a greater sense of belonging, a greater sense of dignity and recognition of their worth as individuals and as respected members of the industrial community.

I cannot lay down a formula for accomplishing these ends. However, I would like to suggest a frame of reference that can serve as a guidepost. Actually, we have ready at hand, as a deeply ingrained part of our thinking, the ideas that can motivate our efforts. These are simply the ideals of the democratic society, ideals that are fundamental elements of our culture and are broadly accepted by management and workers alike.

These ideals are usually expressed in terms of rights—the very word "rights" implying their essentially moral and ethical nature. Some of the more significant of these rights can be briefly stated:

1. The right of every man to be treated as an individual and respected as a person.

2. The right of every man to a voice in his own affairs, which includes his right to contribute to the best of his ability in the solution of common problems.

3. The right of every man to recognition for his contribution to the common good.

4. The right of every man to develop and make use of his highest capacities.

5. The right of every man to fairness and justice in all his relations with his fellows and superiors.

These democratic ideals are not platitudes but working principles of effective human organization. Their validity has been proved over and over again, both in our historical experience and in modern research in the social sciences. These ideals, in fact, are at the very basis of the "free enterprise system" and are responsible for many of the achievements of that system.

In our own company, in cooperation with the University of Chicago and Dr. B. B. Gardner, we have conducted extensive research into the nature of effective organization and the factors that make for cooperation in human relations. Throughout all this research, we have been impressed with the extent to which the fundamental notions of our democratic society have been validated.

We have been impressed with the number of times the notions of participation, human dignity, freedom to speak one's piece, and the right to advance on one's own merits have proved crucial factors in the maintenance of high levels of teamwork and cooperation. These are not merely ideals; they are working principles on how to live and work in a free society.

Another thing we have learned is that an organization with an extensively developed supervisory hierarchy is more rigid, less adaptive, and less satisfying to the employees involved than a "flat" organization that places considerable responsibility on the individual and keeps supervision and formal controls at a minimum. In an organization where there are many layers of supervision, employees feel restricted, controlled, and policed. There is little opportunity for creative effort and the development of ideas. In an organization with fewer layers of supervision and fewer controls, there tends to be higher morale, better feeling, more creative effort, greater adaptability and flexibility, and a higher development of cooperation between employees and management. I hardly need point out that this latter type of organization more nearly approximates the democratic ideal than the former.

If we are concerned with the preservation of "free enterprise" in America and freedom in the world, we must strengthen it by extending its principles more effectively to the internal organization and administration of our own companies. Democracy and the "American Way" cannot be preserved by exhortation or by slick advertising and propaganda campaigns. The system must work effectively, and it cannot do that unless it does a better job of tapping the creative resources, ability, and productivity of its individual members.

The system must retain the spontaneous loyalty and acceptance of the great masses of the American people, most of whom are members of the system in the capacity of employees. Loyalty cannot be bought, nor sold to people the way we sell toothpaste. Attitudes, including attitudes toward management, are largely a product of experience. If the worker's experience on the job causes him to dislike and distrust management, no amount of "education" will change his feelings or behavior.

In a sense, the problem is one of management leadership. If management is to retain its leadership position in American life, it must develop a higher order of managerial skill. This skill, to be successful in our kind of society, must be developed along democratic rath-

er than authoritarian lines, in accord with the deep-seated sentiments and values of the American people. Much of management's
present difficulty is directly traceable to its failure to organize and
manage its business affairs in accordance with these sentiments
and values.

The preservation of managerial leadership will require the creative thinking and intelligent action of management people
throughout business and industry. The work of this Industrial Management Institute is a start in that direction and an encouraging one
for the future. It is my earnest hope that similar efforts can be made
by other groups, particularly through closer cooperation between
business and the universities.

The challenge we are facing is no less than the preservation of
all the things we value most as Americans. If we can meet this challenge successfully, if we can develop ways and means for applying
our democratic principles more effectively within business itself,
we will not only preserve our system but confidently expect a release of creative and productive energies that can be as great as
those released by the rise of democratic states during the eighteenth
and nineteenth centuries.

In closing, I want to return to the *Fortune* editorial with which
this talk began and to quote, as my conclusion, the final paragraph
of that statement. I would like you to view this paragraph, however,
in the somewhat broader frame of reference I have tried to set forth
this evening: "To the degree that Americans are clear about their
system and insist on its fundamentals they will remain productively
strong at home and able to discharge their immense responsibilities
abroad. The stakes are large and the outcome by no means guaranteed. The U.S. began as a unique experiment. The experiment never
ends. But is it safe to say there never has been a time when success
of the American meant more to free men everywhere."[2]

Notes

This talk (without General Wood's covering memorandum) also appeared
in *Advanced Management* 14:1 (Mar. 1949): 16–21.

1. *Fortune,* vol. 37, no. 1:2.
2. Ibid.

18

Education for Business Leadership

Schools of business have come to play an important role in the American educational and business systems. With some 370,000 students of business administration in 1950 (more than double the number ten years before), education for business has become "big business." With all this activity a certain amount of stock taking would seem to be in order, not merely by the schools of business but by business itself, for business has a tremendous stake in the kind of education being provided for future leaders of business.

More and more, progressive business organizations are turning to schools of business for the men and women they hope to develop for future executive responsibilities. Sears, Roebuck, for example, has hired well over six thousand people during the last twenty-five years from colleges and universities, about four thousand of them since 1945. Other companies have had similar recruiting programs. It has been Sears' experience, and I know it has been that of many other companies, that a major share of executive trainees are hired from schools of business. This, you may say, is as it should be. But let us analyze the situation a little further. Here I shall draw not only on Sears' experience but on my knowledge of the recruitment activities of a good many other organizations.

By and large, I think it can be said that there are two primary reasons why so much business recruiting is done through the schools of business. In the first place, in hiring business school graduates a company can be reasonably sure it is hiring people who really want to be businessmen, not frustrated lawyers and doctors. In the second place, schools of business generally have their placement work much better organized than do most other schools and do a better job of cooperating with interviewers sent out to do the actual recruitment work.

Now the interesting—and significant—thing is that neither of these reasons has anything to do with what the students have learned in business school. In fact, many companies have definite reservations on that score. There are exceptions, of course, but it has been the experience of many businessmen that, by and large, what people learn in business school is of little value to them in business—often quite the contrary. One reason for this is an undue amount of specialization and an undue emphasis on techniques. The schools do a fairly good job of developing staff and technical people but not top people. They are good at teaching business *methods* but not in preparing men for leadership. They produce many "experts" but few "statesmen." In part this stems from the difficulty schools have had in determining what to teach and how. The problem of curriculum-planning is a very real one. It is far easier to develop a course in, say, credit management than to develop one dealing with the role of business in modern society. It is easy enough to teach the techniques of personnel or of time-and-motion study but something else to teach the nature and skills of administration.

Business itself must bear a considerable part of the responsibility for the schools' failure on this point. Business organizations have become so highly systematized and specialized that much of their demand is for people who have been trained in specific techniques or who can fit readily into specialized compartments of the business structure. Training of this kind often meets the immediate needs of business, but its longer-range value is questionable. It may serve to get men off to a quicker start, but it is likely to limit them later on. Many schools give the impression of having followed too slavishly the expressed desires of business without exercising real leadership themselves. This has been unfortunate, because often the schools' chief contacts have not been so much with genuine business leaders as with staff specialists, with the result that the schools have tended to receive a somewhat distorted picture of the real nature and the real needs of business.

In any event, it is clear that in too many cases the schools themselves have failed to provide the kind of leadership the circumstances require. The relationship of the schools of business to business is quite different from the relationship of the schools of medicine and law to their respective professions. Professional schools such as these do far more than merely prepare newcomers for entry into particular occupational careers; they provide active leadership to the professions themselves, they establish standards, they synthesize experience, they formulate principle. They endeavor not only to keep abreast of developments within their respective professions but to keep ahead of them. Business is sorely in need of similar leadership from the schools of business.

One respect in which such leadership is particularly needed is the development of a broader understanding of the role and responsibilities of business in modern society. Business, after all, is the dominant institution of our times, and far more is at stake in business management than merely the health and survival of individual businesses, important as that may be. Private enterprise occupies a unique place in America. To an extent that is true of no other country in the world today, the social and economic welfare of the American people depends upon the wisdom and skill of those who direct the affairs of private business organizations. This is not to gainsay the responsibility of other groups, but in this area management's responsibility is most immediate and most direct.

Under these circumstances, the businessman must act not only in terms of his responsibility to his particular business but also in terms of his responsibility to the society in which business plays so crucial a role. He cannot safeguard his own business effectively unless he also works effectively to safeguard the total system. He must see the problems of his own business in their national—and perhaps international—implications, which may be very different from seeing them solely in terms of an individual enterprise. And in the course of running the affairs of his own business he must consider the possible ramifications of his actions over a range much wider than the area of immediate concern. Freedom requires knowledge and intelligence as it requires integrity and courage.

The proper function of the schools of business should be conceived as that of developing the future members of one of the key— perhaps *the* key—leadership groups of modern American society. This will require a program that will be more educational and less vocational than that of the typical school of business. It will require a program that seeks to impart to future leaders the fundamental values of our free society; a program that will inculcate a better understanding of that society and the forces at work within it; a program that will help the businessman understand his place in the scheme of things and his responsibility to the whole; and, above all, a program that will emphasize the crucial responsibilities of leadership, because only through understanding and accepting—and effectively discharging—its responsibilities can any leadership group long survive.

All this represents a function quite different from developing accountants or personnel managers or traffic experts, although training in specific skills is important and should have a place in any realistically oriented school of business. What is chiefly required is a conception of the primary function of business education as preparation for social and not merely technical leadership and for the development of curricula and faculties that will adequately support that conception. This is not the place to go into any detail as to what such curricula should include; that is an exceedingly complex problem and one, in any event, that will have to be worked out by the business educators themselves. Certain crucial areas, however, may be noted to illustrate my point.

There is, for example, the problem of change. If our free society is to retain its dynamic qualities—which is another way of saying "if our free society is to survive"—it must continue to change, because change is the very essence of its being. The schools of business, however, have often done little to prepare businessmen to understand the changes going on around them or to accept change as an essential characteristic of what we prize as the American way of life. On the contrary, the schools have tended to emphasize the static aspects of business and in doing so have often served to confirm and strengthen the social prejudices of their students. This has been a factor in aggravating the sometimes rather marked unwillingness of businessmen to go very far in proposing means for dealing with problems as they arise. Many things that are now universally accepted as right and proper were initially established in the face of strong resistance from business. Classic examples are workmen's compensation, social security, and minimum wage legislation.

This is a dangerous position for business to continue to assume. One measure of that danger is the extent to which business lost out during the 1930s and 1940s in the struggle for political power. Business enjoys a more favorable position under the new Eisenhower administration, but that fact merely adds to its responsibility. As members of a leadership group, businessmen must assist in developing policies that will deal effectively with the changing problems of our times. Not to do so, or merely to resist change, is to abdicate, to allow others through default to exercise the initiative. If the schools of business are to serve their proper function, they must deal more realistically than most of them have so far done with the problem of change.

One aspect of the too-frequent tendency of the schools of business to emphasize the static rather than the dynamic aspects of business and society is their failure to appreciate the importance of history. Here again the schools have followed business itself rather than strike out on their own. American businessmen as a group display remarkably little sense of history—at least so far as business is concerned. This is a curious fact because with respect to other aspects of their past the American people, including businessmen, have a well-developed historical sense. However, the failure of businessmen to appreciate—indeed, even to be aware of—the history of their own institution is potentially dangerous, because no leadership group can survive for long without the sure touch and sense of direction that comes from awareness and knowledge of its own history. What is needed is not preoccupation with the past but a better understanding of how the present evolved out of the past and how the future is in process of evolving out of the present. The businessman needs a more acute sense of where business is going, and he cannot have that in proper degree without knowing where it has been. Herein lies a particularly critical failure of the schools of business, because the study and teaching of "business" history as distinct from "economic" and "social" history is a comparatively recent and still restricted development.

If the schools of business are to play their proper role, they must achieve a much closer integration than most of them have so far achieved with business itself. Two avenues are available—among others—that should be especially useful for this purpose. These are: (1) the further development of programs for people already holding responsible positions in business, and (2) the development of more vigorous and more creative research.

One of the crucial problems of business education is the difficulty of teaching the realities of business to people who have had no experience with business. There is growing doubt, in fact, as to whether most of the business schools are not missing what might well be their most important "student body," whether more of their efforts might not be properly directed toward serving the needs of people already in business and hence in a position to assimilate and utilize the instruction the schools are uniquely qualified to give. This is not to minimize the importance of business education at the graduate and undergraduate levels; there are great and vital needs in this area that must be served. The schools can, however, make a special contribution to people already in business, and in many ways this contribution can equal and perhaps even outweigh the contribution they are making to people preparing to enter business. A number of encouraging experiments along this line are already under way. Especially significant is the Executive Program at the University of Chicago. Significant, too, are such undertakings as the Sloan Scholarships at the Massachusetts Institute of Technology and the Advanced Management Program of the Harvard School of Business Administration. A number of serious problems must be overcome before the needs for adult business education can be met, but the experiments now under way are encouraging. They constitute, in fact, the most significant development since the inception of the business school idea toward the end of the last century.

Adult business education can be particularly valuable to companies that adhere closely to the practice of promotion from within. The development of executives within a company has many values, both from the standpoint of good human relations and of gearing developmental activities more closely to company needs. But promotion from within has one serious shortcoming: the tendency toward provincialism, toward narrowness of outlook and perspective. Furthermore, in companies offering substantial, long-range promotional opportunities it often happens that people with humble beginnings progress quite far up the ladder but find their further progress blocked by limited education. In both these matters, effective facilities for adult business education can render important services.

Over and above the values of adult business education per se, programs for executives can be highly useful as a means for integrating the work of the schools more closely with the realities of business. Furthermore, such programs can serve as channels of communication to the business community that will assist the schools in exerting the influence and the leadership that, as professional schools, they have an obligation to provide.

Research represents a further means for the exercise of professional leadership. The schools of business should be constantly studying the problems of business and doing so in meaningful and creative ways. The results of such research should be used to enrich the content of business courses and should be communicated by a variety of means to the business community. The example of the schools of medicine suggests the vital relation of research to the leadership role within the medical profession. Research can and should serve a similar function for the schools of business.

Much of the business research now being conducted falls short of the quality necessary on this score. The personnel department of Sears, Roebuck is often asked to furnish information for research purposes or otherwise to cooperate on research projects. In consequence, I have had an opportunity to see a good many examples of what currently passes for business research. Much of it is extremely limited in concept and inept in method, dealing largely with the description of procedures or the tabulation of practices and only rarely involving ideas or problems of more than incidental significance. One suspects that the aridity of these efforts reflects a fundamental and far-reaching ignorance on the part of many business school faculties as to the real nature and problems of business. It also reflects a lack of knowledge of progress that has been made in the social sciences during the last quarter-century. One has the impression, in fact, that much of the thinking of the schools of business still rests implicitly on the work of Herbert Spencer. There have been tremendous developments in psychology, sociology, and anthropology—to name only a few—that are potentially of great significance to business, but there is little evidence that many business schools are even aware of them.

There should be attractive opportunities for cooperation in research between the various social sciences and the schools of business. For one thing, rather large sums of money are being expended for research in the social science field, and the business schools are missing what could be an excellent financial advantage. But they are missing far more than this in failing to channel a larger portion of the total research efforts of the universities into areas of importance not only to business as such but to the community at large. Above all, they are missing the opportunity of enriching their own knowledge of the fundamental problems of man and society, which are the proper concern of institutions charged with responsibility for educating future (and present) businessmen.

More active cooperation in research between the schools of business and other branches of the universities can also serve an important need of higher education in general. One of the great problems of modern education is the lack of effective integration among the various specialized disciplines. The bodies of knowledge in the various fields have grown so vast and are so complex that cross-fertilization of ideas is becoming increasingly difficult. The schools of business are in a position to assist in overcoming this problem. Business by its very nature has to deal with the subject matter of many different specialized fields. But whereas the psychologist abstracts out of a total situation the aspects that are of interest to him and the sociologist abstracts out the elements that are of interest to him, and so on, business has to deal with the situation as it is, as a totality. This special role of business offers attractive possibilities for closer integration, through the schools of business, of disciplines that are otherwise growing more and more specialized and more and more divergent in points of view. Integration in this manner would also serve to keep research more action-oriented and thus more realistic than much of the current research in the social sciences tends to be. The benefits of such a course as this both to business and to the specialized disciplines should be great, as would be the contribution to education in general. Not the least consequence would be a vast enrichment of business scholarship and a considerable enhancement of the professional status and leadership potential of the business schools themselves.

Imaginative and creative research can also be an important means for integrating the schools of business more closely with the business community as such. American business tends to be singularly research-minded, and cooperation (including financial assistance) is likely to be fairly readily forthcoming, provided the research projects are properly conceived and provided the business community has sufficient confidence in and respect for the institution conducting the research. The long-standing relationship between Sears, Roebuck and the University of Chicago is a case in point.

Businessmen, understandably, are likely to be much more interested in "practical" than in so-called pure research. But the importance of pure research in the physical sciences has been demonstrated so dramatically in recent years, and so many industrial research laboratories are devoting portions of their staffs and budgets to pure-research purposes, that appeals for the support of pure research in the field of business may not fall on entirely deaf ears. Before this can happen, however, the concepts for such research will have to be developed to a far higher degree than they have been to date. The fact is that the conceptual framework within which most schools of business operate is still in such a rudimentary stage that it is scarcely possible to visualize either the subject matter or the methodology of pure research in business. Until this limitation is overcome, it is useless to talk of the possibilities of anything but applied research. But applied research properly conceived and executed and its findings imaginatively evaluated can be the means for constructing the conceptual framework within which pure research can become possible. And pure research, in turn, can be the means for informing and guiding applied research into more creative and constructive channels.

Education, whether business or otherwise, is concerned with ideas. Any leadership group, as businessmen are, must be concerned with "great ideas." One of the essential functions of insti-

tutions charged with the preparation of members of leadership
groups must be the effective communication of the great ideas that
guide those groups. There are great ideas that underlie American
business, ideas that set it off sharply from European business. There
is the idea of a management itself, the idea of setting up a special
group within the enterprise that is carefully chosen for its competence and responsibility for the success of the enterprise. This is a
far cry from much of European enterprise, which is controlled by
absentee owners but actually run by clerks and technicians. There
is the idea that business exists for purposes broader than merely
earning dividends for absentee owners, that the rewards of increased productivity must be shared with customers in the form of
lower prices and with workers in the form of higher wages, that an
adequate portion of profits must be utilized for such essentially
social purposes as improvement of facilities and equipment and not
merely for the personal enrichment of owners. There is the idea
that business is *accountable* (that is, "answerable") for its steward-
ship not only to stockholders but to customers, employees, and the
public. There is the idea of the "mass" rather than the "class" market, the constant effort to make the good things of life available to
more and more people. In this respect there is a strong ethical component in the American idea of mass production that distinguishes
it dramatically from the European. Closely related is the idea that
markets are not static, that business through competition creates
markets, and that competition broadens the market for all. The cartel system has never taken hold in this country in any important
way simply because it is highly uncongenial to an environment
permeated with ideas such as these. There is the idea that diversity
and experimentation are good in themselves because they reflect
and express the spontaneity that is so basic an ingredient of American life and character. There is the idea that all relations with
employees must be based on deep respect for human beings—not
human beings in a hypothetical mass but individual, flesh and
blood men and women—the idea that people must be treated not
merely as means but at the same time as ends in themselves.

These are "great ideas," ideas that are essentially ethical in nature and that spring from the Judeo-Christian tradition as enriched
and unfolded by the special circumstances of American history. It
is ideas such as these, and the ethical tradition they express, that
more than any other factor—more than our tremendous natural resources, more than our vast free market, more than our mechani-

cal and inventive ingenuity—account for the economic progress this country has enjoyed.

There is evidence that we Americans often do not really understand our own system and what makes it work. Businessmen themselves are sometimes prone to ascribe the success of the system to factors that are largely irrelevant, if not downright wrong. It is dangerous for a leadership group not to understand itself, for it may be led through ignorance to courses that jeopardize its position and undermine the basis of stable and progressive social order. The definition, elaboration, and refinement of the "great ideas" of American business and the communication of these ideas to the rising generation of businessmen represent perhaps the most important task that needs to be performed by the schools of business.

Note

Reprinted by permission of the University of Chicago Press from *Journal of Business* 28:1 (Jan. 1955). © 1955 by the University of Chicago. All rights reserved.

19

Management's Approach to Human Relations

From its inception, the human relations movement has been viewed with considerable skepticism and mistrust by persons outside the ranks of management—particularly by leaders of organized labor and by students of labor problems. Those who seek to criticize management on this score, however, find themselves in a difficult position, for obviously they cannot argue against good human relations as such; to do so would be like arguing against virtue. Besides, their own stock in trade has in large part been a protest against management's sins of omission and commission in its relations with its workers, and it sets with little grace for them to attack management for trying to overcome some of the shortcomings for which they themselves have taken management so roundly to task.

There is a curious reversal of roles here that the critics of management find troublesome. By trying to improve worker satisfactions, psychic as well as material, through use of the insights of human relations research, management seems to be moving into an area that its critics have traditionally and temperamentally regarded as peculiarly their own. And in truth, it must be disconcerting for people with a well-staked-out field of interest to find their supposed adversary playing on the same field but with his own equipment and according to his own rules. Something, the critics seem to feel, is radically wrong with this picture of management trying to "improve human relations." It is perhaps only human to conclude that what is wrong is not so much *what* management is trying to do but *why* management is trying to do it.

Typically, therefore, the attack is on management's motives. Under the common stereotype of management, all managerial action must be in terms of the self-interest of managers and owners, with only such consideration of the interests of workers as may be enforced by law or custom or union regulation, or as may be dictated by a prudent regard for possible adverse consequences. So if management adopts a policy or pursues a course of action, it can be designed for only one purpose: to serve the needs of management, conceived only as broadly as circumstances may require.

So with human relations, the line of reasoning runs, management cannot be interested with the well-being of its workers but must be seeking more effective means of manipulating and controlling them for its own selfish ends. This effort is seen as particularly heinous for it seems to debase and prostitute the results of scientific research. And precisely because the methods of human relations are to some extent based on validated scientific procedures, they are likely to be more effective in achieving their aims than the traditional rule of thumb devices management has used in the past. Things were bad enough when management employed straightforward techniques of manipulation and control, even of coercion. But now management is going scientific!

Motivations of Management

But management's interest in human relations is something less than a monstrous plot. There is no denying management has economic motives, that it sees in human relations techniques a means for improving its organization, for reducing friction at the workplace, for increasing quantity and quality of output, for reducing costs. Management is concerned with such matters; after all, they are among the primary functions of management, and if the application of human relations concepts promises to aid in their achievement, management can hardly be blamed for wanting to use them. Nor has management ever sought to disguise the utilitarian aspects of human relations; quite the contrary. If anything, it has overemphasized such aspects and thereby oversimplified its real motivation.

One of the early and most significant of the findings of human relations research was that workers are not motivated solely by economic considerations, that there are many so-called nonlogical factors (that is, *noneconomically logical* factors) that strongly condition their attitudes and behavior. It is curious that this insight has never been extended in any important way to management, that while it is now axiomatic that workers are complex and many-sided, management is still seen as the corporate embodiment of economic man. But if the motivations of workers are complex and often "nonlogical," the motivations of managers are hardly less so. Managers no less than workers are members of groups that strongly influence their behavior, play roles that are socially defined, are members of a culture with a rich and elaborate system of values. Managers no more than workers are motivated solely by economic considerations. Not that economic considerations are unimportant in either case, but other factors of great significance are likewise at work. Managers, in a word, are "human" too.

One characteristic of managers is a concern for good relations with their employees, partly because such relations are considered important from the standpoint of the economic aims of the enterprise, but partly for other and considerably more complex reasons as well. This is not to suggest that all managements strive to maintain good employee relations at all times, nor even that those who do so strive are consistently successful in their efforts. Nevertheless, the record is reasonably clear that, by and large, American management has shown a marked concern for good employee relations, for reasons growing out of certain peculiarities in the history and traditions of this country.

Chronic Labor Scarcity

For one thing, American business enterprise has been faced with a persistent shortage of labor from colonial days forward. Whereas in other countries (for example, Great Britain a century and a half ago and India today) industrialization has generally arisen under conditions of large-scale labor surplus, American managers, with only occasional and temporary exceptions, have had to build and maintain their enterprises in the face of chronic labor scarcity. The special American penchant for mechanization reflects the need for conserving the available supply of labor. The special American genius for organization reflects the need for utilizing scarce skills in the most effective manner possible. Likewise, the special American concern for maintaining good relations with employees undoubtedly reflects the necessity for making employment as attractive as possible to people who are in a position to pick and choose among places of work.

It makes a profound difference, psychological as well as technical, whether workers are easily come by or hard to find and keep. Scarcity always enhances value—and respect. And that which is valued and respected is better cared for, particularly when lack of care may lead to loss. Scarcity has conditioned the minds of workers as well as managers. Just as American workers have grown to expect and demand good wages, they have grown to expect and demand good treatment. This, too, has strongly conditioned the thinking of realistic managers.

Without doubt, stringency in the supply of labor has been one of the highly significant factors in the development of American capitalism that has tended to differentiate it markedly from the capitalism of other countries. This aspect of American industrial history deserves far more study than has yet been given it. Particularly deserving of study is the manner in which labor scarcity has helped mold the psychological and cultural climate of American industrial society and the attitudes and practices of American industrial managers.

Authority in an Egalitarian Society

Other and more subtle factors have helped sharpen still further the interest of American managers in the quality of their employee relations. One of these is a rather ambivalent attitude toward the authoritarian role they must play in the hierarchy of industrial organization.

The lack of a high degree of social stratification in this country, the relative ease with which people have been able to move from one social class to another, and above all the strong egalitarian elements in American culture have tended to deprive members of the managerial group of a full sense of sureness in the rightness of their authority in relation to their subordinates. Where lines between social classes are more definitively drawn, authority tends to be exercised as a matter of unquestioned right, and to be so accepted by the workers themselves. Americans, on the contrary, are likely to be troubled by vague feelings of unease when placed in positions where they must behave in ways of superiority toward other Americans who by all standards of the American tradition are their equals and whose position of inferiority in the business enterprise in no way detracts from their essential equality as citizens and persons.

This unease helps explain the peculiar sensitivity of the American employer to what his employees think of him, as expressed, for example, in his widespread use of such devices as "morale surveys" and employee opinion polls. But while this sensitivity and the use of such devices may be sources of wonder or amusement to foreign observers, they reflect an important characteristic of American industrial life: the conflict between a deep-seated egalitarianism and the functional necessity for a certain degree of authoritarianism in relationships within the industrial organization.

These feelings of unease are likely to be particularly strong when "good native Americans" find themselves in positions of authority over other "good native Americans." The same compunctions are often strikingly absent, by contrast, when the same "good native Americans" are in positions of authority over less favored groups, such as Negroes or immigrants. Here the "good native American" is likely to feel secure in his superiority and to have few qualms about the "rightness" and "naturalness" of his authority. In such relationships, the American manager is more likely to think and act in ways similar to his counterparts in other societies that take for granted the prerogatives of members of "superior" classes to command their "inferiors." Superordination in such cases is not merely functional; it implies and assumes that the superiors are also better men.

Influence of Immigration

This tendency to differentiate in attitudes toward subordinates according to their social and ethnic characteristics goes far toward explaining some of the seeming contradictions in the history of American industrial relations. For despite the concern for employee good will postulated above as a distinguishing feature of American management, this country has been torn by some of the bloodiest and most intractable labor strife of any modern nation. Much of this strife has arisen, however, in industries that have employed large numbers of immigrant laborers, such as steel, mining, lumber, and automobiles. Here, the inevitable stresses and strains of emerging large-scale enterprise and the equally inevitable conflicts of economic interest were further and often intolerably aggravated by the conflict of cultures, the lack of adequate means of communication, and above all, a widespread feeling on the part of owners and managers—who were likely to be "good native Americans"—that their laborers were "naturally" inferior.

All this, however, was a passing phase, at least so far as the European immigrants were concerned. It continues to exist with respect to Negroes, Japanese, and others whose achievement of status as "good native Americans" is seriously impeded by visible racial differences still read by Americans, in their current conventions, as imposing barriers to acceptance that even the most thorough acculturation cannot dissolve. But the great tide of European immigration has been cut off for more than a generation. The proportion of foreign-born workers in the population is declining rapidly, and even "first generation Americans" no longer occupy the fairly conspicuous place they once did. Second and third generation Americans are thoroughly acculturated, with only the most tenuous connection or identification with the countries of their ancestral origin. The "melting pot" has done its work well. Names like Larson, O'Rourke, and Emmerick have long been as good as Adams, Burgess, and Townsend; names like Novak, Pagano, and Nemechek are acquiring an easy familiarity. And the same compunctions that through our history have fostered a degree of circumspection in the behavior of an Adams toward a Barker, and a couple of generations ago tempered his behavior toward a Baehr, now condition his behavior toward a Bielski.

One wonders what would have been the course of American labor history—and the state of labor relations in the United States today—if, during the formative years of modern American industry, the labor force had been largely composed of the same "good native American" stock that so largely comprised the owning and managing groups. One suspects that the history would have been quite different than it was, and the present state of labor relations would be quite different than it is. For the tide of immigration left its mark, and many features of management thinking and practice that have had so unfortunate an influence on the course and character of American labor relations had their origin in the period when much of the labor force of the emerging large-scale industry was composed of "obviously inferior" breeds of men. Given the egalitarian American tradition, restrictive in its scope as it undoubtedly was, matters would probably have been different if workers as well as owners and managers had been "good native Americans" all.

But now the wheel of history has turned another full cycle, and the sons and grandsons and great-grandsons of the once "inferior breeds" are fully as "good" and "native" and "American" as those of the men for whom their forebears worked. And their bosses are beset by the same feelings of diffidence that have generally characterized those imbued with the egalitarian American tradition when placed in positions of functional superiority over their "equals." It is not without significance that the modern "science of human relations," which has won such wide attention in management circles, first emerged in the mid-thirties, which was about the time the last wave of immigration began to be fully digested.

Rise of Organized Labor

Neither is it without significance that at this same time the labor movement in this country entered into the period of phenomenal growth that has made it so powerful a factor in modern industrial life. For the labor force was no longer composed in important parts of elements once labeled Bohunks and Polacks and Wops, but of people who had acquired the elements of American culture, who demanded to be treated as self-respecting, upstanding American citizens, and who found their deepest sentiments violated by management attitudes and practices that were a carryover from an earlier period. And so, as self-reliant American citizens, they revolted and sought to create through the device of unions the means for enforcing respect and consideration.

This "revolt of labor" was deeply shocking to management. Among other things, it hastened the change in management's attitudes that was already underway but that had not moved fast enough to keep pace with the substantially complete "Americanization" of the labor force that so closely followed the closing of the doors of immigration. The emergence of a powerful union movement provided a further incentive to management to take stock of the quality of its employee relations.

Quest for Better Ways of Life

But the external pressures of the union movement, the exigencies of competing for a scarce supply of labor, and a peculiar sensitivity to worker attitudes growing out of the egalitarian American tradition do not entirely explain the special concern for good employee relations that is characteristic of American management. To these must be added management's own search for a better way of life for itself and its employees.

American history from its earliest beginnings has been instinct with the search for better ways of life—not merely better ways of earning a livelihood but better ways of *living*. This applies not only to the early settlers, not only to those who fought the Revolution, founded the Republic, and preserved the Union: it continues to this day as one of the strong, persistent themes in American history and a distinguishing characteristic of American society. American management is an integral part of that society and shares that characteristic.

One expression of this is the value placed on being a "good employer." The public evaluation of an enterprise is strongly influenced by its reputation in this respect. Businessmen take pride in having their firms known as "good places to work," not only by workers but by the general public and their fellow businessmen; in formulating their business policies, they are likely to take this factor very much into account. This is not a new development but a feature of our entire industrial history.

This historical theme has been expressed in a variety of ways: in utopian ventures a century and more ago to "uplift" the economic and intellectual status of workers, in the development of the now outmoded concept of "welfare capitalism," in the introduction of a wide variety of employee benefit plans—group insurance and hospitalization, profit sharing, paid vacations and holidays, retirement allowances, paid sick leave, regularized employment, and a host of other measures designed to provide greater present and future security for workers and their families. Measures such as these were not the inventions of the unions; they were originally developed and installed by managements, usually at their own initiative and of their own free will, in an effort to assist in meeting the needs of workers in modern industrial society. The unions have taken these plans over as their own and considerably extended their application, but in doing so they have merely followed a pattern already well-established by progressive, forward-looking managements.

Reconciliation of Roles

In developing plans such as these, management has been motivated by more than economic self-interest, although it has managed fairly well to disguise that fact even from itself. For under the accepted canons of business enterprise, businessmen (including managers) are *supposed* to act only in terms of monetary considerations. Everything they do is expected to pass the test of whether and how much it contributes to profits. The businessman's and the manager's role is very clearly defined in these terms not only by themselves but by the society of which they are a part.

Actually, they seldom carry out literally the injunctions of their official creed. As with workers, owners and managers have never acted strictly in the terms of narrow self-interest ascribed to them by economic theory. There has always been a system of human relations as well as a system of economic relations. The two systems function in terms of two different and sometimes conflicting sets of values, with the result that there is often confusion as to the role the businessman is actually playing at any particular time.

It is amusing to observe the extent to which the businessman will sometimes go in his efforts to explain in terms of self-interest an action he wants to take for perhaps quite different reasons, some of which may be definitely generous and unselfish. But because generosity and unselfishness are explicitly outside the frame of reference within which the businessman, *as a businessman*, is supposed to operate, he feels it necessary to explain himself in other terms. One such term is likely to be "enlightened self-interest." One suspects that the frequency with which enlightened self-interest is appealed to reflects the difficulty of relating certain acts to self-interest at all, and that the adjective "enlightencd" serves merely to suggest a relationship that might be exceedingly difficult to trace out in credible detail.

In any event, the justification of generous acts in terms of self-interest, whether "enlightened" or otherwise, helps soothe the businessman's conscience for acting contrary to his socially defined role—or, perhaps more accurately, helps reconcile the requirements of his role as a businessman and the requirements of his role as a citizen. The businessman's role in society is much more complex than his business role alone, and very often other and conflicting roles take over in what may appear to be strictly business situations. But when this happens, the businessman is likely to find himself very uncomfortable unless he can find a way of explaining his actions as really selfish after all. Under these circumstances, the device of *enlightened* self-interest is a useful one indeed.

This circumlocution also helps make the action more palatable to those who benefit from it. Workers would be very suspicious if the act were presented as anything other than self-interest. They too know the behavior appropriate to management's role and are likely to feel uncomfortable, and perhaps resentful, unless the behavior is carefully defined in terms of that role. Their own role as workers, in turn, makes them dislike being indebted to management for favors. Presenting the act as merely selfish behavior on management's part thus gets better acceptance than if it were presented in some other guise.

Conclusion

The special concern of American businessmen and managers for good employee relations may thus be accounted for in a variety of ways. It springs in part from factors that may be grouped broadly under the heading of self-interest, with or without the adjective "enlightened": the need to reduce friction and promote teamwork as an aid to efficient production, competition for workers in a tight labor market, the pressure of a strong labor movement. But it owes its unique character to factors that transcend any realistic definition of self-interest: the egalitarian American tradition, and the simple desire of those in strategic positions within the business system to create an industrial way of life that comports more nearly with their sense of the fitness of things.

Given this background, the interest of American management in the science of human relations is understandable. Human relations is by no means the first, and certainly will not be the last, of the methods adopted by management to promote better relationships with its employees.

Note

Reprinted by permission of HarperCollins Publishers from *Reseach in Industrial Human Relations: A Critical Appraisal*, ed. Conrad M. Arensberg, James C. Worthy, et al. (New York: Harper & Brothers, 1956).

20

Labor Relations Policy

To: Clarence B. Caldwell
From: James C. Worthy
Date: February 12, 1952
Re: Labor Relations Policy

Sears should continue to make every effort to avoid any further extension of unionism within the organization, but our approach should not be the negative one of "trying to stay out of trouble." Our aim should be the building and maintaining of a sound and effective organization.

We should avoid the temptation of doing things or not doing things "to keep the unions out." Our yardstick should be whether a policy or line of action is right or wrong. Expediency may decide how we do something or when we do it, but never *what* we do. "Keeping out the union" is expediency. To subordinate our approach—and even more important, our policy—to the end of "keeping out the union" perverts the policy and impairs its integrity.

We must avoid using the bogeyman of unionism as a means for getting things across to our field management, things that are good in themselves and ought to be done anyhow. The temptation to do so is often very great because it is the one argument that almost always gets quick results. But this is really worse in the long run than a policy that conceives of keeping out the union as an end in itself. First, such an approach would mean that we lack the ability to "sell" our programs to our managers honestly and have to play on their fears, and that would undermine our integrity within the management structure and endanger our relationships with our management associates. Second, such an approach would mean that managers would stay "bought" only as long as we continue to be nonunion but remain under the threat of unionization. As soon as we either became unionized or passed from under the danger of unionization, support for the programs put across as defense against unionization would be seriously impaired.

Another point we must keep in mind is that unionization when it comes to a store or plant is a terrible shock to the management of that store or plant. Substantial unionization of the company as a whole or any major segment of the company, if and when it should ever come, would be a traumatic experience for top management and a harsh blow to its self-confidence. The shock would be especially severe if our rationale for trying to be a good employer was to keep the unions out. The fact that we could be unionized nevertheless might persuade us that nothing we have been doing is worthwhile. We have seen companies where this kind of shock destroyed the good things management had built up over years of effort and shattered its esprit de corps for a decade or longer.

None of this is to suggest that we abandon our well-grounded belief that Sears will not be unionized. But we must not subordinate our policies or attitudes to the aim of "keeping out the union." We should certainly continue to look at all policies with the question: Are they likely to increase the company's vulnerability to unionization? But we must add to that the question: If unionization should come, what would be the effects of this policy? Above all, we must strengthen in our own minds as well as in the rest of our management confidence that unionization, if it should come, will not change the company's basic attitudes, convictions, and policies, and will never be allowed to damage the self-respect of Sears management or paralyze its nerve and muscle.

If we look on union relations as a fire-fighting activity, we will have nothing but trouble in the long run. Our goal should continue to be simply that of building and maintaining a sound and effective human organization.

Note

Memorandum to Clarence B. Caldwell, personnel vice president, Sears, Roebuck and Co., February 12, 1952, in author's files.

21

Overachievement at Work

We hear a great deal these days about workers soldiering on the job and doing careless and sloppy work. In this paper I will present a contrary thesis, namely, that the natural bent of men and women is to do to their work as well as their abilities and circumstances permit. This is not to deny the existence or importance of underachievement; there is, in fact, a considerable literature on restriction of output, one form of underachievement. I will argue, however, that this fairly common phenomenon is more a consequence of the way work is organized and compensated than of worker predilection.

In the course of my personal experience I have found overachievement at work more the norm than the exception, and have often been amazed at the degree to which individual men and women will extend themselves beyond the strict requirements of their jobs or what they are paid to do. This occurs far too often to be merely aberrational or idiosyncratic. Actually, it can be explained in rather straightforward terms.

Psychologists, psychiatrists, and others have long identified as a normal human impulse the tendency for men and women to place great value on their images of self and to strive for favorable self-images. Attitudes of low self-esteem, in fact, are recognized as indicative of mental ill-health. Because people spend more of their waking time at work than at any other activity, the work a person does is a significantly important part of his or her image of self. It is only natural, therefore, that people would rather take pride in what they do than deprecate it; in taking pride in their work, they take pride in themselves. It is difficult for a person to take pride in careless or sloppy work; a minimal requirement of pride in work is a feeling that it is being done as well as the individual is capable of doing it, given conditions on the job, training, and experience.

The need to take pride in work is common to all levels of occupation. I can remember, as a boy when ditches were still dug by hand, watching a man digging ditches and having him explain how important it was to handle the shovel just so and to have the sides of the ditch exactly straight and perpendicular. Similar behaviors are observable in virtually all lines of endeavor: stenographers, salesmen, machinists, professors, managers, lawyers, engineers, preachers, doctors. . . . The reason for this is simple: to do work well is to think well of oneself.

People are especially likely to try to do well jobs they see as in some way essential to the work of the enterprise or otherwise significant. It helps greatly for them to feel that what they are doing is important, that their personal efforts contribute in some consequential way to the accomplishment of tasks that are themselves important. This favorable influence is especially marked where the purposes served are larger than those of the enterprise itself—for example, munitions production in time of war.

In significant degree, work gives meaning to a person's life; it is natural for people to wish to enrich that meaning and to resent deeply anything that tends to impoverish it. Anything that increases pride in work tends to have a positive impact because it helps increase pride in self. Conversely, anything that depreciates or destroys pride in work has a destructive impact because it sabotages pride in self. The *meaning* a job has to the person doing it is highly important. Unfortunately, people sometimes see their jobs as necessary evils, merely a means of livelihood, an unpleasantness to be endured for lack of a better choice.

There is irony of considerable symbolic and practical significance in the use of the term "compensation." The dictionary defines the verb "compensate" as "to make up for or offset, to make equivalent or satisfactory reparation." Deeply ingrained in our culture is the assumption that work is a cost, a disability, a sacrifice that must be "compensated for" by some means external to the work itself. Also deeply ingrained in our culture is the notion of getting as much as possible for as little as possible. Under these circumstances, *the meaning of the job to the worker* may sometimes be, "take as much as you can get, but give as little as you can get away with." Where jobs have this kind of meaning, workers may take positive pride in doing work poorly—only well enough to keep from getting fired. In these circumstances, the real meaning of the job may be a way to get even. Ability to "screw the boss" may become the worker's source of pride, and "screwing the boss but good" may be one form of overachievement.

Absent factors that have the effect of depreciating, in the minds of workers, the importance of their jobs or their value to the enterprise, people have a natural tendency to take pride in their work and do it well because of the strongly positive effect this has on the images they hold of themselves.

The work people do is an important part of the image they have of themselves, of the kinds of persons they consider themselves to be. People would rather think well of themselves than otherwise. A farmer takes pride in being a *good* farmer, a housewife in being a *good* housekeeper, an auto mechanic a *good* mechanic, a programmer a *good* programmer—and so on. And the better one is at one's work, the higher esteem one is likely to have for oneself. There is one important condition: the product of the work must be identifiable and attributable to the efforts of the worker.

I therefore state as a general principle: *In the absence of factors in the job situation that negate a positive relationship between work and the worker's self-image, workers will seek to do their work as well as circumstances and their abilities will permit.*

And to that principle I add this corollary: *Overachievement is a more natural form of human behavior at work than underachievement.*

Note

Excerpted from an address to the Academy of Management, August 16, 1986.

22

A Working Philosophy of Personnel Management

As my last official act as an officer of the Industrial Relations Association of Chicago, I would like to outline some of my thinking as to the proper role of personnel management in the modern business organization, and to suggest some of the lines along which, it appears to me, personnel thinking and practice may be profitably directed.

The task of management has changed considerably during the past fifty years. During the nineteenth century, the great problems of management were those concerned with physical production and distribution. There was a continent to be occupied, railroads to be built, natural resources to be developed, productive capacity to be provided. Closely related to these were the problems of securing capital for a rapidly expanding economy, and the tasks of creating distributive channels capable of handling the vast increase in physical output. Given these circumstances, it is understandable that management's attention in that period was largely preoccupied with matters of production, finance, and sales. And it was inevitable that the production man, the financier, and the salesman should occupy the key positions in industry and that business thinking and practice should bear the impress of their special points of view. Men like Henry Ford, J. P. Morgan, Julius Rosenwald, and Marshall Field were the prototypical figures of this era, for they offered solutions to the basic tasks of management at that time.

The major challenge to management today is not production. Neither is it finance or distribution. All of these offer continuing problems, but not crucial problems. We have the skills and the administrative machinery and we have an adequate conceptual framework in which to exercise these skills and operate this machinery to meet any demands that are likely to occur in these areas for some time to come. The really great task confronting management today is that of building and maintaining the kind of teamwork and co-operation within the organization that will keep the wheels of in-dustry turning smoothly and efficiently. It is in this area that mod-ern management is finding its most difficult problems and where progressive management is devoting an increasing share of its en-ergy and thought. And this is the area where we in personnel, if we are worth our salt, can make a tremendously valuable contribution, not only to our managements but to the health and survival of our system of democratic institutions.

We need a more realistic conceptual foundation than we now have for the development of effective organizations. By "effective organization," I mean one that taps the human resources of its peo-ple, maintains high levels of employee morale, fosters good will and cooperation between management and workers, and achieves the purposes of the organization because it meets the needs and expec-tations of its members. Assuming reasonable technical compe-tence, such an organization is "effective" from the standpoint of both workers and management.

At a broader level of consideration, the challenge we face is learning how to deal with the vast collectivities that have grown out of modern technology, and at the same time preserve individu-al integrity, adaptivity, and character. In a word, the problem is learning how to adapt the fundamental democratic ideals of our society to the realities of the work place. The overriding question is, how are we to preserve the essentials of human freedom within the framework of modern industrial society, a society characterized by huge organizations, by machine production, by impersonal, in-stitutionalized management-worker relationships; how to fit men and women to the requirements of large-scale production without sacrificing their individualities and basic freedoms?

In the simple, agrarian society of Jefferson's day, political free-dom was enough because, to a large extent, political freedom meant economic freedom as well. But as economic relationships have grown more complex, political freedom alone has grown less and less adequate. Political freedom as such has less and less bearing on the ways people make their livings. Political freedom is the start-ing point, the foundation, but political freedom alone is not enough in a world of complex social organization. Under modern condi-tions, to be more than an empty phrase political freedom must be reenforced by economic freedom.

Without necessarily subscribing to theories of economic determinism, it is clear that the ways people make their living have a profound influence on all aspects of their living. Industrial experience can stimulate the development of human potentials—or it can stultify growth and stifle the human spirit. Industrial organization can enrich and embellish individuality—or it can degrade men and women to dull and common levels of mediocrity. Industrial practice can strengthen the underpinnings of democracy—or it can riddle them to a hollow shell.

The record of American business in these respects is mixed. It is better than it has often been given credit for. But it could have been better than it has been. And it needs to become better than it is.

All of this has profound significance for the preservation of the essentials of democracy. Democracy depends on strong, self-reliant individuals, people who are capable of handling their own problems. It is a tragic fact that the methods of business organization have greatly increased the psychological dependency of members of business organizations—workers and executives alike.

We need a science of management that will not have the weaknesses implicit in the effort to apply engineering concepts to human organization, but will integrate into company practice the findings and the special contributions of modern-day social sciences.

Important beginnings along this line have already been made, but a great deal more needs to be done. Any adequate science of management must be a science of human organization. For this reason, it is essential that full use be made of the bodies of knowledge and the special insights of the social scientists who are studying various aspects of the problems of human organization. More than that, business must assist such scientists, not merely by financial support (although that too is important) but by making itself available for closer study for its own benefit and for the advancement of a more adequate science of management.

The growth and wide popularity of so-called human relations is encouraging. It represents an effort on management's part to secure a better understanding of what is going on within its organization and to develop higher orders of skill for dealing with its immediate and long-range problems. But here I want to voice a special word of warning. There has been a tendency, in the last few years, to allow "human relations" to degenerate into a sort of "be nice to the guy" school of thought. Being nice to people is all well and good, but it is not enough. Sometimes management has to do things that are painful to people, and if its only hold on the loyalty of workers consists in having been "nice" to them, it will not retain their loyalty or support for very long when the going gets rough. Under such circumstances, people are quite likely to look around for someone else who promises to be "nice" to them. This "be nice to people" version of human relations is brittle indeed. It will not stand up against a blow of any real severity, and it will be repudiated by workers and discarded by management with little ceremony.

Any realistic science or philosophy of management must be tough-minded. There is a place in it for sentiment but not for sentimentality. It must be founded on fundamental Judeo-Christian ideals, but like Judaism and Christianity themselves it must not mistake the easy life for the good life.

In a real and special sense, the preservation of our democratic way of life depends on the skill and foresight with which management handles its problems of human relations. We in personnel have a great opportunity and a great responsibility for assisting management in this task. We will be foolish indeed if we allow ourselves to be sidetracked by issues of little moment.

We are moving into a time of great opportunites for advancements in the arts and sciences of management. Influential elements in the upper ranks of American business are seeking to come to grips with the pressing problems of our industrial ways of life. Our task as personnel administrators is to assist our managements—as in a real sense only we can assist them—in their efforts to work out in practical, realistic terms the means for making *industrial* society the *good* society. Anything less than this will be tragically short of our historic challenge and our historic opportunity.

Note

Excerpts from "Farewell Address" on completion of term of office as president, Industrial Relations Association of Chicago, June 11, 1951.

Biographical Note

Ronald G. Greenwood

The career of James C. Worthy has been a checkered one, alternating between government, business, and education. He served two tours of duty in Washington, once as assistant deputy administrator in the early years of the Roosevelt New Deal, and again twenty years later as assistant secretary of commerce in the rather differently oriented Eisenhower period. His work in private business spanned twenty-three years with Sears, Roebuck and Co., where he rose to the position of vice president, and ten years as regional partner in the international management consulting firm, Cresap, McCormick and Paget. On retiring from the latter position in 1972, he was appointed to a professorship in the newly established Sangamon State University in Springfield, Illinois, a post he held until reaching the state's mandatory retirement age in 1978 when he joined what has since been named the J. L. Kellogg Graduate School of Management of Northwestern University as professor of management. Over his years in business and education he has served as director of a number of corporations and until recently continued to act as consultant to business and academic institutions. In addition to his career responsibilities, he has been active in numerous civic and professional affairs, and through it all has found time to do a good deal of writing and to be a good husband and father.

Educated at Northwestern University (class of 1933), Worthy began his working career as one of the first employees of the National Recovery Administration, where by dint of good fortune and the accident of being in the right place at the right time he was soon named assistant deputy administrator in the Apparel Section of the Textile Division. After the Recovery Act was declared unconstitutional by the Supreme Court in 1935, he stayed on to help write the history of that failed New Deal agency, following which he served briefly as personnel manager for a Milwaukee department store be-

fore joining Sears, Roebuck in early 1938 to head a newly created research and planning function in the headquarters personnel department. Again, time and place were propitious. The company had weathered its early and trying years in the retail business. Basic merchandising and operating policies had been hammered out, a stable structure of organization was in place, and Sears was not only in fit trim for the difficult war years that lay ahead but for the period of explosive growth that in the years immediately following the war would catapult the company into first place among the merchandising enterprises of the world. In all this, Sears' corporate personnel department was to play a critical role and Worthy was to find a unique opportunity.

Largely through trial and error, General Robert E. Wood, Sears' guiding genius, had gradually evolved a philosophy of decentralized management to which he was firmly committed. In accordance with that philosophy, unusually wide ranges of authority and responsibility were delegated to those at the operating levels of the company. Wood recognized that for such an organization to work it was imperative to make administrative provision to assure that decision-making positions were filled by carefully selected and well-trained people. For very practical reasons, this meant a strong headquarters personnel department. Worthy joined that department just as it was beginning to take definitive form under the leadership of Clarence B. Caldwell. Responding to the challenge laid down by Wood, Caldwell recognized the need to develop a rational body of principles and a strong factual and conceptual base for the company's personnel policies and manpower planning programs. With responsibility for the new personnel research and planning function, Worthy was well-placed strategically to participate in and help fashion a human resources management program that in retrospect was one of the most advanced and effective to be found in American business at the time.

From his initial base, Worthy's responsibilities steadily expanded to include the design and administration of the company's wage and hour policies, employee benefits, training, executive development, and employee relations programs, the latter embracing the entire range of company policies and practices in dealing with its far-flung and rapidly growing organization. The World War II and Korean War periods created serious personnel problems for Sears, in the resolution of which Worthy was closely involved. As the scope of his work grew, he took care to strengthen his original research and planning base, which indeed became the axis for his widening areas of responsibility.

One of his most productive moves for this purpose was the establishment during the World War II period, and the maintenance for some years thereafter, of close working relationships with the University of Chicago. Two of those relationships warrant special note.

In an effort to develop more objective and reliable standards for selecting future executives, an ambitious program extending over a period of several years was undertaken in cooperation with Professor L. L. Thurstone of the University of Chicago, one of the country's leading psychometrists, to identify the psychological traits associated with executive success. From this research, batteries of tests were designed that proved exceptionally useful in helping build the executive staffs needed to support the company's ambitious postwar expansion program and that formed the basis for the selection and placement procedures still in use in the company today.

A much broader and more significant program of research was undertaken in cooperation with the university's Committee on Human Relations in Industry, chaired by Professor W. Lloyd Warner, a noted cultural anthropologist best known for his work on the class structure of American society and as designer of the Bank Wiring Room Study of the Hawthorne Experiments. Executive director of the committee was Dr. Burleigh B. Gardner, also a cultural anthropologist, who had been director of personnel research at the Hawthorne plant of the Western Electric Company. Early in his personnel research work at Sears, Worthy had been intrigued by the interplay of social and cultural forces in the workplace, and the concepts and field methods of cultural and social anthropology espoused by Warner and Gardner offered new and more productive insights into work-place phenomena than those provided by prevailing theories of management and organization. Warner and Gardner for their part welcomed the opportunity to pursue their research interests with a large, complex company whose management was sympathetic with and responsive to the points of view and values they and their group represented. Again, the fruitful confluence of time and place—and people.

During the years 1943–52, a series of research projects were undertaken that proved to be of great value to Sears, not only in respect to employee relations per se but in the broader field of management itself. Warner's and Gardner's interest in social structure led naturally to an interest in organization structure and to the influence of structure on working relationships—not only the relationships of management and workers considered as abstractions but those of all participants in the total enterprise.

In the conduct of the various research projects undertaken, Worthy was not merely the contractor for services but was actively involved in the design and supervision of much of the research itself, particularly in the drawing of generalizations for application to the practical affairs of the business. Some of this work attracted the attention of organizations such as the American Management Association, the Academy of Management, and the Industrial Relations Research Association, of which Worthy was an early officer, as well as a number of major universities. Beginning about 1946, he was frequently invited to address business and academic groups on the results of the Sears research, and papers prepared for such purposes often found their way into business and professional journals.

An unanticipated consequence of these lecturing and publishing activities was Worthy's second tour of duty in Washington. Early in 1953 Sinclair Weeks, who had been named secretary of commerce by the newly elected president Eisenhower, offered him the key post of assistant secretary for administration, explaining he was doing so because of the reputation Worthy had gained as a practitioner and theorist of management. Sears granted him a leave of absence to accept the appointment, and the following two years proved richly rewarding in terms of close and responsible involvement in governmental operations at high policy and administrative levels, and this added learning is reflected in many of his writings. The learning extended to political affairs as well because as a presidential appointee responsible for the administrative affairs of a major executive agency he was called upon to deal with members of the White House staff, elected state and federal officials, and the Republican National Committee. In addition to his departmental work, he served as a member of the President's Committee on Government Contracts, chaired by vice president Nixon and responsible for administering the antidiscrimination provisions of contracts with the federal government.

In early 1955 the poor health of Sears' vice president for public relations led to that officer's early retirement. The post was offered to Worthy on condition he cut short his government leave and return to Sears without undue delay. Sears' approach to public relations was markedly different from that of most corporations, and based on the premise that the best—in fact, the *only*—way to win and hold public confidence and support was through the way the company ran its business and its behavior as a corporate citizen; much of the task of monitoring that behavior and discharging the company's corporate civic responsibilities was vested in the public relations department. Worthy's experience in the development and refinement of Sears' personnel program, his knowledge of government, and the numerous contacts with external groups and interests built up in the course of his government work and extensive writing and lecturing gave him special qualifications for moving into this, for him, apparently new field of work. In point of fact, he found the essentials of this work not at all new but an easy extension of much of what he had been doing for some years past. In particular, the insights gained from his studies of structural relations in the workplace proved as useful in dealing with the external affairs of the company as they had already proved in dealing with the internal.

On returning to Chicago from Washington in 1955, Worthy had been caught up in fund-raising work for the Republican party, and in 1958 he was elected president of the United Republican Fund, at that time the party's official financial arm in Illinois. In that capacity he was actively engaged in the presidential campaign of 1960. Nixon's narrow loss disturbed him deeply, especially the evidence it disclosed of grave weaknesses in the organization of the Republican party in Illinois. By this time his interest in the political affairs of the country had come to overshadow his interest in business, and he left Sears to devote full time to the task of revitalizing the Republican party in his home state. For this purpose, he founded and became the first president of the Republican Citizens League of Illinois. Despite high hopes at the outset and strong encouragement from national party leadership, this proved a frustrating and unsuccessful undertaking, and within a year he began to look about for ways to reenter the business world. By another well-timed stroke of good fortune, he was invited to join the international management consulting firm, Cresap, McCormick and Paget, as partner in charge of the firms's regional office headquartered in Chicago. This was a prospect that had never occurred to him but he accepted with alacrity. Thus, at age fifty-two, he embarked on a wholly new career.

The new course was not an easy one for him. While he had an extensive knowledge of both business and government operations, he found the work of the professional consultant sharply different from anything with which he was familiar. He faced not only the challenge of learning a new and fiercely demanding kind of work but of rebuilding the practice of the firm's central region that had been without resident leadership for some time. Through arduous effort, both challenges were met. Worthy developed into a skilled professional consultant, and in due course the region for which he was responsible was restored to superior levels of performance. His practice brought him into contact with a far wider range of industries and organizations than he had previously known, including not only business but governmental and educational institutions as well. One result was a deepening and broadening of his understanding of the complexities and idiosyncrasies of organizational and institutional behavior.

Despite the pressures of his managerial responsibilities, Worthy was able to devote a fair amount of time to public and civic activities. In Washington, through his work as a member of the President's Committee on Government Contracts, he had developed a keen concern for the problems of race relations, and soon after returning to Chicago he joined the board of the Chicago Urban League, from which vantage point he played an active role in efforts to ease tensions in that racially troubled city. Because of the reputation he gained as a political fund raiser, he was appointed by President Kennedy as one of the four Republican members of his bipartisan Presidential Commission on Campaign Costs, the first major effort to bring a degree of order and control to the chaotic field of political finance.

The most important of his extracurricular activities was his work in the field of education. Early in the 1960s the state of Illinois established a procedure to formulate a master plan for public higher education that called for creation of a series of citizen's committees to consider various aspects of the problem. Worthy was appointed chairman of the Committee on Governing Structure, which through extended hearings and deliberations devised a plan for public university governance that is unique among state systems and has met successfully the stresses experienced by all higher education during the last third of this century. Five years after the work of the original committee, he chaired a similar committee that made recommendations for further improvements.

The success of his work in reorganizing the governance system led to his appointment to the Illinois State Board of Higher Education, which gave wider scope to his long-standing interest in education. The Illinois legislature in its 1967 session authorized the establishment of two new senior institutions, but left to the Board of Higher Education the politically delicate tasks of determining the missions of the two schools, deciding where they were to be located, and placing them in their appropriate places in the governing structure. Worthy was appointed chairman of a special board committee to resolve these complex and inherently controversial issues, a task that called on all his skills as a political realist and hard-headed negotiator, as well as his by-then extensive knowledge of the needs and opportunities of public higher education. The two institutions that emerged from this process were Sangamon State University in Springfield, capital of the state, and Governors State University on the southern fringe of the Chicago metropolitan area.

In July of 1972 he joined the faculty of the newly established Sangamon State University as professor of public affairs and management, and soon thereafter he was appointed chairman of a faculty committee that had been working for some months on the design of an undergraduate business program for the new university. Worthy had been following with approval the growing sentiment in influential academic, business, and governmental circles that "business" and "government" by themselves were bases too narrow for educational purposes, and that schools of business and public administration should begin moving toward education in the basic managerial and administrative functions common to virtually all forms of organization. He agreed with those who felt, "we should get rid of the adjectives," and persuaded his committee to move in that direction.

The result was a *management* program built on the principle that management is a general study and focused on concepts and skills common to all forms of organization. A significant feature of the program was its "liberal" orientation with emphasis on the critical evaluation of alternatives within a framework of human values. Worthy greatly enjoyed teaching and being with young people, and found the intellectual environment stimulating and satisfying. He was pleased to discover that much more of his previous experience than he had realized was relevant to his teaching. In the early 1930s when he himself was in college, management as a defined body of knowledge was too rudimentary to have been included in his own formal education, and after leaving school his work was too demanding to permit any systematic study of the growing corpus of management literature. Joining a faculty and charged not only with teaching but with designing an entire generic management program greatly broadened his conceptual perspective and provided new insight into the significance of much he had learned in his business and government careers. He especially enjoyed and profited from the opportunity to work with faculty from other fields, which further enriched his understanding of the institutional structure of society and of the role and importance of management in human affairs. Sangamon State was a meaningful period in his life.

On reaching the state's mandatory retirement age in 1978, Worthy was offered a "post-retirement" appointment as professor of management at what is now the J. L. Kellogg Graduate School of Management of Northwestern University, an appointment he still holds. His formal duties are light but the Kellogg relationship provides a solid base from which to pursue his still-widening intellectual interests. He finds the Northwestern environment different from that of Sangamon: much richer in resources and academic amenities but lacking in the freshness and excitement of a new school in process of establishing itself and finding its identity.

Over his years in management consulting and education, Worthy served as a director of a number of companies, notable among which was Control Data Corporation. The founder and head of that company until his retirement in 1986 was William C. Norris, one of the most interesting and creative leaders of modern American business. Worthy was especially intrigued by Norris's conviction that the best way to solve social problems was to find ways to convert them into business opportunities, and the manner in which he sought to broaden his business base by using the company's technological and managerial resources to establish positions in nontraditional fields that he felt offered hopeful opportunities for the company's future growth. The task proved more difficult than anticipated, but Norris's aim captured Worthy's imagination and broadened his concept of the vocation of business in contemporary society.

One of the roles Worthy has played over the years has been interpreting in more communicable terms for a wider audience some of the things companies with which he has been associated have been doing. This was true first at Sears, where much of his writing was devoted to formulating general principles from observed practices; to some extent, Worthy helped explain Sears to itself, as General Wood on more than one occasion explicitly recognized. Later, as a director of Control Data Corporation he sought to aid Norris in his efforts to explain his unorthodox policies to a skeptical business public.

In the course of his career, Worthy has received numerous awards and honors, among which are three honorary doctoral degrees. In 1964 he was one of the first nonacademics elected as a Fellow of the Academy of Management, of which he is now Dean of Fellows Emeritus. He is also a Fellow of the International Academy of Management.

Now eighty-four years of age, Worthy continues to work six to eight hours a day five or six days a week at his computer or in the magnificent library of Northwestern University. The publication of his "Selected Papers" at this time may be premature. There are more to come.[1]

Note

1. More detailed biographical information may be found in Worthy's chapter, "From Practice to Theory: Odyssey of a Manager," in Arthur G. Bedeian, ed., *Management Laureates: A Collection of Autobiographical Essays* (Greenwich, Conn.: JAI Press, Inc., 1993).

Index

Anthropology, social: basis of employee survey research at Sears, 15; studies of companies as social systems, xxiv, 57. *See also* Organization, industrial; Weber, Max; Worthy, James C.

Bureaucracy. *See* Organization structure
Business schools, 184–93; adult business education programs in, 188–89; and communicating ideas, 191–93; and developing future leadership group, 186–87; role of research in, 189–91. *See also* Worthy, James C.

Caldwell, Clarence B., 12, 171; and personnel administration at Sears, 7–9; and research/planning function within Sears' personnel department, 12–13, 19; and need for factual and conceptual base for Sears' personnel policies, 215. *See also* Personnel administration, Sears
Committee on Human Relations in Industry, 11, 18–20, 23, 59, 216; creation of, 57. *See also* Gardner, Burleigh B.; Warner, W. Lloyd; Worthy, James C.
Consultants. *See* Management-employee relations
Control Data Corporation, 221. *See also* Worthy, James C.

Employee attitude surveys: use of questionnaire and personal interviews, 59–60; use of non-directive interviewing techniques, 58–59; at Sears, 13–18, 23–24, 27–36, 56–61. *See also* Management-employee relations; Morale questions; Morale scores; Morale surveys
Employee benefits, Sears, 71–72; and profit sharing, 72–73
Employee compensation: problems of, under factory system, 94–96. *See also* Taylor, Frederick W.
Employee morale at Sears, 70–72; as by-product of sound organization, 80; and quality of supervision, 73–74; and size of operating branch, 75–76, 156–59; in X and Y group stores, 118. *See also* Morale questions; Morale scores; Morale surveys
Engineering, industrial. *See* Management, scientific; Taylor, Frederick W.
Engineers. *See* Management, scientific; Taylor, Frederick W.

Factory system, 94–98; and piece rates, 94–96; and range of income concept, 95
Federation of merchants, 141. *See also* Merchandising organization, Sears; Rosenwald, Julius
Functionalization, principle of. *See* Management, scientific; Organization size; Organization structure; Taylor, Frederick W.
Functional specialization, theory of. *See* Merchandising organization, Sears; Organization structure

Gardner, Burleigh B., 11, 18–19, 57–58, 216; and Committee on Human Relations in Industry, 23–24; and fundamental democratic ideal, 181–82; and Western Electric Co., xxiv–xxv,

14–16. *See also* Social Research, Inc.; Worthy, James C.

Group maladjustment, 55–56. *See also* Malfunction, organizational

Hawthorne plant experiments. *See* Gardner, Burleigh B.; Western Electric Co.

Human engineering. *See* Management, scientific

Human relations research. *See* Employee attitude surveys; Management, scientific; Management-employee relations; Worthy, James C.

Houser, Theodore, 140. *See also* Rosenwald, Julius; Sears, Roebuck and Co.; Wood, General Robert E.

Interviewing techniques, non-directive, 58–59; modification of, for Sears' organizational survey program, 64–65. *See also* Employee attitude surveys; Gardner, Burleigh B.

McGregor, Douglas, xxvi, 89. *See also* Worthy, James C.

Malfunction, organizational, 81–82. *See also* Group maladjustment

Management: ambivalence toward authoritarianism, 197–98; assumptions about human behavior, xxiii; authoritarian aspects of, 177–80; conflicting attitudes of, between European immigrants and racial minorities, 198–99; and free enterprise system, 174–76, 180; and improving lives of workers, 200–202; influences on, during 1940s and 1950s, xiv–xvi; philosophy needed to solve organizational problems, 211–12

Management, scientific, 93–96; acceptance in Soviet Russia, 114; desire to control organization's functions, 112–14; and findings of social science research, 211; and human organizations, 98–99, 105–6, 112, 176–77, 211; influence on specialization processes, 100–105; and worker spontaneity, 114–15. *See also* Anthropology, social; Organization

structure; Taylor, Frederick W.; Worthy, James C.

Management-employee relations: attitude of management toward people, 80, 123–24; role of business executives, consultants, and social scientists in, 83–87; usefulness of employee attitude surveys in improving, 86–87. *See also* Employee attitude surveys; Management

Management engineering. *See* Management, scientific

Management process at Sears: personnel selection as essential to, 7. *See also* Personnel administration, Sears

Managerial decentralization, concept of: under Wood, 3–6; revealed in Sears' X and Y study, 124–26. *See also* Sears, Roebuck and Co.; X and Y group stores; Wood, General Robert E.

Managerial leadership, 182–83. *See also* Business schools; Management; Worthy, James C.

Managers, scientific. *See* Management, scientific

Merchandising organization, Sears, 127–38, 151–53; and development of competent/responsible individuals for, 151–52; early development of, 140–42; structure and departmental functions of, 127–29; structure of, compared to X stores, 131; theory of functional specialization applied to, 136–38. *See also* Organization structure; Sears, Roebuck and Co.; X and Y group stores

Midvale Steel Co. *See* Taylor, Frederick W.

Moore, David G., 14–16. *See also* Employee attitude surveys; Gardner, Burleigh B.

Morale questions: answers to, 36–38; percent of employees responding to, in manner indicated, 43–44

Morale scores: by age and length of service, 48; by age groups, 47; comparison of, by sex and functional group, 46; comparison of, for selling and non-selling employees, 41; comparison of, for selling employees, by

classification, 44; distribution of, by type of operation, 40; by functional group and length of service, 48; individual distribution of, 41; individual distribution of, by classification, 45; for individual selling and non-selling employees, 42; by length of service, 48; for non-selling employees, by sex and job classification, 47; by previous experience and length of service, 49; by previous experience groups, 49; for salespeople, by sex and job classification, 46; for selling employees, by classification, 44; by type of operation, 40
Morale surveys: geographical distribution of, by type of operation, 39

Norris, William C., 221. *See also* Control Data Corporation; Worthy, James C.

Organization, formal. *See* Management; Management-employee relations; Organization, informal; Organization structure
Organization, functional. *See* Organization size; Organization structure
Organization, informal: advantage of, 80; unit size as influencing factor of, 156; within Sears' merchandising organization, 135–36
Organization, industrial, 50–54, 99–100; engineers as chief developers of, 98–99; and free enterprise system, 174–76; and learning from mistakes, 120–21; and status symbols within work groups, 51–53, 157. *See also* Anthropology, social; Management, scientific; Taylor, Frederick W.; Worthy, James C.
Organization, integrated. *See* Organization size; Organization structure
Organization, internal. *See* Organization, industrial; Organization structure
Organizational survey research. *See* Employee attitude surveys; Organization surveys
Organization behavior. *See* Organization structure
Organizations, flat and tall. *See* Orga-

nization structure; Sears, Roebuck and Co.; Span of control; Span of management
Organization size: and delegation, 161–64; and resistance to change, 146; and technological change, 159–60; and work influenced by, 157–59. *See also* Organization, industrial; Organization structure
Organization structure, ix; and bureaucracy, 146–48; and group maladjustment, 56; and high morale, 17, 182; levels of supervision, 78–80; personality as influencing factor of, 85; role of functional specialization in, 137–38, 147–48, 160–66; within Sears' merchandising operation, 131–32; X and Y group stores, 125. *See also* Management; Organization size; Sears, Roebuck and Co.; X and Y group stores
Organization surveys, 62–69; and unions, 171, 194. *See also* Employee attitude surveys; Gardner, Burleigh B.; Group maladjustment
Organization theory: autonomous work units as alternative to, 154; unit interdependence encouraged by, 153–54
Organization X and Y, theory of, xxvi, 91n. *See also* Theory X and Y; Worthy, James C.; X and Y group stores
Organized labor, 200; and Sears, 204–5. *See also* Management; Management-employee relations; Organization surveys; Worthy, James C.

Personnel administration, Sears, 7–9, 215–16; Clarence B. Caldwell and, 7–9; and promotion from within, 9, 74–75, 135; Reserve Group Program, 8–9; and selection of key employees, 7; and X and Y study of store operations, 117
Personnel management. *See* Management; Management-employee relations; Personnel administration, Sears
Piece rate system, 94–96; differential proposed for, 97. *See also* Factory system; Taylor, Frederick W.

Putting-out system. *See* Factory system; Piece rate system

Rosenwald, Julius, 1, 11, 209; role in finding highly qualified people to fit loosely structured organization, 139–40, 143. *See also* Personnel administration, Sears

Sears, Richard, 1
Sears, Roebuck and Co.: approach to public relations, 217; as chief merchandiser during 1940s and 1950s, ix–xi; and centralized buying, advantages of, 127; and decentralized management structure, xii, xxvii, 1–6, 76–78, 124; early challenges to organization structure, 143–45; early organizational development, 140–45; employee morale and loyalty as company growth factors, xii, 27; findings of survey programs, 70–80; human relations research, 11, 23–25; organizational flexibility during early years, 139–43; and promotion from within, 74–75; X and Y study, 117–26. *See also* Caldwell, Clarence B.; Management process at Sears; Personnel administration, Sears; Wood, General Robert E.; Worthy, James C.; X and Y group stores
Social Research, Inc. (SRI), 18–21, 59
Social scientists. *See* Management, scientific; Management-employee relations
Span of control: factors determining optimum, 149–50; as practiced at Sears under Wood, 6, 78; in Sears' merchandising organization, 130–32; theory of, xxv–xxvi, 137, 164–65; in Y group stores, 118. *See also* Organization size; Organization structure; Span of management
Span of management: theory of, xxv–xxvi, 150–54; defined, 149. *See also* Span of control
Specialization of workers. *See* Management, scientific; Organization structure; Taylor, Frederick W.

Taylor, Frederick W.: personal view of

control, 111–12; mechanistic view of the individual, 98–99, 107–10; and Midvale Steel Co., 93–97; and mutuality of labor-management interests, 96–97; philosophy of management, xxii; and traditional managers, 111
Theory X and Y, xxvi, 91n. *See also* McGregor, Douglas; Organization X and Y, theory of; Worthy, James C.

Unions. *See* Organized labor

Warner, W. Lloyd, 11, 18–19, 57–58, 216; and concepts of social anthropology, 15. *See also* Anthropology, social; Gardner, Burleigh B.; Social Research, Inc.
Weber, Max, xxiv. *See also* Anthropology, social; Employee attitude surveys; Management, scientific
Western Electric Co., 1–2, 53, 216; and Burleigh B. Gardner, xxiv–xxvi, 14–15; and employee behavior research, xxiv. *See also* Moore, David G.
Wood, General Robert E., 11–13, 140; and decentralized management at Sears, xii, xxvii, 3–6, 215; and employee relations philosophy at Sears, xxii, 173; influence of employee relations research on, xxii; role in transformation of Sears, 1–3. *See also* Personnel administration, Sears; Merchandising organization, Sears; Sears, Roebuck and Co.
Worthy, James C., xii–xix; career of, 213–22, 222n; and educational quality of business schools, 169–70; and hierarchical, goal-oriented enterprises, xxvii, 180–83, 210–11; and research on organization structure, xix–xxii, 14, 24; and Social Research, Inc., 19–21; views on formal and informal relationships in business organizations, xxv; views on scientific management, 89, 98, 104–10, 114; views on worker overachievement, 206–8. *See also* Anthropology, social; Business schools; Employee attitude surveys; Gardner, Burleigh B.; Organization surveys;

Organization X and Y, theory of; X and Y group stores

X and Y group stores, 117–26; comparison of flat and tall organization structures in, 151–53; and managerial attitudes toward staffs of, 123–24; range of differences between, 118–22. *See also* Personnel administration, Sears; Sears, Roebuck and Co.

JAMES C. WORTHY was employed by Sears, Roebuck and Co. from 1938 to 1961, where he rose to the position of vice president. During this time, on leave of absence from Sears, he served for a two-year period as U.S. assistant secretary of commerce. Subsequent to his Sears employment, he was for ten years a regional partner in the international management consulting firm Cresap, McCormick, and Paget. In 1972 he was appointed professor of public affairs and management at Sangamon State University, and in 1978 he joined the faculty of the J. L. Kellogg Graduate School of Management at Northwestern University as a professor of management. He is the author of numerous articles and has published five books, including *Shaping an American Institution: Robert E. Wood and Sears, Roebuck* (1984) and *William C. Norris: Portrait of a Maverick* (1987).

RONALD G. GREENWOOD is the F. James McDonald Professor of Industrial Management at GMI Engineering & Management Institute in Flint, Michigan. He has twice served as chairman of the Management History Division of the Academy of Management and as president of the Midwest Management Society. He is the author of *Managerial Decentralization*, and has coauthored *The Evolving Science of Management* and *Frederick Winslow Taylor*.

DAVID G. MOORE is the coauthor of three editions of *Human Relations in Industry*, the *SRA Employee Attitude Survey*, and *Organization Makers*. He worked with James C. Worthy in the 1940s on the research that provided the basis for Worthy's observations about organization structure and employee motivation. At Cornell University he was dean of the New York State School of Industrial and Labor Relations and later he served as executive vice president of the Conference Board in New York. He is currently retired from the University of North Florida as professor emeritus.